Copyright BackPage Press 2012

ISBN 978-0956497161

A catalogue record for this book is available from the British Library.

Cover by Freight Design, Glasgow

Designed and typeset by BackPage Press

Illustrations by Dave Alexander

Printed and bound in Poland by Totem

www.backpagepress.co.uk

HENRIK, HAIRDRYERS AND THE HAND OF GOD

EXTRAORDINARY TALES FROM THE PRESS BOX

Edited by Brian Marjoribanks

CONTENTS

CONTENTS

FOREWORD

By Brian Marjoribanks

I n early September 2011, I had a dream that my soon-to-be-born son was destined to score the winner for my beloved Falkirk against Rangers in some far-off Scottish Cup final.

Most parents get at least until the teenage years before their aspirations for their children begin to intersect with reality. For my wife Jennifer and I, however, our dreams and hopes for Andrew were cruelly extinguished before we even had the chance to meet him.

Jennifer went into labour on September 11, only for us to find out on our excited arrival at Forth Valley Royal Hospital that our baby had suddenly, and inexplicably, bled to death.

Some 24 difficult hours later, our perfect-looking little boy, who weighed in at a whopping 9lb 2ozs, arrived stillborn; five days before he had been scheduled to make his official entrance into this world.

One week later, as dusk fell on the day of my boy's funeral, a Falkirk team packed full of promising kids would knock Rangers out of the League Cup. I felt nothing; it's hard to feel anything when you've just carried a tiny white coffin containing the body of your little boy to his final resting place.

Over the coming weeks and months, sport began to provide increasing comfort to Jennifer and I as phone calls, texts, emails, cards, flowers and letters containing moving and deeply personal experiences flooded into our home in Falkirk from across the football-writing fraternity. Each new message increased the sense of belonging to a family; the kind more readily associated with successful sports teams and not my much-criticised trade.

There and then came the idea for this book: a celebration of sportswriting and all the talented people who are privileged enough to do this beautifully bonkers job for a living; with all proceeds going to Sands, the stillbirth and neonatal death charity whose support helped Jennifer and I through the toughest spell of our lives.

The aim of the book was to tell terrific sports stories first and foremost, while giving the reader a peek behind the curtain at sports-writing as a job. I especially wanted the articles to tell 'the story behind the stories' in the hope of giving readers a unique insight into a career that fascinates many and enrages even more.

Sportswriters get a bad press, if you excuse the pun, but I believe it shines through in this book that each article (all were kindly donated for free) is the work of gifted professionals and good people, who love their job, adore their sport and are passionate that what they do for a living matters.

There is, sadly, an undeniable 'end of empire' undercurrent running through many of the articles, relating to the state of Scottish journalism as well as Scottish football. While some writers are not entirely comfortable with the way journalism is going, and the wilful neglect by some of the trade's custodians over the years, all, however, remain fiercely proud of their place on the rollercoaster on what is never less than an exhilarating ride.

And while my baby boy will never score the winner against Rangers in a Scottish Cup final, this book in his memory will raise money to help try and prevent similar tragedies in future.

In this small way, sport will provide Andrew with his legacy after all. There could be no more fitting tribute to my son; there could be no prouder father.

Support Sands at www.uk-sands.org

KIRK BROADFOOT DOES NOT WANT TO BE INTERVIEWED

By Tom English

I was born in March 1969, which, journalistically speaking, was about 30 years too late. By 1969 I should have been in my 30s and I should have been in America, hanging around with Norman Mailer and Jimmy Cannon, Gay Talese and Mark Kram, and all those other brilliant chroniclers of the heavyweight fight scene. I should have had an 'I was there' wisdom about the night Cassius Clay shook up the world by beating Sonny Liston in Miami in 1964, I should have been in the Garden when Joe Frazier beat Ali, should have been in Kinshasa when Ali beat Foreman, should have been right there at the 'Thrilla in Manila' when Ali and Frazier damn-near killed each other in the third and final act of their unforgettable blood feud.

Everybody wants to be younger. Sometimes, I just wish I was older. Back then there were no agents, no publicists, no sponsors getting in the way, no press officers hanging about and making a writer's life difficult. You had Ali talking for hours in his hotel room, in his training camp. You had access all areas. A magazine writer phoned Ali once and said, "Muhammad, would it possible to get an interview with you for an hour? I know it's a lot to ask …"

Ali said no. "No way. What I've got to tell you is gonna take way more than an hour – unless you've two hours, don't bother coming!"

Everything's changed. If you're a football writer nowadays you don't get much in the way of exclusive access, you don't get many players talking openly. Most of them have nothing to say in any case. You ring up the press officers at the football clubs and ask for an interview with one of their players not because you think he has anything remotely interesting to tell you but because it will sit well with the boss, it'll give the editor something to flag up on the front page. 'Exclusive interview with new Celtic/Rangers striker …'

I want to tell you about a week in September 2008. On the Tuesday morning I emailed Rangers with a request to speak to Kirk Broadfoot for a piece for Scotland on Sunday. I look back now and I wonder what the hell I was thinking, but it must have seemed like a good idea at the time. On the Thursday I had a mission in Aberdeen. And I was nervous as hell. I could count on the fingers of one hand the amount of times I have been jumpy going into an interview and this was the one that made me jumpiest of all for I was meeting Joe Frazier that day; I was getting a glimpse of what it must have been like back in the 1960s when these remarkable sportsmen were accessible and compelling.

Joe was sitting in the corner of the restaurant when I arrived. Lunch was being served. He took my hand and we said a prayer. Then we ate and shot the breeze. He asked if I had a wife and I said I did. He asked if I loved her and I said yeah, champ, I do. He asked if I'd kids and if I'd gone in the delivery room and I said yeah again, both times. Joe had lots of kids, but had never been around when they were born. "That damn tape switched on?" he asked. "Well, switch it on, man. Switch it on."

Joe was talking and transporting us back to the poverty of his youth in South Carolina and his rise to heavyweight champion of the world. He was talking about time spent with Martin Luther King and Malcolm X, but mostly he was talking about Ali and the poison that existed between them. Joe was good to Ali when Ali was banned from boxing. Gave him money for one thing. Called on the authorities to lift the ban for another.

Joe was telling a story about what he did for Ali. "I went to Tricky Dicky," he said. And I'm thinking, Tricky Dicky – who's he talking about here? Then it dawns on me. He's talking about Richard Nixon, president of the United States.

"Tricky says, 'Come on in, Joe, how ya doin' champ?' We're in the White House now. 'Sit down, Joe, what can I do for ya?'

"I says, 'Mr President, I'd like to ask permission for Muhammad to get his licence back.'

"Tricky says, 'OK Joe, how do you feel about that?'

"I says, 'I feel I can clean him up, I can beat him, no doubt about it.'

"'All right, Joe, I tell you what I'm gonna do. First thing tomorrow morning I'll put a call in and have him get his licence back.'"

In return, Ali betrayed Joe, said many unforgiveable things, called him an Uncle Tom and turned black America against him through the force of his own personality. Joe always hated him for it. In Aberdeen he was talking of Ali's Parkinson's disease. "Ali did a lot of dumb stuff in the sight of the Lord and the Lord didn't like it. See what the Lord did? He sent me to get him. He fixed it so Muhammad can't talk anymore. When the Lord speaks, ain't nobody gonna get a word in, right?"

Two hours with Joe were the two most engrossing hours in my 20 years of writing about sport. Later he signed the cover of the Life magazine I'd kept for the longest time, an edition from March 1971 that told the story of the Fight of the Century at the Garden when Joe beat Ali. 'To Tom. Right on! Joe Frazier.'

I left Joe as he was talking to people in the foyer of his hotel and posing for photographs with men who were dumbstruck in the presence of sporting greatness. I switched on my phone. There was a message from Rangers. "Sorry," said the press officer in response to my request earlier in the week. And in words that will never leave me, words that are emblematic of changed times in the sportswriting game, she said, "Kirk Broadfoot doesn't want to be interviewed."

Tom English is the chief sportswriter with Scotland on Sunday and has been Scottish sports feature writer of the year on five occasions. His book, The Grudge, won rugby book of the year at the British Sports Books Awards 2011. He comes from Limerick and still pines for the Guinness in Myles Breen's bar.

THE ACCIDENTAL SPORTS JOURNALIST

By Graham Spiers

I never believed I'd ever be a sports journalist. I never had any ambition to be a sports journalist. To compound all this, there are plenty people out there who will tell you I've never been one, either.

Given my own career experience – a vast junket which has involved attending big football matches for free and getting to flounce around places like Wimbledon and Augusta National – I feel it could be instructive to offer a piece which might best be titled: How To Accidentally Become A Sports Journalist And Go On To Make A General Hash Of It. I hope, for younger readers of this book, this might make a worthwhile and useful career tip.

First off, I loved football. From about the age of about four I lived every day to play football. I was born into a Baptist manse and, apart from a prolific knack for writing sermons, the other thing my father loved was football. He played it, he went to watch it, and he opined endlessly about it over our dinner table.

We lived in Anstruther in Fife for a few years when I was a wee kid and one afternoon, when I was about four, my father walked into our house and said to me, "Wee fellow, look what I've got." Out of a large, brown-paper bag he produced a brand-new football. Exactly 60 seconds later Dad and I were playing football in the little park right across the road from our East Neuk home and, for me, it was the start of a lifelong love affair with the game.

But becoming a sports journalist? Don't make me laugh! The

thought never entered my head. I went to school (average), I conned my way into university (distinctly average again) and all the time I played the game: for school, for St Andrews University, for my own Sunday league team. But, as much as I hollered at and despised TV football pundits and their half-wit views, and argued and debated football endlessly with pals, being a 'sports journalist' was something that never once crossed my mind.

Then it slowly, accidentally, almost blunderingly began to unfold. I remember the night I graduated from university. I came away with a degree in theology – I mean, what the heck do you do with that? Many of my football mates already had jobs lined up – in banking, in industry, in commerce, in medicine, in education – and here was me thinking, "So what the hell am I going to do?"

Following my Dad into the church had been very briefly considered – about as briefly as the time it took to order a 58p pint of Skol back in 1984. It was never really an option. But that graduation night my old divinity professor, a little the worse for wear, bumped into me and said, "Ah, Graham my boy, so what are you going to do with yourself?" I came clean and told him: "I don't know, sir."

Well, the months rolled by, and the post-student period kicked in. You realise your childhood, your carefree years, are truly over. Student life was immense, quite terrific: football, pub, girls (occasionally) and minimal study. When all of that suddenly ends a slightly quashing sense of adult responsibility hits you. The word 'career' began to be heard in my vicinity and I suddenly felt I'd better get my hands on one.

So what to do? Well, one afternoon, and a tad bored at 22 years old, I sat down and wrote a piece about student life under Margaret Thatcher. For a laugh I posted it off to The Herald's office in Glasgow. Two days later a bloke at the paper phoned me and said, "We really like this piece ... we're running it in tomorrow's paper." I was beside myself. Not only that, but about three weeks later I received a cheque for £125, for a piece that had taken me precisely one hour to write.

I thought about this for a moment ... one hour's work at a rate of 125 quid per hour? Maybe I should think about this!

I knew about two things: football and the church. Now the latter, I didn't think, would be a money-spinner in print. So I wrote more stuff off the cuff, about Graeme Souness and Rangers, and about the Scotland international team, and out of nowhere I began getting more pieces published. Then one afternoon a national Scottish newspaper phoned me up and said: "Would you like to come in and speak to us about a job here?"

I said, "Look, I need to tell you … I have no journalism training whatsoever. And I have never wanted to be a journalist at all."

The guy said, "Doesn't matter. Come in and see us. We think we've got a role here for you."

That was 23 years ago now. Since then I have covered World Cups, European Championships, Champions League finals, Wimbledons, around 20 Open Championships and maybe 12 or 13 Masters in Augusta. It has been one great, vast, intoxicating jamboree. And the one constant throughout has been this: I am an utterly hopeless journalist.

There are two lessons, I believe, in this tale of The Accidental Sports Journalist. First, it doesn't matter if you have any journalism training or not. Instead, here is the question: can you write? If you can, and if you have a slightly withering edge to your writing, then you'll make it.

Don't get me wrong, I'm not knocking proper journalism training – that can only be a good thing. But it is not the half of it. Indeed, it might not even be the third of it.

Second, sportswriting is about judgement, opinion and values. If you do what I do – which is blunder around in an opinion-making minefield – then you have to have a sense of values: a sense of what things mean, of what is 'the right' and 'the wrong', and be able to say as much. To look at a footballer, a golfer, or a sporting occasion, and place it in some kind of context, is the challenge.

I'll give you one brief example. In 1995 I went to Augusta to cover what turned out to be 43-year-old Ben Crenshaw's second Masters win. What was amazing about that Crenshaw triumph was this. First, his form that early season had been woeful: missed cuts here and tied-40th there. Second, his great mentor of decades, Harvey Penick, had died eight days earlier, and Crenshaw went from being a pallbearer on the Tuesday to a Masters champion on the Sunday.

How did this happen? How was this possible? What was the strange link between mourning and winning? If you were a sportswriter at that 1995 Masters this was all a captivating and thrilling challenge. It was great just being there. The question was simple: can you write it?

So I urge all budding sportswriters today: don't think about your career. Don't plan it in advance. Don't apply for journalism college. Indeed, scarcely give it a second thought.

Instead, just sort of blunder into it. It's the way to go.

Graham Spiers has written for the Times, The Herald and Scotland on Sunday during a 20-year career in sportswriting. He is also a regular broadcaster. Spiers has been honoured seven times at the Scottish Press Awards, including being voted sportswriter of the year on four occasions.

TO ABSENT FRIENDS AND A GENTLER AGE

By Chick Young

Hughie Taylor, bless him. And John MacKenzie, the Voice of Football. Legends in a day when the football writing business was just about everything it isn't now.

They were good to me when I was battering at the door of journalism trying to get in. Hugh, whose infectious laugh sucked through his teeth; it sounded like air brakes on a lorry. And as for the Voice, how good is that – to be known, even on social occasions, by your byline!

It was a gentler world then. And much the better for it, I'll wager. No mobile phones nor internet. Nor the curse of social media where every kid who can't tell an apostrophe from a catastrophe thinks he is Carl Bernstein or Bob Woodward. Not that I suspect many Twitterholics would know much about Watergate. Probably think it is something at the bottom of a reservoir. I'm talking late 1960s and 1970s here, when Hughie and John were kings at the Daily Record and Daily Express. I hung on their every word and they let me into their world. I have been unable to tunnel out in the years since.

It was a football writer's life for me, right from the start. I wanted to be a player of course, but I lacked one vital commodity: ability. And for once I showed a bit of foresight and volunteered to become the only male in the shorthand and typing class in fifth and sixth year at school. Pitman's and perfume, an awesome combination which played havoc with my hormones: happy days.

I applied for jobs from Kirkwall to Cowdenbeath, but one

summer's day in 1969 two letters dropped on the doormat. One from the Stornoway Gazette and one from the Daily Record: one rejection, one interview offer. And not the way round you would think. Aye, the good people of Lewis have no idea how lucky they got.

So, after a summer toiling for British Rail loading parcels on to trains at a depot in Glasgow, off I toddled for a princely £4 a week into the Hope Street offices of the Record which, at the time, was just overtaking the Express as the biggest-selling newspaper in the country. I was on my way. Maybe not quite sure where to, but at 18 years old I cared not a jot. Bright lights, action, at the very least Fleet Street, surely?

Well no, actually. What I had to settle for in the early '70s was Girvan, for the now defunct and sadly missed Carrick Herald, and Irvine, for the Irvine Herald ... taking the scenic route to stardom, I suppose. The late Ken Gallacher, another legend of Scottish football writing taken from us far too early, was another who steered my professional life. He pointed me in the direction of my first fulltime football-writing job, with Charles Buchan's Football Monthly in London.

A theme was beginning to emerge. The Carrick Herald had closed while I was working for it and in June 1974 they locked the door on the magazine. There were plenty of similar cases to follow including Scottish Football Weekly magazine and the Scottish Daily News. I wanted a reputation as a good reporter. I was getting one as a jinx.

It was with the Scottish Daily News that I enjoyed my first foreign assignment, to Iceland with Celtic. Marvellous. And none of this nipping in the night before and straight back after the match. We flew out on the Sunday and came back on the Thursday, and despite strict instructions from Messrs Taylor and MacKenzie to have a quiet debut abroad, there was an embarrassing scene with two Icelandic girls, a lift door and a game of poker. But I won't bore you with that tale for the time being ...

To be honest, in my personal life I have made a few dodgy decisions, should have turned right instead of left on more than one occasion, but a football writer's life was the one for me.

I've seen the world and cried shamelessly – never the neutral observer when the national team play – when I watched Scotland win the European Youth Championships in Finland in 1982 and when much the same bunch of lads reached the quarter-finals of the under-19 World Championship in Mexico a year later.

World Cups in Spain in 1982, Mexico 1986, Italy 1990, France 1998, Germany 2006 and South Africa 2010 were great, even if my nation failed to qualify for the latter two.

Maurice Johnston signing for Rangers – maybe Scottish football's most extraordinary hold-your-breath moment until the same club went into administration, other clubs dying (some of shame), European finals, owners who had never been anywhere near the Wild West turning clubs into cowboy outfits and scenes of shame from Copenhagen to Cordoba; I've reported on most of them and been involved in a few.

I wonder sometimes about what Hughie and the Voice would have made of what I made of their legacy. To be fair they couldn't stop laughing about the night in Reykjavik and the Icelandic ladies. They were the first to tell me you can't be at the coalface of journalism for every hour the good Lord grants us.

It's a different world now, Scottish football spiralling spectacularly out of control, death threats and bullets in the post to managers, machinations, madness and mayhem. Fun? Sometimes I think they couldn't spell it any more. I honestly think I have seen the best of the old business, timed my run to just about perfection. We've lost too many old friends and too many newspapers.

And don't blame me. There were one or two in whose downfall I played no part at all. Just a couple.

Chick Young has been at the coalface of football journalism – newspapers, magazines, radio and television – for more than four decades. He has watched many of them close around him but claims that at least one was not his fault. But he still prefers to be known as the captain of the legendary charity football side Dukla Pumpherston, the drinking team with a football problem.

THE CHANGING MAN

By Ron Scott

Having started with the Sunday Post in 1968 before most of my present-day colleagues were even born, I thought it would be enlightening to reveal what it was like working in the days before the advent of tape recorders and laptops. And let me tell you, some of us have still not moved on from the swinging '60s!

The introduction of computers undoubtedly changed the way newspapers are produced beyond recognition for those of us old enough to remember the hot-metal days transforming into an all-electronic age. However, an equally major change in my lifetime is the way we obtain stories.

Back in the '60s press conferences were unheard of while press officers had not even been invented. You were lucky to be allowed over the front doorstep of a football club to talk to players and managers when I started. I vividly remember trying to catch a word with the then Aberdeen manager Eddie Turnbull as he headed for his car after a game at Pittodrie. "What the f**k do you want?" was the norm, especially if the Dons had not won.

Players were easier to track down. They were mostly of my own age so I knew their favourite watering holes after matches. Mobile phones had not been invented then. In fact, very few players even had telephones at home although those who did were normally listed in the phone book. No ex-directory numbers then.

Most of us knew where players lived so it was common to doorstep them. I had a sports editor who insisted you waited until your target returned home otherwise you were not allowed back into the office. Sometimes you were camped outside someone's house till all hours. The usual approach was, "Can I have a quick word?" Martin Buchan famously replied, "Velocity."

Mostly you ran an idea past your target without even taking a note, never mind a tape-recording. Once you realised the player was on the same wavelength, you were off and running. I was never accused of misquoting anyone; it was not only shorthand typists who transcribed. I remember stunting a picture to go with Jocky Scott sending Dundee a written transfer request. My photographer actually snapped him posting the letter. Years later, when Jocky was manager of Dundee, I had to remind him of this when he wasn't too happy at me reporting one of his players wanted away.

My early days were when journalists were used to tap players for other clubs. Agents hadn't been invented then either. When Richard Gough was emerging with Dundee United he quickly became a prime target for a move to a bigger club. As soon as I let him know Tottenham Hotspur were interested, Gough was determined to move. Having helped bring player and club together I waited for my pay-off. It arrived one Saturday night when Spurs manager David Pleat phoned to tell me their £750,000 offer had been accepted and that the player had been given permission to travel south to thrash out terms. I was feeling happy with myself after seeing the Sunday Post's headline the next morning, as I met up for an inter-club golf match between my club in Dundee, Downfield, and Aberdeen's Murcar. 'Gough signs for Spurs today' it said.

I'd no sooner boarded the bus for Aberdeen than someone said I'd taken a big chance. He'd been out the previous evening with among others Gordon Wallace, then coaching at Tannadice. My golf partner was able to tell me Chelsea had matched Spurs' offer and that Gough was off to London to talk to both clubs.

No wonder I started six, seven, seven at Murcar; my mind was all over the place. I didn't relax until I phoned home to be told by my wife big Richard had phoned to say he had indeed signed for Tottenham. You can imagine the first place I headed for.

The Scottish Football Writers' Association has gone a long way in improving working conditions by ensuring we are all allowed access to managers after games. However, these all-in press conferences make it very difficult for anyone to land a story to him/herself.

One of the most amusing incidents I've been involved in was with Alex Ferguson long before he became a knight of the realm. Aberdeen were defending the European Cup Winners' Cup in Budapest against Ujpest Dozsa. They played the Hungarians off the park yet still contrived to lose 2-0 thanks mainly to some profligate finishing from Mark McGhee.

Fergie was furious and told me he was going to sort McGhee out once and for all by signing Charlie Nicholas from Arsenal. In fairness the Dons boss had had a few by this time.

When we arrived back at Aberdeen Airport the following day, Fergie asked me if I wanted my usual few minutes with him at the baggage reclaim. I reminded him he'd already given me a good line the previous evening. Initially he said that was off the record but his mind quickly moved into overdrive. "Aye, go ahead and use it. We've still got the second leg to come and it might inspire McGhee to get the finger out," he said.

Fergie's tactics worked – and how. The Reds won the second leg 3-0 to make it to the semi-finals for the second season in succession thanks to a McGhee hat-trick. Nicholas did indeed sign for Aberdeen but not for another three years.

No-one will ever be able to stand in the way of change. Like myself though, you don't necessarily have to agree. Most of my colleagues know where I stand. And I certainly get more enjoyment looking back, that's for sure.

Sunday Post chief football writer Ron Scott has spent his entire working life with DC Thomson, having started straight from school in 1964. He's covered three World Cup finals, two European Championship finals and more games abroad than he cares to remember. He always says the key to conquering the job is knowing how to enjoy yourself!

RONALD WAS A DUTCH OF CLASS

By Michael Baillie

Sometimes getting a great interview can simply come down to being in the right place at the right time, as I once discovered while sitting in the lobby of the plush Grand Hotel Krasnopolsky in Amsterdam's Dam Square.

As I waited for the check-out desk to clear before moving on to another city hotel to join the rest of the Scottish press pack assigned to follow then SPL champions Rangers on their pre-season trip to Belgium and Holland, a galaxy of multi-million pound football stars started to appear. Clarence Seedorf was waiting in the queue to check-out while the De Boer twins, Frank and Ronald, were milling around the lobby as well as former Celtic striker Pierre van Hooijdonk. Suddenly the majority of the Dutch squad for Euro 2000, who had fallen to Italy on penalties at the semi-final stage of the finals in their homeland, were in the lobby of the five-star hotel.

What were they all doing there? Well, they had all been guests at their international team-mate and then Barcelona star striker Patrick Kluivert's wedding reception the previous evening.

If only I had known that when I returned to the hotel in the wee small hours after enjoying a Saturday evening in Amsterdam, I could have attempted to gatecrash the wedding of the former Ajax 'Golden Boy' who had climbed off the bench to bag the winner in the 1995 Champions League final against AC Milan.

What a story that would have been but sadly it never materialised as instead, none the wiser that the party was taking place in the hotel, I made my way to bed. Now, though, just two months into my career at the Scottish Daily Mirror, I had the chance to interview some of the biggest names in European football.

After rummaging through my computer bag for my Dictaphone I approached Frank de Boer to see if he'd be willing to spare me a few minutes' chat. In hindsight Frank probably wasn't the best one to go and ask as he was standing on the front steps of the hotel about to walk to his car and leave.

One knockback, but there were still plenty more to ask. My next target was Van Hooijdonk and I approached and introduced myself to the Dutch international who had starred for Celtic for two years before departing to Nottingham Forest in 1997. I explained that en route from the Belgian city of Genk, where Rangers had won a pre-season friendly 3-1 on Friday evening, I had a few days in Amsterdam before moving on to Enschede which would be the press pack's base for the second leg of the Ibrox outfit's pre-season break, and asked, would Pierre be up for an interview? Pierre was charming but because of his connections to Celtic he very politely declined my interview request. It probably wouldn't be the best for him to speak about Dick Advocaat's ever-growing Dutch colony at Rangers.

Two down, but undeterred I then approached the second De Boer twin Ronald, who was then starring for Barcelona alongside his brother and a number of Dutch internationals, including the player whose wedding he had just attended. Ronald was willing to give me an interview. Result.

The Dutch master waxed lyrical about Advocaat and the number of players from his homeland that were starring for Rangers, which had grown that summer by the signings of Bert Konterman and Fernando Ricksen. He chatted about Rangers' chances in the forthcoming Champions League and how with Advocaat at the helm and with his international team-mates Artur Numan and Giovanni van Bronckhorst they had a great opportunity of making a major impact in Europe's premier club competition.

It was great stuff from Ronald, who just a few weeks later would add to the Dutch contingent at Ibrox when he made the switch from

Barcelona to Rangers; as the Scottish press would discover he was always an engaging character to interview. He was never short of an opinion and, unlike far too many footballers these days, was not afraid to express it.

With a back-page splash and spread secured from my chat with Ronald I was rather chuffed with myself as I checked out of the Grand Hotel Krasnopolsky, and then made my way to join up with the rest of the Scottish press pack. As I made my way to their hotel, however, I realised I now had a dilemma. Do I share my exclusive interview with the rest of my daily colleagues or do I keep it for myself? Naturally I would have been entitled to keep it to myself; after all it was my interview. The question was whirring through my head as to what I should do as I joined up with the press guys, checked into a new hotel and then headed out for lunch and to watch the men's Wimbledon final between Pete Sampras and Pat Rafter.

As my colleagues and I enjoyed a few refreshments we were discussing what we would send back to our various sports desks the following day. Rangers were not arriving in Holland until Tuesday and while Andrei Kancheslskis had been interviewed in Genk, this was for the Monday's papers. This meant there was one day we were short of copy. At that point my decision was made and I piped up that I had an interview I'd be willing to share with my colleagues to get them out of their predicament. As I was new to the job and this was my first pre-season trip I thought it would be better to share my Ronald de Boer interview and ingratiate myself to the press pack. I explained about Kluivert's wedding and the Dutch squad being there and how Ronald was only too happy to speak about Rangers and their chances in the Champions League. Needless to say a celebratory round of drinks was ordered.

As I said earlier, sometimes getting a great interview comes down to being in the right place at the right time. It was just luck that I was staying in the Grand Hotel Krasnopolsky for that one night rather than with the rest of the media. I used my good fortune to conduct an interview with Ronald de Boer and rather than keep it for myself, as the Scottish press pack were away for the next 10 days together with Rangers I thought it would be better to pass it round to my colleagues.

It helped them accept me and, in return, they helped me out during the rest of the trip.

So, while I could have had my first superstar exclusive, I have never doubted that I did the right thing.

Michael Baillie has reported on Scottish football matches for 17 years and has worked full-time in sports journalism for 12 years; for the Scottish Daily Mirror and as a freelance reporter for the past six years. His articles regularly appear in the Daily Express, Daily Star, Sun, Daily Record, Daily Mail and The Herald.

MEETINGS WITH REMARKABLE MEN. AND DAVID CAMERON

By Kenny MacDonald

One of the perks that comes with being involved in this dodge is that from time to time it affords you what the American humorist SJ Perelman used to call "a brush with the quality".

Perhaps the high-water mark of this came in October 1993. Me and the Sunday Post's Doug Baillie, larger-than-life doyen of Scottish reporters, had come out of a press conference in Glasgow's Hilton Hotel and gone into the elevator. The doors began to close. Just as they almost met, two very large hands pushed them back open and we found ourselves looking at a couple of huge, dapper men. Between them came an older, smaller, somewhat hunched black man, who nodded imperceptibly at us, and was joined by his two bodyguards for the ride down to the foyer.

I'd like to report I asked Nelson Mandela – for it was he, in town to be given the Freedom of the City – what it was like on Robben Island, how he survived his ordeal, and what he thought of that Special AKA record about him. Instead Doug and I just gawped at the back of his head – the hair black but greying – like a couple of schoolboys. Then the lift doors opened and he was gone.

To go briskly to the opposite extreme, one day a few years ago, in the perceived manner of Sunday newspaper reporters everywhere, I was catching up on staring vacantly out of the window when, loping down the office towards me like some ghastly apparition, came the future Prime Minister of our country. David Cameron, then Leader of the Opposition, was being ferried around the News International premises and had washed up at the News of the World.

In that blokey way he has – the one guaranteed to set your teeth on edge – he brayed, "Well, guys, what's Boruc been up to this week?" The then-Celtic goalkeeper's private life had at the time been followed enthusiastically by the News of the World's news reporters.

Cameron – who you just knew wouldn't have known Artur Boruc from Arthur Askey – was surrounded by a gang of jabbering sycophants and you could tell the conversation that had taken place between them before he'd set foot in the office … "That's them – that scruffy, dozy looking lot down there. They're the sports desk. Here's what to say to them …"

Another surreal encounter was with Uri Geller. I'd heard all the stories but, like most people, thought it was all a bunch of guff. Then, one night in Tel Aviv three of us – from memory, Darrell King of the Evening Times, former Rangers striker Derek Johnstone and I – got in tow with the generously haired one. Yes, just like that. We struck up a conversation and before anyone could say 'complete charlatan', Geller dashed into an adjacent hotel and emerged clutching a spoon. Then, before our very eyes, he rubbed it for a matter of seconds and it flopped backwards like limp spaghetti. What made this spectacle even more notable was that Derek got on his mobile and rang back to Radio Clyde, whose football show was still on air, and described the whole spectacle, complete with Uri interview, to a bemused west of Scotland audience.

Singer Loudon Wainwright III, a hero of mine, proved to be as easy-going in what psychologists term 'real life' as he was on a stage. Over a latté nearly 30 years ago – in those days a beverage of quite mind-boggling sophistication, available only in Glasgow's West End – he cheerfully admitted the question he was most often asked was, "What is Alan Alda really like?" This was a reference to the appearances Wainwright made in the TV series MASH in the mid-70s. (The answer, incidentally, was, "Very nice – though I don't think he's ever had a Martini in his life").

Similarly in the exciting world of the popsters, in the early '90s I got it into my head that what the world badly needed was for some-one to track down the obscure, largely forgotten 1970s songwriter David Ackles. At the time it was almost 20 years since he'd made a record.

The labyrinthine process of locating him to his farm in Tujunga in the hills above Los Angeles was duly documented for a magazine called, inexplicably, Ptolemaic Terrascope, who were quite under-standably thrilled that some mug had found one of their idols, writ-ten an article about him, and didn't even want paid. A few months later a letter popped through the door from Ackles himself, thank-ing me for taking the trouble to find him and complimenting me on the article. I haven't had many letters like it from SPL players.

The late John Peel was another gent. My friend Muz and I took him for an Indian meal in Islington in the late '70s, to interview him for a fanzine we were running when we both should've been work-ing. He told us a story from the '60s about a conversation he'd had with Jack Bruce, bassist of famed lumpenrockers Cream. Peel was complaining about having to go and see some dodgy hippie-dippie flower-power band, probably called something like the Twitterlings of Thredsnody, and how he was dreading the prospect. Bruce leaned over conspiratorially and slipped a couple of small, pill-like ob-jects into Peel's hands. "These'll get you through them OK," he said knowingly.

Peel, not wishing to appear dim, nodded and slipped them in his pocket. In the weeks that followed, with no idea what the things were, he sought out the opinions of experts in hallucinogens. None had seen anything like them before, though one habitué of the phar-macological world poked at them for a bit and tried to set them ablaze before finally proffering the opinion they were probably some sort of opiate.

Time passed with Peel none the wiser but finally, he grasped the nettle. Probably while listening to the first Soft Machine album, he popped the two of them in his mouth, swallowed, and waited for either nirvana, the rapture or vomiting.

Nothing much happened and one night soon afterwards Peel

was at the famed UFO club and there in a corner was Bruce. The thirst for knowledge overpowering our hero, he sidled over and got into conversation with the musician. Eventually, he said, "Do you remember a few months ago you slipped me something you said would see me through the Burblenurfs of Rhapsodia be-in I was going to?" Bruce replied that he did.

"Well," confessed Peel, "I'm not terribly up on that whole scene, man, and I was just wondering, well, exactly, er, what they were?"

Bruce looked at him with a puzzled expression on his face, leaned over, and said, "Earplugs."

Kenny MacDonald started what is hysterically referred to as his career in 1977 at the Weekly News, before slithering acrobatically up the greasy pole to the position of sports editor of the Irish edition. He subsequently worked for the News of the World and is currently living the dream at the Scottish Sun. His proudest talent is an ability to recite the alphabet as a word.

TELEVISION MAKETH THE MAN

By Liam McLeod

I t springs to my mind every time I arrive at a football ground, be it Albion Rovers' Cliftonhill or Manchester United's Old Trafford.

The 'it' was round about the turn of the year 1996, from recollection. That would have made me 16 years old and in fifth year at secondary school. My classmates and I were awaiting news of where our work placements were to be. Some had gone for shop assistant, some mechanic, some simple office worker.

I, of course, had to be different.

As an Aberdonian living in Dyce and in the shadow of the neighbouring heliport, working on the rigs, or learning a trade – unlike the vast majority of my school friends – was not for me. Because I was never the footballer I wanted to be and because nobody wanted me to drum in their rock band, I decided I wanted a career in the media. It was kind of obvious to me that sport, and more pertinently, football, would be the way forward. My attitude was, 'If I can't play the game, I'd be as well talking about it'.

So, that takes me back to that Biology classroom on the ground floor of Dyce Academy in '96. As the heady days of Britpop raged outside those walls, was it to be a case of broken dreams inside them? The teacher began reading out who had been assigned what, as I waited in anticipation of confirmation that I would be going to Grampian TV, the BBC or Northsound Radio. Mr Large then read out my name and, in a laughter-stifling voice, said: "Liam, we couldn't get you anything in television."

My classmates found this highly amusing. They weren't being nasty; the laughter was for the fact that I had even considered applying for that as my placement, not that I had failed to get it. Nope, I was off to Halfords instead. Archie Macpherson's job was safe.

Undeterred, I went off to college and spent the ensuing years travelling between Aberdeen and Edinburgh. Playing an important role at this point was Andrew Cotter, the now familiar voice of the BBC's rugby, golf and tennis coverage. He was then the sports editor at the now defunct Scot FM in Edinburgh. A simple 10-minute chat he afforded me the day after Scotland defeated England at Wembley that ended in eventual Euro 2000 play-off disappointment, had me cranking doors open at last. I would subsequently go on to annoy him and his successors for months into giving me opportunities I had thought were only pipe dreams after the disdain with which my work experience request had been treated.

So eventually the opportunity came and I was off on the train to do my first game for a radio station with the job of collating post-match interviews from Love Street where St Mirren were taking on Dundee. It was the sunny Saturday of August 19th 2000. Finally, I had arrived. I had no idea what I was doing. Where was I going to sit? I was thinking of questions to ask the managers before the game had even started. I saw people like Chick Young sat there watching me, wondering who this new upstart was. I felt like a wildebeest just before the lions close in.

It finished 2-1 to the hosts, with Steven McGarry scoring a late winner. It was then time for my big moment. I had been warned previously that the then Dundee boss Ivano Bonetti liked to greet you with a hug. What was this, The Godfather? While not quite a hug, Bonetti's warm reception for me was to prove a red herring when dealing with a beaten boss in the future.

Such an example arrived a few months later as then St Johnstone manager Sandy Clark – a colleague these days – gave me a very public dressing down for daring to ask him about the future of his star striker Keigan Parker in front of the old main stand at Easter Road. The 3-0 hammering his team took that day at the hands of Hibernian didn't help my cause. The commentaries would come five years and lots of knock-backs later, after involvement with a BBC/RNIB initiative to provide football clubs with commentators for blind and partially sighted supporters.

The first game I ever covered for the BBC was a match between Livingston and Falkirk. Donald Garden – the interviewer who had famously incited Alex Ferguson to slaughter his Aberdeen side after a 1-0 Scottish Cup final win over Rangers – had handed me the opportunity to work at this game for BBC Radio Scotland's Sportsound programme, having met him on a course. I had listened to Sportsound all my life; the voices of Alastair Alexander, Derek Rae, David Begg, Bob Crampsey and Richard Gordon were my Saturday staple when Aberdeen were away from home, so this was something of an honour. But I spent the 90 minutes more concerned about poor Donald to my right. I have never seen a man more nervous as he was that day. He would deny this, but with every mistake I made, he'd jolt out of his seat.

I've been doing radio commentaries ever since and upsetting managers ever since too. Jim Jefferies, for example, heard me describe his team as fortunate to secure a 0-0 draw in a game at Rugby Park. The following week, as I snuck into the Kilmarnock dressing room to ask him for his team for their next game, I was given an almighty dressing down. So much so, this caused his Killie players in the vicinity to enjoy my demise with one piping up, "Good, it's not just us then!"

Since then, frighteningly, I have been able to commentate on matches for both radio and television, following in the footsteps of Jock Brown and that Archie bloke I mentioned earlier. The irony being that I'd not really considered the TV option since Mr Large's scathing tone.

A similar scathing tone was heard when Scotland manager Craig Levein commented as I asked for his team to play Wales in a Nations Cup match in Dublin, "You should know, you picked it!"

He was referring to something I'd said about Charlie Mulgrew being deserving of a Scotland call-up in one of my commentaries.

To be fair, Mulgrew was picked for Scotland less than a year later; maybe I am in the wrong vocation after all.

And no, I didn't do the placement at Halfords.

Liam McLeod has commentated for BBC Radio Scotland's Sportsound since August 2005 and Sportscene since 2007. He spent some time with Scot FM and Northsound radio before a brief spell with STV. He also works as a broadcast journalist on Radio Scotland programmes such as Good Morning Scotland and Newsdrive, and has also presented Sportsound.

HOW CAMERON DIAZ JOINED THE SCOTTISH PRESS PACK

By Lisa Gray

It's fair to say that being a female football reporter has its moments but I have to be honest and admit that moonlighting as a Hollywood celebrity isn't usually part of the job description.

Unfortunately for me, my spare time is not generally spent straddling a motorbike driven by Tom Cruise or counting the likes of Justin Timberlake among my conquests.

So you can imagine my surprise when, in Seville with Rangers for a Champions League game in December 2009, I was accosted by a local radio journalist demanding I go live on air and pretend to be none other than Cameron Diaz. I was up against the clock. I had Walter Smith quotes to file ahead of deadline. I had a mixed zone to get to and players to blank me. But the request from my new Spanish friend seemed simple enough. Apparently, the only requirement for the job was an ability to speak English so insert your own gag about having a face for radio here …

Diaz and Tom were in the city filming Knight and Day, and were VIP guests at the Estadio Ramon Sanchez Pizjuan (trying saying that after a few sangrias) while taking a break from their hectic schedules. And, having managed to give the paparazzi the slip afterwards, it was left to me to save the day. Which is why listeners of a late-night Seville radio show were treated to the dulcet tones of 'Cameron' declaring: 'Hi! I'm Cameron Diaz and I just LOVE Juan Fernandez and his fabulous show!'

Speaking of brushes with celebrity, there was also the time I travelled to Israel for a Uefa Cup tie, again with Rangers. Then assistant manager Ally McCoist raced over to the assembled media at Glasgow Airport and, bursting with excitement, informed us that none other than Bruce Dickinson would be flying the plane to Tel Aviv!

Yup, I had no idea who he was talking about either.

However, the rest of the hacks looked suitably impressed and, thinking it might be a famous former player and not wanting to look like a total idiot, I nodded along eagerly, murmuring, 'Wow. Bruce Dickinson, eh?'

Turns out he wasn't an ex-pro from way before my time or a perma-tanned antiques expert from Dickinson's Real Deal (that was my second guess) – he was actually the lead singer with Iron Maiden. Now, if you'd told me Robbie Williams would be donning a pilot's cap and getting behind the controls, I might have been excited. But an ageing 1980s rocker? He didn't even have long hair or wear black leather, and I had more tattoos than him for goodness sake.

Myself and my colleagues bumped into Bruce and his cabin crew in a bar later that night. I've always been more of a Wham! kind of girl to be honest but, after a couple of large Chardonnays, I decided to get into the spirit of things and request his autograph on my exposed shoulder in what I thought was a very rock n' roll fashion.

The next morning I awoke to find said scribble smeared all over the pristine hotel bed-sheets and realised to my horror the 'pen' I'd proffered was actually my new Chanel khol eyeliner. For male readers, think the equivalent cost of about five pints. Worst still, there wasn't even any chance of flogging the autograph on eBay.

At least I'd asked for that one. Unlike the time when, as a rookie reporter covering lower-division games for the Daily Record, I crossed paths with Godfather actor Robert Duvall at, of all places, an Albion Rovers match that had attracted all of about 100 spectators. He was researching a film he was making about Scottish football and I was looking for a story. "Mr Duvall?" I enquired nervously. He took one look at me, grabbed my notepad, scrawled his name and sauntered off into the Coatbridge night without a backwards glance.

Months later when I watched A Shot at Glory, I couldn't help but think Duvall should have put more effort into his Scottish accent. Then again, some might say my own shot at glory as Cameron Diaz wasn't much better.

Lisa Gray joined the Press Association in May 2000, becoming chief Scottish football writer six years later. She has braved Old Firm derbies, covered Scotland's representatives in Europe at home and abroad, and watched Rangers lose the Uefa Cup final in Manchester in 2008. Unfortunately, Scotland's dismal qualification record in recent times means working at the Euros and the World Cup has so far eluded her.

TELL ME SOMETHING I DON'T KNOW

By Gordon Waddell

Tell me something I don't know. Rule No.1 of interviewing. First advice ever given to me, and still the best. Premise being, if it's something you've seen, and I've seen, and all I'm doing is getting someone else to talk about it, I'm telling you nothing you don't already know. So what's the point, right?

What's the point in watching a player slide on his knees across a sodden park, roll around like a puppy in an Andrex factory, pretend-pee on the corner flag and be swamped by delirious team-mates, only to ask, "How did you feel about the goal, Dave?"

So tell me something I don't know.

What happens in dressing rooms. On training grounds, in homes, hotel rooms, on flights, in the physio's. They're the places readers don't get access to. So get them access.

Like George Burley's office at Derby. Walls completely bare apart from three frames.

You'd think his, 'I was the best manager in England' award from 2001 would be one of them, the one he bagged ahead of a title-winning Sir Fergie and Liverpool's cup treble-winning boss Gerard Houllier.

You'd be wrong. All the things he'd done in his career, and two of them, weirdly, were Scottish Cup Man of the Match certificates from games against Clydebank and Motherwell.

The other was a picture of long-time No.2 Dale Roberts putting their Ayr United players through a gruelling session – a poignant daily reminder of a friend whose life was heartbreakingly cut short by cancer. And a doorway into an emotional interview we'd never have done if it hadn't been hanging there.

Every so often, though, you stick your head through a doorway like that and BAM! – some bastard clatters it shut in your face. Like Duncan Ferguson.

It's the 1995 FA Cup final. Everton have just beaten Man United thanks to Paul Rideout's winner. It's in the days before mixed zones and media officers, and players wearing noise-cancelling, journalist-cancelling headphones. At the end of the game, you just went down the old tunnel at Wembley to the dressing room door and took your chances.

I was there for the Sunday Mail, Bill Leckie was there for the Record, and out walks Big Dunc. Only Scot in the winning team, only real target for us.

It's a week before he's due to be sentenced for the headbutt on Jock McStay which would eventually see him in Barlinnie.

Still …

"Big Man, Big Man … Dunc, over here!"

Eye contact. Good.

Malevolent narrowing of eyes upon recognition. Baaaad.

"Can you spare a word for the Scottish guys, Big Yin?"

"Aye, I'll spare you two – F**k yez."

No chip on the shoulder there, then …

But not exactly getting the paper filled on deadline either. So God bless the legend that is Neville Southall, who walked out at Dunc's back, shook his head, came straight up to us and said, "Can I give you something, lads?"

We ended up getting half an hour with him out on the pitch, chapter and verse. Top man, top set of quotes.

The postscript came 17 years later – and it cost me the grand sum of a Mars Bar to finally get Ferguson to speak to a Scottish journalist for the first time since he'd done a piece with Fraser Mackie in the Rangers News in 1994. It came from a call to the SFA's Jim Fleeting to find out who was at Largs doing their badges in June.

"Big Dunc's doing his 'A' Introductory."

"Next …"

"How, what's up with the Big Yin? He's fantastic, a real enthusiast; guys love him."

"There's more chance of Howard Hughes interviewing Lord Lucan sitting on top of Shergar."

"Ah'll get him tae speak tae ye."

"No chance. Won't happen."

"Bet me a Mars Bar …"

"I'll bet you the deeds to my house."

About a week later, the phone goes. "Bring a Mars Bar …"

And there we were, stood in the blazing sunshine at Inverclyde, the man looking every inch the same at 40 as he did at 20. Except without the angry force-field around him. "The baby that everyone remembers," he says, "that young man, he's gone."

And in his place was a grown-up, humble, aspiring coach, a doting dad of three, a loving husband. He was terrific. They say a leopard never changes his spots, but can they find their inner pussy cat? Who knows …

All I know is it was value for money at 60p.

But then again, so was George Graham, and he cost a bloody fortune.

I've not interviewed many people who can genuinely make the piano player stop simply by walking into a room, but he could. The room was the famous Langans Brasserie in Mayfair, the wallet-emptying result that comes of a rookie saying "you choose" to a man who oozes upmarket through every stitch of his Armani suit.

I booked the table in my name, arrived sharp (Rule No.2 of journalism: if you're five minutes early, you're 10 minutes late) and was greeted by a maitre d' who managed to raise an eyebrow into a question mark and look down his nose at me all in one remarkably well-honed, keep-the-plebs-on-the-pavement welcome.

"Ah yes, Mr Waw-DELL [pet hate, right there], you're at table 4352 – up the stairs, past the gents, out the fire exit, round the corner, down two flights … just look out for the golden arches …"

So I say I'll take a seat at the bar and wait for my dining companion.

In walks George. Piano player stops. So does the maitre d'. Hugs him like a father would a son. Then steps back with a look of bafflement. Points at the reservations list. Shrugs. Can't see his name anywhere. Until George points over at me. And the maitre d' has a heart attack at the realisation that he is about to send Graham for a happy meal.

So he comes over. "Mr Waw-DELL, there seems to have been a mistake with your table – this way, sir." And off we go, front and centre. But as he's walking me there, I feel his hand dig into my bicep. "'Ere," he says, "y'didn't tell me you wuz bringing f**king ROYAAALTY for lunch. NEVAAAH do that t'me again!"

Turns out Michael was a Spurs fan. The marbles in his mouth were clearly inserted every morning, not inherited at birth.

Again, though, Graham himself was fantastic. Cover piece for the magazine, back page for the paper – and a win for the deputy sports editor in the sweep for how big the receipt for the expenses chitty would be.

It's all the wee things, the details, the background colour that make for the best interviews.

Like speaking to Paul Sturrock about his Parkinson's disease while he's getting a haircut in the living room of his mate's house.

Like Gordon Strachan on the 9.03 from Southampton Airport to Waterloo, with two octogenarians listening to every word. One of those tiny old-school compartments. It was like he'd been transported back in time.

"See when I was at Dundee," he grins, "we used to get trains like this from Edinburgh all the time.

"The compartments had four seats. And if you were really lucky you could stretch out and get a kip [Like he'd have needed FOUR seats!]. There was usually a crowd of us. I'd get my hands all burnt because I was the kid who got sent for the tea and bacon rolls. Then I'd blow my £13-a-week wages on the cards!

"I'd have no money and always end up getting a loan from Bobby Robinson. What a lovely man he was. Didn't drink, didn't smoke

– should never have been in football, should he?"

And he tails off. "He died of cancer at 47 …" snapping him out of his reverie.

He'd just turned 47 a week earlier.

The third-best journalist in his family, Gordon followed in dad Ken and brother Bruce's footsteps after a spell finding out that a career in accountancy would have seen him gouge his still-beating heart out with a rusty melon scoop through sheer boredom. He started out as a copy boy at the Sunday Scot before joining the 7-Day Press agency and writing for the cult Scottish Football Today magazine. A brief spell in London with Today ended with a call from the Sunday Mail in 1994, and he's been in the building ever since, including a four-year stint as the youngest-ever Sports Editor of the Daily Record.

THE (SECOND) BEST JOB IN THE WORLD

By Pat Nevin

There are some jobs you land about which you are never allowed to complain and in my working life I have rarely had much to moan about. If there is a better job than being a professional footballer I haven't come across it, but if there is one that comes close then it is being paid to sit and watch matches, then have a chat about them.

I had 19 years of playing followed by over a decade as a pundit; let me make it perfectly clear, I know how lucky I am. If there is one downside then it is being away from my wife and kids more often than I would choose, but plenty of others have to suffer just that scenario while doing jobs they deplore.

I prefer to consider the positives. Sitting in a remote studio analysing is thoroughly enjoyable and even testing when you work for a company that allows you to treat the viewer like an intelligent adult. Analysis that shows the watching fan something he or she might not have witnessed from the position of a former pro can be a fulfilling role. Even the programmes in which nothing is allowed other than the crash-bang-wallop of goals, saves and debatable refereeing decisions can still be fun if a little less rewarding.

The real joy however is being at the stadiums. As I write I am in a hotel room in London getting prepared to cover Arsenal v Manchester United. Last week I was in Barcelona and halfway through the season I have already covered over 40 games all over the UK and in Europe. Being away from the family may be a bit of a drag but fortunately I love travelling, seeing new places, meeting different people and sampling various cultures. The question I am thinking about right now is, which was the best/most enjoyable game I ever covered as a pundit?

It is a tough one to answer; it certainly isn't going to be a game that Aston Villa played in eastern Bulgaria a few years back. That one included the TV truck being involved in a fatal accident, and myself twice almost being killed by a taxi driver who clearly had no idea how to control his car over 40 mph, which was a concern as he flew the 81 miles between Bourgas and Varna at an average speed of about 100mph. It also included terrible grub, the ensuing bout of food poisoning, and a pistol being drawn on one of my colleagues, then placed against his right temple as I was chatting to him in a bar after the game. Strangely enough I can't recall much about the game itself, not even who won. I just wanted to get home alive from Europe's modern-day equivalent of the Wild West.

Moscow doesn't have too many good memories either. Chelsea v Man United in the Champions League final was supposed to be the glory day. My former club Chelsea is my favoured English side, so losing on penalties after the skipper had a chance from the spot to win the trophy wasn't fun. A further problem was that I had just had a new hip inserted three weeks previously, was obviously still on crutches and was supposed to be resting instead of traipsing around the continent on Aeroflot. It turned out to be 60 hours without sleep and indeed rarely the opportunity even to sit down other than during the cramped flights there and back overnight. Standing on an airport bus for four hours outside the airport throughout the second night to allow the VIPs, the likes of Blatter and Platini, to swan through customs without having to wait beside or even see any supporters, just about took the biscuit.

It didn't actually take the aforementioned biscuit, that was heartily consumed the next day when both men went public to say that, "The organisation was a triumph and we did not see any logistical problems with playing the game in Russia, transportation was perfect as were the hotels."

Of course you didn't see any problems; you were ferried between the airport, the stadium and your five-star hotels in blacked-out limos while tens of thousands of others were herded on to freezing antiquated charabancs on the other side of a runway so as not to spoil your view. I hope they enjoyed their slap-up meal after the game with the other VIPs, while we had to wait for them to finish, gutted by the result, hungry, cold, exhausted and increasingly furious.

Strangely those occasions do live in the memory and can be laughed at (eventually), but Scotland being hammered by Holland 6-0 to crash out of the play-off for Euro 2004 is a wound that is still painful. It was bad enough going out, it was depressing to get so royally battered but I had to analyse it not for BBC Scotland but for Channel 5. As such there was a good chance there were quite a few English people watching and some of them would have enjoyed watching me squirm on behalf of my entire nation. The hope I/we displayed at the start of the game with our single-goal advantage was in stark contrast to the desolation at the end.

Isn't this very Scottish, I am trying to write about the highlights and I haven't even begun to get there yet. There have been plenty of great days. Last season in the space of a couple of weeks I went to see two Clasicos, an Old Firm derby, Liverpool v Man United and Chelsea v Arsenal. It gave me the opportunity to compare and contrast not only the styles of play but also the buzz around some of the world's greatest games. For noise, passion and pure atmosphere it wasn't even close – an evening game at Celtic Park between the Old Firm was streets ahead of the rest of them. I know many people hate the Old Firm games and I have my issues with it too, but I also love much of the extreme passion and the unequalled power cascading down from the stands. Even a common-or-garden league game between these two can assault the ears as much as a European semi-final between Real Madrid and Barcelona.

Talking of Barca, maybe they should provide the best single memory, after all they are arguably the greatest club team in the history of the game and it has been a privilege to cover them on numerous occasions. In Messi they have the finest player alongside Maradona that I have ever witnessed in the flesh, but they also have Iniesta and Xavi. This will be looked back on as a golden era with a golden team, but no, my favourite game doesn't involve Guardiola's gang; there was a better moment and it was in Korea on June 8th 2002.

BBC Radio 5 Live had kindly sent me out for the World Cup to crisscross the country for the month, catching a host of games in what was a joyous event for the locals in particular. A wonderful, friendly, honourable and respectful people, they provided some of the greatest spectacles you could imagine. After South Korea somewhat surprisingly won their first game, millions of people flooded the streets of Seoul to celebrate. At 3am I looked out of the 23rd-floor window of my hotel room to see a carpet of humanity, all wearing exactly the same 'Be The Reds' T-shirt, and to a man and a woman, almost all had the same jet-black hair. It looked like something Hollywood had fixed up on CGI; it was a sea of humanity which took the breath away.

I stared for a while amazed and then forced myself back into bed knowing that I had an 8.30am flight for my the next game. My last thought before nodding off was, it is going to be carnage down there in the morning after that party. The taxi arrived at six and as it took me through the now deserted city I couldn't believe what I was seeing. There wasn't any broken glass, not a single discarded fast-food container, no beer cans and I eventually started staring at the ground to see if there were even any used cigarette stubs. But no, the place was gleaming.

Imagine the same scene four hours after a multimillion-man party in the UK; it would look like a war zone. I asked the taxi driver what had happened. How could so much partying lead to so little mess, to which he casually answered, "In our society we all just clean the mess up on our way home." I love Korea.

Even so, that wasn't the moment; it actually came when I was down in the beautiful island of Jeju. Picture the scene: we were there for three days, it was constantly at a very pleasant 87 degrees. Our five-star hotel was on the top of a cliff and at the bottom was an endless, almost empty beach with crashing six-foot waves rolling in all day long. I love swimming and this was my idea of heaven.

The only work I had organised was for the last night when we had to amble down the road about half a mile to reach the most beautiful stadium I had ever seen. Then we just had to watch Brazil beat China 4-0 with a joyous display of exhilarating samba football. The scorers were Rivaldo, Ronaldo, Ronaldinho and Roberto Carlos. After the game the stadium was the venue for the most dramatic fireworks display I have ever witnessed. Half an hour later I wandered lazily back to the hotel alongside the commentators John Murray and Jonathan Pearce, both great friends of mine. As we sat outside on a warm, starry evening, sipping a particularly nice dry white wine, we simultaneously realised the madness of it all – we were actually getting paid for this!

We raised our glasses and I would like to do the same now and thank the Brazilians, the Korean people, the BBC and everyone who pays their licence fee. I promise you all, I never took a moment of it for granted.

In a 19-year football career, Pat Nevin played for Clyde, Chelsea, Everton, Tranmere Rovers, Kilmarnock and Motherwell. A gifted winger, he won 28 caps for Scotland. Since retiring he has worked as chief executive of Motherwell FC, as well as a football writer and broadcaster with BBC Radio Five Live and BBC Sportscene, among others.

NO BUSINESS LIKE SHOW-BUSINESS ...
EXCEPT FOOTBALL

By Brian Marjoribanks (Senior)

I t is spring of 1982, 11.30 on a Saturday morning and the recorded radio interview has just finished.

But Jock Stein is steadfastly refusing to leave the BBC studio. Is the Scotland manager waiting to challenge me about something I'd said recently on television? He did once, at Ayr Racecourse after I'd tipped Hibs to beat Celtic in the Scottish Cup final. But no, this time Stein just wants to talk. And over the course of a marvellously indiscreet hour Scotland's greatest-ever manager gives an unprompted and revealing insight into his personal football philosophy, and the intriguing characters that populated his teams.

Who was the biggest womaniser? Which player would he place on the bench with the sole purpose of introducing in a gladiatorial role whenever the opponents resorted to physical intimidation? The thickest? The biggest troublemaker? Nothing was off limits.

After the man who brought the European Cup home to a northern European club for the very first time had given me the privilege of an off-the-cuff guided tour through his stellar career, I could not help but think: how on earth had my own professional life taken me here?

And even 50 years on from taking my first steps on the road which would eventually lead to the BBC's sports department, it remains a tale the corporation's script writers would surely reject on the grounds of being too fanciful.

The story goes back a long way to a sunny July Saturday in 1961. I had auditioned that morning for entry to drama school in Glasgow and when I returned home there was a Jaguar car parked outside my home in Falkirk. The then Hearts manager, the legendary Tommy Walker, was waiting for my return and offered me a contract with the Tynecastle club.

I had already agreed to meet with the Hibs chairman, Harry Swan, the following Tuesday and decided to procrastinate on the Hearts offer. On the Monday morning I received a letter from Glasgow Drama School offering me a place and on the Tuesday night signed a two-year contact with Hibs. I naively thought that there was a vacancy at Easter Road for a centre-forward with Joe Baker having just departed for AC Torino!

I did manage to make my first-team debut for Hibs after five reserve-team games, scoring in the Edinburgh derby against Hearts at Tynecastle. I was training full-time at that point and became the first student to phone drama school to request three days off for an Inter Cities Trophy match in Lisbon against Belenenses.

Travelling from Falkirk to Glasgow then to Edinburgh to train quickly proved a problem and I switched to Edinburgh Drama School. Like many young professional footballers at that time, being a student and playing part-time also proved difficult, and despite moving to join Hearts it did not resolve the problem. At the end of my final year at drama school I was offered a season's contract at the Gateway Repertory Theatre in Edinburgh and decided to quit football. I was unaware of the media interest in such a move.

Every Scottish newspaper and many of the English ones carried the story. I was invited on to the Today programme by the late Jack de Manio and interviewed on my reasons for this unusual change of career. At the end of the interview he asked me to do a Shakespearean speech.

That afternoon I received a phone call from a television director in London who was casting an episode of Dr Finlay's Casebook, at that time the UK's No.1 drama series. He wanted a young actor to play the part of a Scottish footballer suffering from osteomyelitis, a bone disease in his leg (as anyone who ever saw me play for Hibs or Hearts will tell you, this was a shrewd piece of casting by the BBC).

The director arranged to meet me in Edinburgh the following day, and after auditioning I found myself one day out of drama school and cast in the leading part of this outstanding series. I had never even been inside a television studio before! I was promptly invited back on to the Jack de Manio programme with Jack rightly saying that his interview had resulted in my casting.

I was released for a month by the Gateway Theatre to do the part which included filming the outdoor scenes at Recreation Park, Alloa, just after Alloa had lost 7-2 to East Fife. The Alloa lads came back on to the field in front of about 200 fans brandishing the banners of the fictional Tannochbrae United.

The English director gave his instruction through a megaphone to the Alloa players: "In the first scene Mr Marjoribanks will waltz round four players, put the ball through the legs of a fifth, then he will smash the ball into the back of the net. However, gentlemen, when you challenge him, you must not make contact."

A supporter from the side cried out, "They wilnae hae tae act. They've been daein' it a' efternin."

At that point, a young makeup lady came rushing on to the park and applied a touch of makeup to my face. The same supporter cried out, "Away ya big pansy!" With a name like Marjoribanks, who was I to complain!

I finished the season in repertory theatre, then joined Jimmy Logan at the Metropole Theatre in Glasgow for a season, starting with me playing Jimmy's son who signed for Celtic – with Jimmy playing a rabid Rangers supporter!

After the Met, I joined the cast of the BBC television series United which was transmitted twice a week in the mid 1960s from their Birmingham studios. I was in the series for six months. It was described as "doing for football what myxomatosis did for rabbits".

It was at this point that the late Peter Thomson asked me to join the sports team at BBC Scotland. I thought that with my background I would have been used as a football reporter or commentator, but instead found myself in the studio, soon to present the radio edition of the television show Sportsreel. I spent 17 years to the day with the BBC and have many fond memories of presenting television sport and then Sportsound as it became with the advent of BBC Radio Scotland which replaced the Home Service.

Looking back two things spring to mind. The limitations of technology played a big part in the set-up. Football matches were generally covered on 16mm film, in 10-minute reels, as opposed to the flexibility of video tape. I recall presenting Sportscene in February 1968 when Hearts beat Dundee United 6-5 at Tannadice in the Scottish Cup and there was a missed penalty kick. The film was sent from Dundee to Glasgow for processing, then an editing job that required at least 13 joints for transmission. The film fell apart several times during transmission.

Similarly, with Sportsound, apart from the main commentary match (with the inimitable David Francey) for which there was a direct line to the ground, all other matches were covered by reporters on the end of a telephone line.

When interviews with managers were introduced, I had to do them from the studio on a match that I had not seen and on which I had only listened to a one-minute report. Was it any surprise that I resorted to a bunch of clichéd questions?

"You were two goals down at half time, Jim McLean, but you won 3-2. What did you say to the lads in the dressing room at half-time?"

The second issue related to Sportsound during the fledgling days of Radio Scotland when the programme expanded in a short space of time to a four-hour programme without the necessary budget or resources to support it. Often we had a guest in the studio to chat with and I was surprised at how many big names from both sport and the wider world of entertainment were pretentious. There were two notable exemptions.

One was the former British Lion Gordon Brown, who had just launched his book, Broon frae Troon. He was so down-to-earth, so vibrant, so entertaining and so much a man's man that I was shocked to hear of his death in 2001 at the age of just 53.

The other exception was Stein. Any manager who could take a team of players from a radius of 30 miles of Parkhead and mould them into a European Cup-winning side must obviously be my sportsman of the century. I suspect that no manager today would speak so openly and informally to a media man the way Jock did after that radio interview. I learned more about football and Jock's psychology in that hour than most people will learn in a lifetime. In those days there was a much more relaxed relationship between football managers and the media. And an unbreakable trust, which means Stein's secrets must remain with him.

Sport has come a long way since those days. Broadcasters now have a large say in the direction the game is heading and finance seems to determine the path ahead.

Are these changes for better or worse? I really don't know. I just feel privileged that I was able to be part of an incredible journey from the 1960s to the present day.

Brian Marjoribanks Senior is a former professional footballer with Hibs and Hearts, as well as an ex-professional actor, broadcaster, and broadcasting administrator with the IBA and later Ofcom. He presented Sportsound on BBC Radio Scotland for 17 years.

MEND IT LIKE BECKHAM

By Brian Marjoribanks

He came from a Galaxy far, far away. And every time AC Milan's star attraction ventured within snapping distance, camera phones lit up the snowy Glasgow night with the kind of flash-bulb explosions more readily associated with the heavenly bodies of the catwalks of the Italian fashion capital or the celestial beings who grace the hotspots of Hollywood Boulevard.

When David Beckham visited Ibrox Stadium in February 2009, he brought with him the kind of midwinter glitz and glamour Rangers fans feared was gone for the season upon their team's brutal Champions League exit at the hands of the unheralded Lithuanians FBK Kaunas six months earlier. The former Manchester United star and ex-Real Madrid Galactico, now a Milan player on loan from LA Galaxy, duly proved box-office gold in Govan as over 45,000 star-struck souls packed Ibrox for a meaningless 2-2 friendly draw.

Beckham would, however, save his most impressive work of the evening for afterwards, as his Dr Henry Kissinger impersonation, as timely as it was unlikely, restored harmony to a bunch of Scottish hacks teetering on the brink of civil war.

I've been a huge admirer of Beckham since his refusal to bow to seemingly inevitable defeat paved the way for Manchester United's Champions League-winning miracle in the Nou Camp in 1999. This is not the tale of some starry-eyed worshipper at the altar of fame, however. Spend long enough as a sportswriter and you become utterly immune to the cult of celebrity. That was quickly knocked out of me within weeks of starting at the Daily Mail in 2004, when the boss I idolised during my formative years, Jim Jefferies, Falkirk's Manager of the Millennium, treated me to the full hairdryer treatment at Glasgow Science Park.

Now managing Kilmarnock, Jefferies had taken offence at an article I'd written, mentioning, for no real reason, that Rugby Park was a hellhole and he was the bookmakers' favourite to be sacked first that season.

"Cutting-edge analysis," thought this fledgling reporter. "You troublemaking little c**t," was the contrary view screamed in my face by a livid Mr Jefferies, who turned out in the long-term to be one of Scottish football's good guys.

That experience toughened me up for two years later when legendary Rangers manager Walter Smith dished out a verbal filleting, complemented, to devastating effect, with his infamous trademark 'Walter death stare'.

Smith had just delivered a lengthy, unprompted, Gettysburg Address-style proclamation on the Ibrox club's need to eradicate sectarianism, only for this intrepid correspondent to destroy the hushed, reverent silence by blundering in with, "Aye Walter, but what about the Thomas Buffel situation?"

Now, having been ordered by my sports desk to enquire after the mediocre Belgian playmaker's future I was determined not to let my boss down on Buffel. But I learned an important lesson that day about the changing nature of the news agenda, which was cemented when a mocking diary piece about my unfortunate line of questioning appeared in that weekend's Sunday Herald.

Those were undoubted career low points, for sure, but there have also been many more memorable moments.

I've shaken hands with Diego Maradona (not THAT hand, sadly); and broken the news to an emotional Brian Laudrup that Rangers, the masters of all they surveyed in his 1990s heyday, had gone into administration and were heading for liquidation.

I've had the happier experience of informing Aston Villa's Barry Bannan of his first full Scotland call-up (although I was technically beaten by 'Cannonball' – an online 'friend' who, seconds earlier, had instant messaged Bannan to congratulate him as they played the computer game Call of Duty.)

I've befriended Uri Geller, to the detriment of my kitchen cutlery, and while queuing at the American Embassy in London for a US visa to cover Celtic's pre-season tour of New York and Boston in 2006, I spent an enjoyable morning with a lovely girl, finding out only as we parted that my new best friend was none other than the rather charming English supermodel and Vogue cover-girl, Cecilia Chancellor.

And I've stood in a Malmo bar next to Craig Whyte, who months before had bought Rangers for £1, as he accepted beers from admiring fans and Ibrox employees, plus several from his young, leggy blonde companion, all bought on her tattered old Switch card, without Whyte buying a single drink for anyone in return. In under 24 hours, Rangers' Champions League exit in Sweden would kickstart the unravelling of the biggest sporting scandal in Scottish history, while simultaneously stripping Whyte, the unlikely emperor of Ibrox, of his new clothes.

This beautifully bonkers job has taken me to weird and wonderful corners of the globe but while travel broadens the mind, hundreds of interviews harden the heart as to the reputation of whichever sports star happens to be sitting opposite. None more so than the weekly press conferences at Rangers and Celtic, which sharpen cynicism levels as disinterested Old Firm players and sceptical reporters face off in the kind of information-excavating experience outstripped only for utter joylessness by your average Guantanamo Bay interrogation. Unlike Guantanamo Bay, however, at Murray Park and Lennoxtown it's often just as painful for the interrogator.

All of which brings us back to David Beckham.

On the night AC Milan visited Glasgow, as deadlines approached, nerves were fraying in the hack pack as, true to form, a succession of Rangers players shunned the press. Temperatures were rising as the little (in both stature and media demand) US winger DaMarcus Beasley, who had been earmarked to speak to the Sunday newspapers, was grabbed by the broadcast journalists, as the desperate dailies also lurked with malevolent intent of robbing him of a quick quote.

Just as the three factions of journalists looked on the verge of tearing each other limb from limb, however, suddenly it happened. Out came Becks. England's poster boy did not descend from on high, accompanied by harp-playing angels. It just felt that way as Beckham emerged to deliver the ultimate masterclass in sports public relations.

The hating and baiting which came with Beckham's status as modern football's wealthiest and most marketable player, with a globally famous pop star wife, obscured the fact he possessed such a delicious right boot he was twice runner-up in Fifa's World Player of the Year. Beckham was a serious talent in his prime and while, at 33, his best days were behind him by the time he arrived in Glasgow, that night the gap in class was just as stark off the park between this true star of the game and the Rangers mediocrities he had just outshone on the Ibrox pitch.

Despite descending into a media maelstrom earlier that day at Glasgow Airport, Beckham showed absolutely no sign of press fatigue and soon had a tough crowd eating out of his hand. He even managed to charm hardened reporters still mindful that his last appearance in the city had been a 2-0 win for England at Hampden in 1999; which effectively kicked off a barren 14 years (and counting) away from major tournament finals for Scotland.

Over the course of the next 45 minutes, Beckham spoke at length and courteously to every single reporter who wanted a word: and gave considered responses to all. Duties done, he signed off by thanking each of his inquisitors for taking the time to show an interest. Self-serving platitudes? Who cares. Here appeared a genuinely decent man who understood the value of the press and its usefulness to him and his brand. That night he broke the news that he wanted to extend his stay in Milan to win a place with England at World Cup 2010, and, with back pages duly filled, there was enough left in our notepads for a follow-up feature the next day on Beckham's thoughts about the-then up-and-coming Ibrox wunderkind John Fleck.

My mind drifted back to David Beckham the other day when a little-known but enormously untalented Dunfermline defender refused to participate in a two-minute telephone interview that would have been little more than a glorified advert for his struggling team's next match. That snub occurred in the very same week it emerged 600,000 fans had stopped attending Scottish Premier League games over the previous five years. At a time when financially stricken clubs desperately need the oxygen of publicity, the Scottish game seems sadly intent on self-strangulation. Even the small- to medium-sized clubs appear oblivious to the reality that open access to players generally equates to favourable coverage and increased sponsorship revenue.

As 2013 approaches, however, it's undeniable that Scottish journalism, just like Scottish football, also finds itself in grave peril. As our game, and our trade, both strive to get people interested once again, there is, perhaps, a solution at hand: why can't footballers and press work once more in tandem, just like that fine frozen evening at Ibrox when Goldenballs performed such effortless public relations alchemy?

Why can't we mend it like Beckham?

Brian Marjoribanks started out on the Falkirk Herald and has written for the Scottish Daily Mail since 2004. He has been nominated for four Scottish Press Awards, twice finishing runner-up, and is a former winner of the Jim Rodger Memorial Award for the best young sports journalist in Scotland. His proudest moment in journalism, however, remains being given a standing ovation by a bar full of drunken Albanians in Tirana after a flawless karaoke rendition of Wind Of Change by the Scorpions.

THOSE UNSUNG HEROES OF THE SPORTS PAGES

By Richard Winton

've never been to the Maracana; never scoured Argentina in search of Maradona; never been bawled at by a puce-faced Sir Alex Ferguson. I've never been to a major international tournament or travelled abroad with the Scotland squad. In fact, the last time the national team reached a major finals, I had to run home from school to see it.

I'm the other kind of journalist; the kind who doesn't write stories but instead sits in a soulless office complaining about those who do.

Actually, that's not entirely true. Not the bit about the moaning – after all, the persistent whine of a sub-editor is often mistaken for an air-conditioning unit – but the bit about not writing stories. For a short spell in my early 20s, I was the target of the gripes during a fleeting stint as a sportswriter for the Sunday Herald and continue to sporadically smite the subs by covering football matches and churning out a weekly column.

That, though, is done in my own time. Instead, my week is spent keeping the writers out of trouble and, from time to time, causing it for them. For example, when one of them is fending off the keyboard warriors amid a message-board flogging because of the headline attached to something they have written, myself or one of my colleagues is to blame. We were the ones who wrote it. It works the other way, too, though. If they get a name, fact or figure wrong – or worse, libel someone – we are the ones who mend the error.

They might not like it – and I know I didn't – but they have to entrust their carefully crafted words to us, the faceless journalists. But who are we? What do we do? And how does the supplement that many readers reach for first come to be?

On occasion, my responsibilities extend to editing that section, so let me offer an insight into how the sports desk was run on one particular Sunday in May. Normally, I would make my way into the office for around 10am with a rough schedule in mind and a coffee in hand, but this day was a little different. By the time I reached Renfield Street, I'd already taken and made several phone calls relating to the 8.45am announcement – my slumber having been disturbed by the insistent beep of my mobile heralding the email – that Charles Green, Rangers' new owner, would be holding his first press conference at Murray Park.

Having agreed with Michael Grant, our chief football writer, that he would make his way to Milngavie for the 10.30am briefing, it was decided to remove him from duty at the Celtic game that day, leaving chief sportswriter Hugh MacDonald to cover the match and presentation of the Clydesdale Bank Premier League trophy.

Given that a four-page advertising supplement had limited us to just 16 pages on an already busy day, finding space was going to be an issue even if, as expected, the news section of the paper would be eager to relieve us of much of what Green had to say. A quick conversation with the duty editor established that they had not sent a news reporter to the conference but were keen to take the majority of the content, with the suggestion of an analysis piece from Michael combined with reaction gathered by the news reporters soon agreed.

With Michael hiving off the best of the football-specific stuff for our front page and writing his column on his first impressions of Green, the first problem of the day was resolved before 11am. Now for the rest of the section. As well as the final three SPL matches of the season and the culmination of the Barclays Premier League campaign, we also had Saturday's football, the fall-out from Glasgow Warriors' Rabodirect Pro 12 semi-final defeat by Leinster, the Spanish Grand Prix and the Scottish Saltires playing the Welsh Dragons to squeeze in alongside golf, racing, tennis and the success of Scottish modern pentathlete Mhairi Spence in the World Championships. Frankly, we did not have enough pages to do it all justice, so sacrifices had to be made.

Still, a heaving schedule was put together and, after a robust exchange of views during the morning conference – a meeting with the various section editors to discuss the content of that day's paper – the order was agreed and pictures arranged. Now phone calls could be made to the respective writers to agree word counts, chew over ideas and commission anything not already lined up.

With the rest of the production staff not arriving until 4pm, the following couple of hours would normally be spent fielding calls, making further arrangements and generally monitoring the unfolding afternoon of sport before overseeing the page design later in the day. However, a shortage of staff meant a head start needed to be made when it came to designing the pages, or at least compiling some of the more fiddly elements of the section, such as cricket scoreboards and football results.

By late afternoon, though, the bulk of the book was drawn, the pictures chosen and the copy waiting for the subs to do their work. Just as well, given the distraction of the epic end to the Premier League title race in England with Manchester City pipping Manchester United to finish on top for the first time since 1968, a conclusion which vindicated the decision to free up more space than normal to accommodate it.

But with everything in hand, it was time to leave them to it and head home with the instruction to phone should anything unexpected develop. Fortunately, though, Sir Alex didn't call and nobody found Maradona …

Richard Winton is assistant sports editor of the Herald in Glasgow, having previously worked as a sportswriter with the Sunday Herald and freelance contributor for FourFourTwo, Real Radio, Talksport and PA, among others.

REBEL WITHOUT A CLAUSE

By Graham Hunter

B ouncing computers, fishnet stockings, French whispers but no
French kissing, barking dogs, Tintin – it all happened so fast.
It was a time (I barely remember it) of naivety.

One evening a friend in Belgium was telling me, en passant,
that Jean-Marc Bosman, who was suing RFC Liege in the European
Court of Justice in order to be allowed to leave the club at the end
of his contract, was paying a terrible cost for his crusade for justice.

He told me that Bosman was bereft of proper support, was verging on alcoholism, had seen his marriage break up and was back
living with his parents. It was nearly 9pm but I phoned my editor,
just to pass on the idea that this seemed like a guy who had been
trampled upon by the system and who might be worth interviewing.

AT Mays was closed by then so I humoured the boss when he
told me that he was so excited by the tale that I'd better be ready to
be on a plane to Belgium first thing the next morning. Daft old git.

Little did I know that there were 24-hour travel companies so by
about 9.45am the next morning I was already in Brussels feeding
centimes into a Belgian phone box and phoning the house of M et
Madame Bosman in Liege. My French, then as now, was eclectic. I
stumbled through asking to speak to Jean-Marc and he came on the
line. "What do you want?," "no" and "no" were his first six words.

He didn't want to speak, he didn't want our support. Basically, I
was screwed. But with the centimes running out and my chippiness
starting to set in, I used the old, "I've come this far and surely a guy

like you should show me a bit of solidarity ..." There was a pause. "Vous avez combien d'argent avec vous?"

I was going to have to pay for access. I'd taken 50 quid with me, needed train fares so I hazarded, "Three hundred francs."

"OK, deal," he told me. "Get on the 11am train to Liege and I'll meet you at the station."

My sense of relief met my sense of humour head-on when the car which pulled up to meet me at the Gare de Liege was a big black new BMW. Bosman's life might be in the dustbin but when a few players' unions around Europe passed the hat around for him long, long after he'd spent months next to bankruptcy, he'd immediately leased a 'cor-blimey' motor to keep up appearances. He was a footballer after all. So we arrived chez Bosman in luxury.

He'd had to sell his flat and all his furniture to fund the case he was running against his former employers, a case which has subsequently ended football slavery and meant that players, like any other employees, can leave for another workplace without restraint at the end of their agreed contract.

It was a tiny, two-bedroom apartment at the top of a narrow, winding staircase. Up we went and once I'd done the niceties with his extremely nice parents (turning down a plate of chips, some luxury chocolates and a Hercule Poirot DVD), battle commenced.

I asked him questions in French and taped his long, articulate, occasionally emotional answers. I got about 60 per cent of the long conversation but knew that there was a long job of translation and transcription in front of me. A very long job.

We spoke for about the length of a football match, a fluke but a nice detail. Into the last half hour of the chat the phone started ringing. And ringing and ringing. His mum fielded a couple of calls but then, inevitably, came through to tell her boy what it was about.

France Football, AFP, Canal Plus, Belgian state television and a gaggle of other media were frantic to speak to Bosman because the interim verdict on his case had just been announced by the European Court. He'd won.

Everyone knew that for better or worse a line had been drawn.

Footballers' rights were about to change irrevocably, the general consensus (from the headless chickens) was that football clubs were all going to go to the wall, instantly, and agents could now afford to build their garden walls out of gold, platinum or clusters of 24-carat diamonds.

It was a shock to be there on this day of days but that was only the first shock. "Tell them I'm not speaking to any of them – tell them that this guy paid for his time and I'm going to honour my commitment."

He did. We spoke on until I was satisfied and I knew that just his passion for the subject, not necessarily my interview skills, meant that he had worn his heart on his sleeve.

We started to say our goodbyes at the top of the stairs and then their MASSIVE Doberman, whose name I was given on arrival but the word Satan is all I remember, lunged at me ... as killer dogs do. I swerved, my bag tipped and the portable computer did a brilliant Barnes Wallis job of bouncing jauntily down the stairs, not missing a step on the way and leaving debris with each impact. Satan and the Bosmans (which would have been a great name for a Belgian rock group) chortled a bit and I left.

The paper arranged for me to meet one of their stringers from the European Parliament whose wife was fluent in French and would do a rush job.

She was, without exaggeration, straight out of 'Allo 'Allo. Cleavage which you would need a ski tow to ascend, fishnet stockings which never saw the back of a trawler (she promised) and a nasty habit of needing to rub her knee on mine as we debated the niceties of Bosman's use of the conditional tense. Oh – by the by, the fact that I'd been sitting with the rebel who had wrecked world football while he told me about his battle with depression and alcohol, his rage at the system, and how his wife had walked out on him (as soon as she heard he was winning she pitched up again, he took her on a romantic 'reunion' weekend to the Island of Reunion , exercised his conjugal rights and then told her to 'conjugal rights'-off) meant that the Daily Mail wanted a 1200-word spread article and a back-page lead by just after 7.30pm. It was 6pm by the time I had all the transcribed words at my disposal, which added just a hint of stress.

We pulled it off. Just. And that day probably had as much impact on my career and subsequent life as it did on Bosman.

Back in my Tintin-themed hotel I treated myself to a plate of chips, some luxury chocolates and a Poirot DVD.

Thanks for being a rebel Jean-Marc.

Graham Hunter is a journalist of international renown and covers Spanish football and FC Barcelona for Sky Sports, the BBC, and newspapers and magazines across the world. He is also the author of the critically acclaimed Barça: The Making of the Greatest Team in the World. He modestly describes himself as "having been nicking a living since pencils were invented."

LIKE FATHER, LIKE SON

By David McCarthy

W e're a lucky lot, sportswriters. We get to meet our heroes, even if occasionally the old adage that you shouldn't holds true.

I've been fortunate enough to sit down with some of the greats over the years. In fact, if I thought long and hard about it, I might just be able to go through the alphabet.

Amoruso (yes, he does count – I wrote his book, LA Confidential, and revealed to the world how he became addicted to Baileys Irish Cream), Beckenbauer, Cruyff, Dalglish (see my second sentence!) ... all the way to Zidane, whom I might say was charm personified at the French training HQ at Clairefontaine a few years back. That was on the same day as Fabien Barthez, who was Manchester United's goalkeeper at the time, refused point-blank to speak English to me. I tried a little French and ended up conducting the shortest interview of my career.

"Ah, Fabien," I enthused, slapping on my biggest smile, "parlez-vous Anglais?"

"Non," he lied and walked away. "C'est la vie," I muttered to myself. "Vous etes merde de toute favon." Or I would have if I'd known "you're s*** anyway" in French at the time.

Jose Mourinho, when he was merely 'the OK One' was fascinating company in the week I spent in Oporto during the build-up to Celtic facing his team in the 2003 Uefa Cup final. Five years later, it was St Petersburg for a week with Dick Advocaat recalling the good old days at Ibrox as he plotted the downfall of Rangers in the final of the same competition.

John Collins netting the penalty in the Stade de France against Brazil and the entire Scottish press corps going as potty as the Tartan Army on day one of France '98 was a particular highlight. As was interviewing my true childhood hero Denis Law for the first time. I half expected him to turn up with his shirttail hanging out and the cuff stuffed into his fingers, but he was immaculately attired and a perfect gentleman.

I could go on forever. So many precious memories locked away, and it's great fun to turn the key and let them out every now and again.

Casting the sporting net further, Rafa Nadal is simply the nicest sporting superstar on the planet. Tiger Woods? He isn't. Paula Radcliffe? Almost, but Rafa just pips her at the post, which is something that usually happens to her only at the Olympics. This year, Paula, please? And, as I say to my boys every day before taking them to nursery: "Will you please go to the toilet BEFORE you leave the house?"

But, you know, for all the big names I've encountered over the years, the experience that I enjoyed the most involved a roofer from Linwood, whom I took on an aeroplane for the first time in his life to see his boy play football.

It was August 1996. Billy Lambert was 49 at the time and had never been abroad, never flown; he was as nervous as a kitten about doing so. But I was asked to fly out with him to Germany to see his son Paul make his debut for Borussia Dortmund against Fortuna Dusseldorf just weeks after the move that launched the current Aston Villa manager from journeyman footballer at Motherwell to a Champions League winner nine months later.

For a man who spent all his working life with his head touching the clouds, Billy is as down-to-earth a character as you'd ever wish to meet. He admitted he cried when Paul won the Scottish Cup with St Mirren at the age of 17, and sitting in the Westfalen Stadion listening to 60,000 fans bellow "LAAAMBERT," after the stadium announcer called out "No 14, Paul ..." Billy's eyes welled up again. Earlier in the day, the three of us had walked upon the lush playing surface, and Billy turned to Paul and said: "If you can't play on this, you want to chuck it."

Paul just smiled. He'd heard it all before. He didn't know the journey upon which he was about to embark and, certainly, Billy didn't. But he was a proud dad that day. An ordinary man, whose boy had made good and it was simply a pleasure to be there with him on the night he saw for himself just how far Paul had come. Lambert Jr has gone on to great things, but he's never forgotten that night either.

Nor has he forgotten where he's come from. Paul's a good lad. He's his father's son.

David McCarthy is the chief sports features writer with the Daily Record. He started in journalism in 1983 and still can't believe he gets paid for going to events like the Olympics, World Cups, Ryder Cups and Wimbledon.

PILGRIMAGE TO THE MARACANA

By Patrick Barclay

The beautiful game? Maybe it was on somewhere else.

I had come to experience the *joga bonito* at its spiritual home, the Maracana, the vast arena in Rio de Janeiro that had been built for the 1950 World Cup. That event ended in disappointment as the hosts lost the final to Uruguay and now, early in 1998, although Brazil were reigning world champions, they were giving every impression of readiness to surrender their crown in France a few months hence.

The beautiful game? So dismally were Brazil performing in a friendly against Argentina that some of the 100,000 in the Maracana might almost have sighed with nostalgia for the plainly effective game that had made them world champions in the United States in 1994. Almost; because for the Brazilian audience, winning is never enough. They had never really taken Carlos Alberto Parreira's team to their hearts. After a massive party, they had consigned it to the cabinet of history, filed under 'B' for Boring.

The Brazilians have a simple requirement from football: they want everything; victory with majesty involving a touch of arrogance and a liberal smattering of back-heels. On this night in '98 they were getting next to nothing and the scorn that cascaded down the Maracana's slopes was palpable. In Brazil, the diminutive tends to be used affectionately – Ronaldo became 'Ronaldinho' as his popularity burgeoned – but, as Argentina secured a merited winner through Claudio Lopez, there was no mistaking the derision. "Timinho," the crowd chanted ("Little Team"). Every touch taken by Brazil's great rivals, whose anthem had been drowned out before the kick-off, was greeted with a self-deprecating "Ole."

How little atmosphere can matter in football when those whom it is intended to inspire are not capable of responding to it. Everything except the team had met a lifetime's expectation of the Maracana. A first visit to a special place – the tombs of the Egyptian kings or the Grand Canal in Venice – can induce a sense of deja-vu. But nothing prepares you for the epicentre of football because noise cannot be photographed and the old Maracana was unique. Whatever modernisation is done before the 2014 World Cup must, while improving the spectators' comfort, sacrifice what made it so.

It was a stadium of shabby splendour that rocked, literally, and defied the traditions of football architecture. Unlike the San Siro or the great arenas of Spain, it was perfectly round and the angle of the terraces reclined languidly, which meant that it did not bear down on the pitch. The nearest spectators sat 30 metres from the corner flags. Yet it fairly throbbed. An hour and a half before kick-off, conversation was a question of cocked ears and snatched gist. Even the moths around the floodlights, it seemed, were dancing with the compelling synergy that is a mark of the Brazilian people.

But the carnival was over long before half-time and thereafter the various factions on the terraces spent most of their passion on calling for substitutions that made no difference. They united in roaring at Rai, the gifted but ambling midfielder, to walk off; he waited for the signal from the veteran manager, Mario Zagallo, which duly materialised. Afterwards, Zagallo said he wasn't too worried: "I won't be reading too much into a friendly."

Pele, as a television pundit, nevertheless doubted that Zagallo would sleep well, pointing out that the midfield players had kept getting in each other's way.

By the time Brazil kicked off the World Cup against Scotland in Paris a few months later, Rai had gone. He was replaced by Cesar Sampaio, who scored after four minutes. Scotland equalised through a penalty taken by John Collins but a Tom Boyd own-goal set the

Brazilians on the road to qualification for the knockout stages, in which they beat Chile 4-1, Denmark 3-2 and Holland on penalties before the bizarre incident involving Ronaldo at the Stade de France. First he was omitted from the final through illness. Then he was restored to the side that succumbed 3-0 to France as if traumatised by concern over their superstar. Even the crowd at the Maracana would have been forgiving on that day.

Four years later, when Ronaldo led Brazil to the title in the Far East, my thoughts strayed to the old rocker. Even on a bad day, it was a wonderful place.

Patrick Barclay is a football writer and broadcaster who has worked for, among others, the Guardian, Telegraph, Times and Independent newspapers. He has written biographies of Jose Mourinho and Sir Alex Ferguson. He is currently working on the life story of Herbert Chapman and is a member of Dees Down South, the club for supporters of Dundee FC who live in and around London.

DON'T CRY FOR DIEGO JUST YET, ARGENTINA

By John Greechan

'**G**o and find out if Maradona is really dying." As direct orders from the sports editor go, it's hardly up there with "Pop along to that Partick Thistle presser."

But that was the very edict issued in January 2000, as this Fleet Street newcomer was despatched to stand outside a Buenos Aires hospital, speak to anyone who could understand my Scots English, ask a load of annoying questions and hopefully produce something relevant – "Make it sing," the guv'nor used to say – on the downfall of El Diego.

To set the scene, Maradona had taken ill in the Uruguayan holiday resort of Punto del Este and was rushed first to a clinic there and then to a hospital back home, where it quickly became clear that years of cocaine use had put his very life in danger.

A player who had enthralled football fans the world over, a character whose excesses fascinated anyone capable of recognising a tragedy in the making, he was always worth writing about. Especially if there was a chance that he was about to shuffle off this mortal coil.

And the gaffer, Daily Mail head of sport Bryan Cooney, believed that applying one of the golden rules of journalism – always shorten the distance between yourself and the story – would pay dividends.

Now, let's put this mad dash to South America into some perspective. I was already in Rio de Janeiro to watch Manchester United in the Fifa World Club Championship. As the boss said at the time,

Argentina was just around the corner, wasn't it? So, after a terrifying twin-prop flight through an electrical storm, during which ice-cool photographer Andy Hooper somehow managed to sleep, we landed in the capital without a single contact or, to be honest, a word of useful Spanish between us.

But things always seem to work out, don't they? First we got chatting to a few English-speaking TV reporters keeping vigil, along with some truly devoted fans, outside the hospital compound.

Then, through a friend of a friend's colleague who just happened to hail from Argentina (seriously, this is how these things happen) we were put in touch with Nacho Dimari, a local freelance journalist who proved as helpful as he was resourceful.

There were obvious obstacles. Maradona's agent, who might have been relied upon to provide quiet guidance or useful background info, wouldn't talk to anyone without receiving a fistful of dollars in advance. To be honest, it wasn't even bothering London with that request. Even if they would have sanctioned it, something in the gut – call it an ingrained Scottish respect for money – railed against paying someone for sharing insight that would surely be overtaken by our own digging.

Stuck behind enemy lines, with only the merest foothold on this hugely important story, we remained confident. Why? Partly because it was Andy who, as well as being a top snapper, remains the ideal wing-man for any reporter landed in an unfamiliar situation and expected to deliver. He knows when to float ideas, knows when to interject – and knows when to stay quiet, because blurting something out might queer the whole deal being negotiated. With Nacho as our guide, how could the dynamic duo of Johnny the Greek and Hooperman, as we jokingly dubbed ourselves, fail to crack this story wide open?

Within a few short hours we were sitting in the studio at La Red Radio, a kind of 24-hour sports and news station that had been transformed into a rolling discussion on the plight of Argentina's national hero. Firstly, they wanted to interview Yours Truly, with Nacho doing the translating, about why a British newspaper should be so moved by Maradona's plight. I tried really hard not to mention the Hand of God. Being invited into the studio really paid off, though, when a stream of Argentine greats – Maradona's former team-mates, old coaches and legendary figures – were either paraded in or called up to comment. All I had to do was sit there and listen to Nacho translate, scribbling particularly furiously as Sergio Batista drew on his own battle with drug addiction to offer advice to his old pal.

We made a couple of calls ourselves, too. Or, to be more precise, Nacho called some key figures and asked questions on our behalf. It was all coming together.

But the real stroke of luck? Someone at La Red putting us in touch with World Cup winner Jorge Valdano, who had just written a piece containing a phrase guaranteed to make headline writers weep.

"It will be tragic and compare this to the death of Princess Diana," said El Diego's old team-mate, summing up the level of desolation felt across Argentina at the mere thought of losing this favourite prodigal son. A story that had been missing a hook now needed merely to be put together.

In truth, the writing was the easy part. How could any hack worth his salt not be inspired to new levels by a tale of national obsession, family tragedy and a self-destructive dynamo who had scaled such heights and sunk to such depths?

Very early the next morning, Buenos Aires time, the phone started ringing. The paper had hit the streets back home – and the story had created quite a stir. First it was the BBC breakfast programme, then ITV, then a couple of radio stations, all wanting to hear about this fascinating tale from someone on the ground. They were all referred to Nacho, with instructions to double their normal fee for an on-air interview; he had earned as much.

Anyway, with a flight to catch that afternoon, and having spent approximately 36 hours in Buenos Aires without seeing much more than a hospital, a radio station and a hotel bar, it was time to play the tourist. First stop? To pay my respects to an earlier figure of Argentinean national obsession, someone whose name had cropped up repeatedly during conversations about El Diego.

No, with all due deference to the great Evita herself, perhaps visiting the grave of Eva Peron wasn't the most exciting way to spend a last few hours in BA. In the circumstances, though, it only seemed right.

After 20 years in journalism, John Greechan has accumulated a wealth of skills that are entirely non-transferable to any other line of work. Given his big break when covering Raith Rovers' 1994 League Cup win and subsequent Uefa Cup involvement, an international debut at the 1998 World Cup convinced him that a career of following Scotland to major tournaments beckoned. In between working at the SPL coalface and dipping into rugby, golf and other events no-one else in the office can be bothered covering, the Scottish Daily Mail's chief sportswriter spends his private time wondering where the years went – and hoping that Caledonia will rise again.

THE TWO FACES OF SIR ALF RAMSEY

By Rodger Baillie

S ir Alf Ramsey didn't like the Scots. If independence had been granted to Scotland during his lifetime the World Cup-winning England manager would have been at the border waving us off.

On one notorious occasion the England team bus pulled up at the imposing entrance to the Marine Hotel in Troon, their squad head-quarters before the biennial match against Scotland at Hampden. Step forward Jim Rodger, doyen of the Scottish press corps, who said in a friendly fashion to the England gaffer, "Welcome to Scotland, Sir Alf," only to be met with the crushing retort, delivered in that strange accent of Ramsey's which was a mix of his native Dagenham and received BBC English: "You must be f*****g joking."

Yet it is only fair to record that, as a Scotsman, I found Sir Alf in private the contrasting image to his public face. I had two direct interviews with him, one face-to-face and one on the phone – and he was polite and helpful. It was a reminder to me how dangerous it is for a journalist to assume preconceived ideas about someone they hope to interview. Sometimes their reaction is surprising.

That first interview in January 1966 seems a lifetime away. The World Cup triumph he masterminded, and his subsequent knight-hood, were still down the line for later that year. I was the Scottish sports columnist of the Sunday Mirror, then a far more influential newspaper than the pale shadow it is north of the border today, and it was a move by the SFA which prompted me to seek out Alf. The Scottish game's supremos were trying to find a replacement as

Scotland team manager to John Prentice, the man they had summarily fired for flying to Canada the previous autumn to investigate the possibility of taking over a club in a new North American league set-up.

Prentice succeeded Jock Stein, who quit as part-time international manager after the failure to qualify for the World Cup finals in England, and Kilmarnock boss Malcolm Macdonald had taken charge as caretaker for two matches. Some of the SFA powerbrokers had never been convinced of the need for a full-time manager; indeed some had never been convinced of the need for a manager at all. Among the doubters was the extremely influential secretary of the organisation, Willie Allan.

He could have doubled as a church elder or a bank manager. He wasn't tall, around 5ft 7in, always wore his trademark soft-brimmed hat, and on occasion was not entirely without humour. But it was rumoured he took the SFA rule book to bed with him every night; it was his bible with which to oversee Scottish football.

There was no doubt this formidable figure was behind the amazing advert for the Scotland manager's post that appeared in newspapers early in 1966 which contained the intriguing job description, "could be suitable to those with other business interests." You hardly needed to be Sherlock Holmes to deduce the SFA favoured a part-time appointment. I decided to seek out the views of the one man in Britain who was a full-time international manager.

Put it down to youthful brashness – I had reached the ripe old age of 25 – but off I flew to London to try to interview Ramsey in his London lair. I actually made the telephone call seeking to speak to him from a public callbox near FA headquarters – and to my utter amazement he agreed to see me. And not only to see me, but to give me more than half an hour of his time for a completely impromptu meeting.

My report the following Sunday started: "The walls of the room in London's Lancaster Gate are an austere grey. There's not a sign of the mascot World Cup Willie anywhere. But it is the most unique room in British football. Its occupant is Alfred Ramsey, the £4,500-a-year team manager of England." £4,500 a year for the man who was to guide England to World Cup glory? I did say it was a long time ago.

Alf expanded on his reasons for firmly rejecting any suggestion of splitting his time between the international side and a club team. "I can only speak for England but I could not do this job on a part-time basis."

At the start of his England reign he was still manager of Ipswich Town and he went on: "We had two internationals in that spell and we lost them both. It produced a lot of difficulties, I found myself at games concentrating on Ipswich so much I couldn't properly weigh up any potential England players in the opposition.

"I also find that not having any club connection I get a franker assessment from other managers on the form of their players. If I were a club manager what a headache it would picking your own players for the international side, you would be accused of favouring them but why should they be excluded?"

Ramsey had full control of selection, a concession granted to Stein but not without grumbling from some members of the SFA selection committee, annoyed that their influence had been curbed.

He stated: "The final decision is mine. I am the sole selector."

His choices were certainly vindicated in the coming summer of that year. No English manager has come close to his World Cup success. Incidentally, the SFA eventually thought better of appointing a manager who doubled as a butcher, baker or candlestick maker, and St Johnstone boss Bobby Brown was appointed in a full-time role.

My second interview with Ramsey, by then Sir Alf, was before the 1986 World Cup finals in Mexico. He had been England manager for the 1970 campaign in that same country and he revealed how impressed he was that Alex Ferguson, in charge of Scotland following Stein's death, visited him at his Ipswich home to discuss dietary needs for the players and the problems of playing at altitude in Mexico.

In his clipped way he indicated how favourably it contrasted with England team manager Bobby Robson. The pair only lived 300 yards apart in Ipswich, they had both successfully managed the local club yet because of a coldness between them they never met to discuss the same details as Sir Alf did with the Scotland manager.

Ferguson recorded: "He could not have been more helpful. I was glad and grateful to hear him say we deserved to do well."

The soon-to-be master of Manchester United had discovered, like myself many years earlier, that maybe Sir Alf didn't really dislike the Scots as much as he claimed.

Rodger Baillie is a veteran sportswriter with over 50 years' experience on national newspapers. Starting with the Daily Record in 1959 he then served on the Sunday Mirror for two decades before returning to the Record. Appointed chief sportswriter of the Scottish Sun in 1995, he allegedly retired 10 years later but since then has worked for the Sunday Times, the News of the World and the Sun again.

THE DARK DRUNK DRIVER

By Bryan Cooney

W e've taken occupation of a restaurant in Suffolk. The gaff boasts not only exquisite cuisine but exorbitant prices. Lunch is now a distant memory and we're currently on the brandies. Large ones, of course.

Staring into arguably the most famous pair of managerial eyes in England's history of football, I'm debating two things: first, what will the managing editor say when he receives the Buffalo Bill? My mind visualises a scaffold being erected and Yours Truly being huckled up the steps in order to test-drive the properties of oblivion. Second, and of far greater import, is there a slender possibility that Sir Alf Ramsey might have had enough to drink? I'm no laggard as regards elbow action, but this man inhabits a different planet. He's had two double gins and tonic, quaffed a vineyard of wine, and is currently giving the Remy Martin a proper seeing-to. I peer once again into those often saturnine eyes. No evidence of melancholy in him to-day. By God, no! We've completed that infernal interview (he's never been Mr Loquacity) and, at this moment, Alf is happily, gloriously, monumentally pixilated.

The young and overworked waiter marches up to us (Alf and I are in the company of photographer Roy Chaplin) and announces, with something close to triumph: "I'm afraid, gentlemen, that the bar is now closed!"

Alf appears to be firmly against the motion, or indeed notion. He summons up the spirit that won England the World Cup in 1966, and responds with great certainty, "Well, f*****g h-open it h-again!"

The poor fellow retreats to the gantry and returns with three brandies that deserve the title of gargantuan. There's an unmistakable glint in the eye of the old master. "Do you know, just another 'our or so and they'll be h-open again!"

At this moment, common sense is invited into my life. It's March 1982 and I've recently been appointed chief sportswriter of the Daily Star. There's a column to be written. Sure, I'd love to continue this bonding session with this most enigmatic of men, but today I should obey the voice of professionalism for once in my aberrant life. I've done damn well in as much as I haven't managed to upset him with my robust questioning, and neither have I mentioned the no-no factor – the sobriquet of Darkie. Alf's nickname has been bestowed on him possibly because of his alleged Romany roots, but more likely because of his swarthy appearance. Apparently, he thoroughly disapproves of it and I've been warned by Chaplin not to speak its name.

So far, so good. I look back at my guest. He may be as pissed as the proverbial parrot, but he's still clinging to his perch. "Sorry, Alf, but we must get back to the office. We've gone way past our time. We'll have to catch the 4.15; otherwise we'll miss our print deadline. We'll get a cab."

If there is disappointment in Ramsey, he proves expert in camouflaging it. "All right then, if you must go, so be it ... but h-I shall drive you there!"

Even through the myriad lairs of alcoholic insulation, this is a prospect without appeal. Alf had picked us up at the station and driven – highly erratically, it should be said – to the restaurant. No, given the choice, I'd sooner take my chances walking down Sauchiehall Street at midnight on a Saturday, rather than get back alongside him in that Saab. I attempt reason. "We would never impose ourselves on you like that."

"Nonsense!" he fires back. "This is not no imposition. I have been your guest. Now you must be mine!"

I see enough horrors ahead for an X-certificate finale, but Ramsey is as sure as he was on the day he decided to leave Jimmy Greaves stranded on the sidelines against the beastly Germans. You can't argue with a man of such unshakeable resolve. I pay the bill and our party virtually gropes its way into daylight. Alf's driving does nothing to exorcise the pessimist in me. It's even more erratic than earlier. Even worse, he is attempting to drive fast, something comfortably beyond his capabilities. There is little traffic around until we near a point where, somewhat incongruously, the dual carriageway ends and the two-way traffic begins. There is a lumbering lorry ahead and Alf's foot is hovering, indecisively, above the accelerator pedal "What shall I do?" he wails. "Do I pass it, or what?"

This is no time for the inauguration of a debating society. It's 4.11p.m and we have four minutes to catch that train. "Pass the bloody thing, Alf!" I implore.

This seems to galvanise him and by now we are level with our tormentor, but the sight of traffic coming the other way seems to impinge on his resolve. If he doesn't put his foot down, we'll miss the train. Alternatively, if he does but isn't forceful enough, we'll hit the oncoming car. I am seized by the forces of hysteria. "Don't stop now! For f**k's sake – go on … Darkie!" I scream.

For one nanosecond, that's all, I swear there is confusion, if not outrage in Ramsey's eyes as they swivel towards me. Then, a toothy, malevolent grin, a la Jack Nicholson in The Shining. Ramsey puts an assertive foot down on the accelerator; we pass the lorry and, with inches to spare, swing over on to the left side of the road as a car, flashing its lights, rushes up to meet us. Eighty is registering on the Saab's speedometer. We have missed certain death by the width of a couple of pubic hairs.

We reach Ipswich station with 30 seconds to spare, with no post mortem on what had been an act of sheer lunacy. Neither is there the hint of recrimination from Ramsey – my terrible, if understandable, faux pas is not even mentioned. You might say it's been an exceptional day.

Aberdeen-born Bryan Cooney worked as a racing sub-editor with the local Press & Journal before moving to news sub-editing with Scottish Daily Express and on to Fleet Street, working for the Daily Mail, Sun and Daily Express as an inside man. He then became chief sportswriter of the Daily Star before becoming head of sport at the Daily Mail. A former three-times sports journalist of the year, Cooney is the author of three books – the John Lowe Story, Celtic's Lost Legend (George Connelly) *and* Fingerprints of a Football Rascal, *and is currently working on a biography of that enigmatic genius, Gerry Rafferty.*

Story adapted from Fingerprints of a Football Rascal *by Bryan Cooney (Kindle: £4.64)*

3

1974: WHEN IT BECAME 'THEM' AND 'US'

By Glenn Gibbons

Talleyrand once observed that only those who had lived before 1789 could have a proper appreciation of what the good life had to offer.

Had the most famous and influential diplomat of post-Revolution France been discussing Scotland's football writers, he would have noted that the watershed year was 1974.

To present-day scribblers, 'travelling with the team' on a foreign assignment is a concept that begins – and virtually ends – with a largely disarrayed huddle around some hapless player in an airport departure lounge, the 'interview' regularly interrupted by loud and unintelligible PA announcements.

Apart from the official media preview conference on the eve of the match, at which the manager and team captain will blandly field banal questions in a free-for-all (newspaper, radio and television interests all served by the same scrum), the next contact between 'accompanying' journalists will be another rushed collision in the sweaty aftermath of the match. This in itself is the prelude to a hairy stampede to the airport, the primary objective of the entire exercise to get the team airborne and heading home as soon as possible.

These fleeting 'contacts' are the consequence of the desire by football's executives, be they representing a club or the Scottish FA, to keep a metaphorical firewall between themselves and the possibly leprous members of the hack pack. The arrangement includes confining the official party and the chroniclers in separate hotels.

In an ideal world, the football people would really prefer the press to book and pay (exorbitantly) for seats on the team's aircraft without their actually occupying them on either the outbound or the return journey. The origins of this segregation ('back of the bus' is entirely appropriate to the status of the football writing corps on these expeditions) may be traced to the 1974 World Cup in West Germany. Or, more precisely, the pre-engagement visits to Belgium and Norway during the most eventful week of this veteran reporter's 45-year career.

Led by the gloriously good-natured manager Willie Ormond, Scotland's heroes were heading for the great jamboree for the first time in 16 years. Commercialism was in its infancy, but there was enough savvy around for the players to appoint an agent, Bob Bain, who would look after their interests. Within minutes of our arrival at our hotel before the match against Belgium, rumours that the SFA intended to dip its toes in the players' pool were addressed by the team manager.

Willie, flushed with the conviviality that sprang from the free bar aboard the British Airways charter, assured the press that there was no way the SFA would be allowed to interfere. He seemed oblivious to the notion that he was making a headline-grabbing declaration of war on his own employers.

That was the first of a series of gifts to the papers. The next came as early as the following day, when we learned that Bain, judged to be a potentially bad influence, had been banned from the training ground.

Following an abysmal performance (ending in a 2-1 defeat) against Belgium, the players were allowed out for what might politely be called a relaxing evening. Because of a coach trip to our 9am flight from Brussels to Oslo next day, breakfast was called for 6.30.

Looking at the casualties of the 'unwinding' session, betrayed by pasty complexions behind dark glasses, it was clear that several beds had passed the night undisturbed. By the time we reached Oslo, the flying champagne bottle in which we were travelling had anaesthetised much of the collective pain.

Having checked into what were university halls of residences vacated for the summer, a colleague, Brian Scott, and I repaired to the wine and beer bar in the basement, there to encounter the two leprechauns, Jimmy Johnstone and Billy Bremner.

As we sat at a pine table with bench seats, Billy at my side and Jimmy and Brian opposite, Willie Ormond, clearly disturbed, entered, walked the length of the room and, leaning between the other two, said sarcastically to Bremner, the squad captain, "Thanks very much!" and left.

It transpired that Johnstone and Bremner had flouted an order to remain in their rooms, out of the public – and the media – gaze. I heard from the team doctor that night that a full-scale meeting was taking place "upstairs," although nothing emerged until the following day.

Then, the SFA secretary, Willie Allan, informed us that two players (whose identities, of course, we already knew) had been severely reprimanded and had come within an ace of being sent home in disgrace. This sensation was so forcefully condemned by John Mackenzie of the Daily Express that he was banned from the flight to the World Cup itself after the match against Norway. John's great friend and rival, Hugh Taylor of the Daily Record, received a phone call from his editor, outraged that Hughie had not managed to achieve the distinction (and heaven-sent publicity) of getting himself banned.

On the night before the match, the Scottish press were not allowed into their own national team's training session, apparently "on the orders of Mr Ormond." That led to more fever and another confrontation the following morning. It was clear that the manager, far too friendly ever to have taken a unilateral decision to ban the press, had been acting under orders.

Predictably – this was, after all, a country notorious for a bloody minded dedication to producing optimum work under the least conducive circumstances – the Scots would beat Norway that night. Furthermore, they would return from the World Cup as the only unbeaten team in the tournament, eliminated on goal difference and celebrated to this day by an adoring public. For those nosey little ink merchants, however, it would be the end of sharing digs as well as flights with the 'precious' ones. Not that anything that occurred in that bizarre week could be ascribed to our efforts. It's just that our proximity to the action allowed us to see what the authorities would have preferred to hide.

Glenn Gibbons is a former sports journalist of the year. During 45 years in the trade, he has written for publications including the Daily Mail, Observer, Guardian and Daily Telegraph, and spent the last 10 years as chief football writer at the Scotsman. Glenn is now a weekly sports columnist for the Scotsman.

WE WERE ON THE MIDNIGHT MARCH WITH ALLY'S ARMY

By Malcolm Brodie

C overing major sports tournaments such as a World Cup or an Olympic Games is quite an exhausting experience – certainly no vacation.

Forget the image of basking in the sun by the pool with a cooling drink or partying every night. It is quite the opposite, believe me, and in 14 World Cup finals I've found it hard, relentless work.

Time differences can make transmitting copy a gamble and, frankly, it can all become quite a nightmare. Prolonged sleep is a luxury.

It is June 1978. The place: Cordoba, Argentina. Scotland, under the wildly optimistic stewardship of Ally MacLeod, had fans indoctrinated this could be the year for their side to win the World Cup. Alas, the Scots were defeated 3-1 by Peru in the opening fixture which proved an anticlimax and the start of ferocious criticism of Ally and the Scots.

This meant constant hammering of the typewriters to satisfy the appetites of the various sports desks. They couldn't get enough of what was a fast-developing story.

By noon of the day after the match I had finished. I lay down on top of the bed in my hotel. Ah, total bliss, I thought, and drifted off to sleep. An hour later my slumber was shattered by the ringing telephone. On the line was Harry Cavan, Irish FA president and influential Fifa senior vice-president. "Come round, I have something

90

to tell you," he said. Somehow I managed to find sufficient energy to take me the few blocks to the luxury Fifa accommodation.

"Come in, take a seat," Harry said as he poured me a large Johnny Walker, which in the circumstances, tasted like nectar.

Then he handed me a telex from Fifa, the world governing body, which had been transmitted from Buenos Aires and revealed a Scotland player, Willie Johnston of West Bromwich Albion, known as 'Bud' to his team-mates, had failed a drugs test. There were indications of the substance fencamfamine in his urine, the result of taking two Reactivan tablets before the defeat to Peru. He maintained his innocence and does so to this day.

I immediately returned to the media centre at the Jockey Club in downtown Cordoba and asked the medical staff to give me a run-down on the drug. Within an hour the world had been informed of the news from the wires of the Associated Press, an American news agency. The result was frantic activity in the Scottish camp with attempts made to obtain interviews with players and officials who, however, were ensconced in the Sierras hotel, nicknamed Stalag Luft III, at Alta Gracia in the foothills of the Andes. The Scots were attending an official reception in the hotel to meet Denis Howell, the UK Minister of Sport. The security was tight, and only those with passes could gain admittance, although Trevor McDonald, the ITV presenter, accompanied by a cameraman, eventually broke through the cordon. Indeed, it was Trevor who informed many of the officials and Johnston just what had happened.

I tipped off two colleagues, the late Hugh Taylor and Stuart Brown of the Edinburgh Evening News, and we decided to visit Alta Gracia in the early morning and hopefully learn from Stuart's mole in the camp what decision had been taken on Johnston. Brown telephoned his mole and was told we were to make the night journey to the camp. Upon arrival, and true to his word, the mole walked down to the gate lodge which also served as a media centre during the day. Only the security guard was there. We had been tipped off that Johnston had been expelled from the camp, his future as a Scottish international was in doubt and that this would all be revealed in a statement in the morning from the SFA – much too late for the evening papers. We discovered a telex machine and persuaded the guard to let us use it, aided no doubt by the accreditation badges hanging round our necks. Somehow we got the device to work and made an agreement to transmit the one story to Glasgow, Edinburgh and Belfast, from whence it would be disseminated to the other papers. We felt exhilarated. It had meant hours of labour and, of course, no sleep.

My last memory of Ally is at the media conference following the pyrrhic 3-2 victory over Holland in the final game. The great man sat on a chair on a platform, patting a huge dog. "You are my one friend in the world," he said. A sad finale for a wonderful character, but one who had really lost touch with reality.

Dr Malcolm Brodie MBE is former sports editor and football correspondent of the Belfast Telegraph and is a long-serving member of the Scottish Football Writers' Association, covering Celtic and Rangers matches for more than four decades. He has also covered 14 World Cup finals.

FAREWELL ALLY, YOU GAVE US A GLIMPSE OF THE STARS

By Brian Scott

H ampden Park on a midweek evening towards the end of May 1978. How could we ever forget the occasion when Ally Mac-Leod and his Scotland team prepared to depart for the World Cup finals in Argentina?

Some 25,000 fans were gathered at the national stadium to bid the team good luck in their quest and Ally, leading his players on to the field, milked the moment as only he could. Then, having exchanged waves with the crowd, the Scotland squad, accompanied by SFA officials and members of the press assigned to the forthcoming trip, exited the scene and boarded a convoy of buses.

A policeman on points duty at the junction of Hampden Drive and Cathcart Road raised his left hand to hold back the oncoming traffic, and gave us the thumbs-up with his right.

Next stop Prestwick Airport which, like every flyover we'd passed under on the way there, was bustling with well-wishers. Those were the best of times for the national team; soon, alas, to become the worst.

Scotland – dare we remind ourselves – flopped in Argentina by losing to Peru, drawing with Iran and then beating Holland by an insufficient margin to progress in the competition. The huge expectation which accompanied them to South America gave way, within a matter of eight days, to abject disappointment and bitter recrimination; much of the latter directed against the hapless manager.

He, Scotland's talisman, stood accused of having whipped the country into a mood bordering on hysteria about his team's chance of doing well at Argentina '78. An anguished Ally later attested to the severity of the backlash he was made to suffer by reflecting wryly: "There were 25,000 waving us off at Hampden ... aye, and 100,000 waiting for me when I got home."

The misadventure which was Scotland's participation in that World Cup is an episode which, save for Archie Gemmill's wondrous goal against the Dutch, would be better erased from our collective memory. But that's not to say we can, or should, forget Ally MacLeod. What a character he was: boundlessly enthusiastic and, if sometimes to a fault, infectiously optimistic.

Stories concerning him abound from his first time around as manager of Ayr United, with this one being a personal favourite. Ally is sitting in his office at Somerset Park, scanning the fixtures for the new season. Ayr, he reckons, are a stick-on to win their first few matches. Then, noting his side are due a visit thereafter by Rangers, he declares dismissively: "They won't like facing us when we're at the top of the league, so that's another couple of points."

I recall once chancing upon a publication which carried an interview with Ally from his time with Blackburn Rovers during the 1950s. What, the writer asked him, did he envisage doing once he stopped playing football. Ally mused in response that he might open a corner shop somewhere. But, had he gone on to do so, Scottish football might have been deprived of one of its greatest characters.

Aberdeen were in need of a lift when, in the late autumn of 1975, they hired him from Ayr United as successor to Jimmy Bonthrone. Who better than this charismatic figure to give them one?

Ally was innovative as well as inspiring; a leader who, quite literally, made a difference from day one by instructing the Dons to kick off in their opening match under him with a long, rugby-style punt towards the touchline. Such a strategy, he reckoned, would immediately put the opposition on the back foot and, at the same time, command the instant attention of Pittodrie fans.

He eschewed tradition in another way, too, by flying the Aberdeen team to games in the central belt rather than having them cooped up on a bus for three hours or more.

Yet, after a good run of results, the Dons suffered a series of set-backs which were serious enough to drag them towards the foot of the then newly instituted Premier Division. History informs us they avoided the threat of relegation, albeit narrowly, before recovering sufficient momentum to win the League Cup in Ally's first (and last) full season in charge.

Therein lies a tale so typical of him. Picture the scene as the Aberdeen party pull away from the hotel on the southern suburbs of Glasgow in which they had spent the night before the final with Celtic. Their bus is approaching a roundabout when the sharp-eyed Ally sees Celtic's one converging on it from a different direction. "Put the foot down," he yells to the Dons' driver.

Ally seemed to reckon that, if Aberdeen could get their noses in front of the opposition en route to the match venue, it would augur well for the game itself. Daft, or what? Yet his side went on to win 2-1 after extra-time.

The SFA were moved to appoint Ally as Scotland manager the following spring. "Surprise, surprise," secretary Ernie Walker said before introducing him at their HQ in Glasgow.

Ernie was joking, of course. Ally had been everyone's best bet for the job since Willie Ormond stood down and, after guiding the Scots to a 2-1 victory over England at Wembley, his stock was destined to soar still higher.

Indeed, Scotland's subsequent qualification for the 1978 World Cup, by dint of their 2-0 win over Wales at Anfield, sent the nation into raptures. Ally positively revelled in the ensuing hype, most of it generated by himself.

One of my newspaper colleagues tells the story of how, with a Scottish League XI in northern Italy for an inter-league match, he was first down for breakfast in their lakeside hotel. The national manager duly breezed in and, thinking he was alone (the said journalist was sitting behind a marble pillar), he began chanting a verse of Andy Cameron's anthem, We're on the march with Ally's Army.

Talk about believing one's own publicity! Still, those were stirring times to be around the Scotland team. They remained so until things went horribly awry in Argentina.

But we've long since forgiven Ally, who passed away in 2004, for taking us there on such an ill-starred flight of fancy. It really was fun… while it lasted.

Brian Scott is a long-time scribe with the Daily Mail in Scotland. After setting out on his journalistic career with DC Thomson, he has covered eight World Cups including the six in which the Scottish national side competed from 1974 until 1998. His work has brought him into contact with many of the game's greatest characters, few more colourful than Ally MacLeod.

BIG IN JAPAN

By Robert Grieve

O saka, Japan 2006. Walter Smith's Scotland were taking part in the Kirin Cup and as usual the daily press boys traipsed along for the ride. We arrived at our hotel and did what we usually do after checking in. We headed out.

Taxis to a British pub for some hot food and cold beers. Nothing unusual in that. But what happened after we left the boozer baffled those of us who were there – and still does now. We'd asked for a recommendation from the guy behind the bar. He was an expat so it seemed a good idea at the time. He was happy to oblige and scribbled something down in Japanese and off we went.

First stop taxi rank. We got to the front of the queue and gestured across to the driver standing on the pavement 10 feet away. Handing over his instructions, four of us waited for a nod of the head and an invitation to climb inside. But wait. The old boy had stopped smiling and now had a look of sheer, genuine terror on his face. Looking at me, then across to his mates, then back to me, the colour drained from his face. I tried to tell him we meant no harm – that we were just looking for a late-night drink – but he was having none of it. He slowly handed back the piece of paper before he shouted something, jumped into the cab and sped off into the night. We laughed. It seemed odd that he'd reacted in such a bizarre way but then we were in a bizarre country. So we carried on.

Around 50 yards along the road there was a doorway with a 20-something bouncer standing, arms behind his back. This is the boy who'll help, we thought. I still had the note so called him over before quickly finding out he didn't speak a word of English. Politely handing him the piece of paper, I still expected him to nod his head and point us in the right direction. But wait. Another look of awestruck panic. He handed me the Post-it sized note like it was carrying a deadly bacteria. Without taking his eyes off me he started walking, backwards, towards his doorway. The four of us all looked at each other and tried to calm his fears. But the open-mouthed, terrified look on the lad's face was there for all to see. He didn't dare take his eyes off us for a split second.

Reaching out behind him for the access button to what was a lift, he couldn't have looked more worried. What did the note say? To this day none of us have any idea. It was ripped up and thrown away there and then. But it must have been something almost unimaginable to provoke such a response. I only wish I knew.

Japan was sensational, though. A real shock to the culture senses but positively eye-opening. Everywhere you looked was just, well, different. But in a good way. The bullet train was 21st-century genius at one end of the scale. The taxis with their windows draped in lace curtains somewhere at the other. But the time we had there was a genuine privilege. Apart from anything else, Scotland were sensational that week. Kris Boyd made his international debut against Bulgaria in Kobe and scored twice in a 5-1 win, Chris Burke also notching a double with James McFadden hitting the net too. Two days later in Tokyo a 0-0 draw with hosts Japan saw us win the trophy. That's not an everyday occurrence so being there to see it was fantastic.

But like any other trip it's the laughs we had along the way which makes it stand out as one to remember. The Osaka incident was mindboggling but the entire trip was unforgettable. We even had a stag night on the Saturday in Toyko for one of our colleagues who was due to get married.

Smith and assistant Ally McCoist turned up for what was one of the best nights out I can remember. "What would you like to drink?" Smith was asked when he turned up.

"Bottle of red," he replied.

For the next five or six hours we all had the time of our lives. The highlights included Walter winding up reporter Neil Cameron about his nickname Spook (he lost his virginity in a graveyard) with the Scotland manager claiming his late granny was buried in the place concerned ... possibly THE place.

Robert Grieve is chief football writer of the Scottish Sun. He was 2009 sports news writer of the year and is a two-time winner of the young sports journalist of the year award. Married to Arleen, they have two children, Melissa, nine, and Joel, seven.

GIORGI ON MY MIND

By Stewart Fisher

O ne of these days one of my children will discover a dusty old
box up in the loft and ask, "Daddy, how did a decorative Georgian sword get in here?"

It is a good question – I don't know how I got it through check-in
either – but a smile will crease my lips when I tell them the tale of
the three-day tour of duty I spent in this conflicted little corner of
the Caucuses in the company of former Dundee midfielder Giorgi
Nemsadze.

The Scottish press are renowned the world over for being a sober,
abstemious bunch. But sometimes our hosts just won't take no for an
answer. The trip to Georgia in October 2007, as Alex McLeish's side
were scheduled to travel to Tbilisi to take on Georgia in the penulti-
mate match of our Euro 2008 qualifying campaign, was one such occasion. The cheap 2-0 defeat which saw Scotland play in maroon and
feature a rather bemused Stephen Pearson in central midfield, would
become little more than a footnote amid the dramatic events which
followed against Italy at Hampden Park the next month. Thanks to
Nemsadze, those 90 minutes would also become something of a detail in our epic eastern excursion.

My itinerary had an accidental quality to it. With its finger typically on the pulse of world events, the Sunday Herald's travel company had waited until every last footsoldier of the Tartan Army had
booked up before deciding that Scotland's best chance of qualifying
for a major tournament in a decade was worthy of coverage. That

meant myself and my wily, wizened colleague Kenny MacDonald of the News of the World travelling via an overnighter in Riga and alighting in Tbilisi a full day before the squad, management, officials and other press men. The choice of dwellings was also limited, with my accommodation split between a family-run bed and breakfast way off the beaten track which could best be described as 'rustic,' and the opulent surroundings of a city-centre Marriott which would have made even Comrade Stalin, that infamous Georgia native, blush.

Undaunted, and showing the appetite for hard graft which characterises the fourth estate, I suggested spending our additional day interviewing Nemsadze, his country's most capped player and a man who had recently been forced by the country's government to decline the presidency of their FA. My colleague secured a number and a reference from his former Dundee boss Jim Duffy, and we duly proposed to meet up for a half-hour interview. Little did we suspect that he had bigger plans for us.

I will gloss over much of the first day which (in no particular order) saw us clambering up a scree slope and narrowly avoiding a sheer drop to reach the first of the day's two churches, each of us being presented with a ceremonial sword, and being force-fed a number of borderline unpalatable Georgian delicacies without spending a single lari for the privilege. But as he dropped us off again after our gruelling day of activity, our host muttered those immortal words: "Same time, same place tomorrow?"

Having absented ourselves from his presence long enough to interview some people and file some stories, events duly culminated the night before the game, when Giorgi insisted that ourselves and three others join him and four of his Georgian friends for a tour of a brandy factory and a Georgian banquet, or 'supra.' Everything was progressing as normal until Giorgi stood up, gesticulated to the balding, broad-shouldered man on his left, and said, "This is our 'tamada.' Who is yours?"

'Tamada,' it soon transpired, is the Georgian word for toastmaster, and we quickly elected the redoubtable Ron Scott of the Sunday Post into this august yet admittedly ad hoc position. With waiting staff deeming it a mortal insult if our glasses were ever allowed to run dry of wine, the night thus descended into a bewildering series of toasts – "I drink to our beautiful country," "I drink to your beautiful country," "I drink to the friendship between our two beautiful countries." The chalice of choice soon grew from a small tumbler to a large horn-rimmed affair, even before hack after hack took over tamada duties in order to give Ron a break, which was a bit like an alcoholic version of the Canadian barn dance.

For diplomatic reasons, I can't say too much more about the events of that night. But predictably, Giorgi didn't take a lari for any of it. And there he was, quietly sitting in the hotel car park waiting for us, same time the next day.

Stewart Fisher is one of a number of battery-fed sportswriters at the Herald and Times group, and his name is synonymous with niche topics such as league reconstruction and unknown Icelandic Under-21 players. He has devoted himself to his art since the turn of the millennium, churning out 60-minute masterpieces on a daily basis yet somehow avoiding the acclaim of the masses. Stewart lives in Gourock with his wife Mairi-Anne, and sons Ewan and Oliver.

ALEX FERGUSON PERFECTED THE HAIRDRYER – ON ME!

By Frank Gilfeather

Those who had close contact with Sir Alex Ferguson during his Aberdeen years will have their own views on if and when, during those early days, they spotted something that indicated he was to progress to become one of the biggest names in football. What was clear from the beginning was that this was no ordinary man.

He may have been left the nucleus of a highly promising squad by his predecessor, Billy McNeill, but the trick of turning them into winners was left as his responsibility. The changes he effected in the side over the two-year period from 1978 when he joined the Dons were significant, and in 1980 he lead them to a 5-0 win over Hibernian at Easter Road on the last day of the season to win the Scottish Premier League championship. It was only the second title win in Aberdeen's history. Here was a coach with special qualities, but who would have thought that triumph was just the beginning of a truly remarkable period for a provincial club?

I was the sports correspondent with Grampian Television, before it morphed into STV, in those heady days and was fortunate enough to follow an Aberdeen side during the Fergie era which brought the club enormous success and with it, inevitably, the reality that he would find bigger fish to fry.

There was no easy ride in those days for anyone associated either directly or indirectly with Aberdeen Football Club. Even as an onlooker you could only wonder at the level of energy and commitment the manager gave to the task of instilling the belief in his players and, indeed, in everyone with an interest in the club, that the tag of also-rans would never be tolerated as long as he was in charge. Alex had ambition by the bucketful – still has, but ambition is impotent without talent, drive, energy, diligence, preparation and application. Put all these into the mix and you have a person who will not be diverted from his goal. Interfere with any of this and you could be sure his opinion of you and your efforts would follow.

Ferguson and I were never bosom buddies – neither of us would have wanted that – nor could I accept the rants he often launched into when the views or questions of a journalist upset him. I have vivid memories of him and me falling out over a variety of issues, but I accepted that he was protecting his interests – his team – and, like a father would a child, defending it to the hilt. There was no doubting the man's dedication and sense of responsibility to those who depended on him, and his nature to control, spread far beyond his brief of team boss.

How well I recall him roaring down the telephone at me one Monday morning after he had discovered that, on Radio Clyde the previous Saturday, I had revealed that Jim Leighton, his international goalkeeper, had been dropped and was not, as Ferguson had claimed, unavailable because of injury. A club director had offered me this intelligence moments before I entered the football ground and it became a major talking point in the preamble to a fixture against Hibs in which Bryan Gunn, Leighton's able deputy, kept goal for the home side. The rage emanating from the telephone was audible enough to attract the attention of everyone in that Grampian TV room that morning. Much of the vocabulary from the Pittodrie hotline was industrial and were I to embellish the tale with a little bit of poetic licence, I would claim women fainted and hardened journalists went weak at the knees. But there was neither swooning nor leg-buckling; just the dropping of jaws and transfixed eyes.

I was told I was banned, not from reporting Aberdeen's home games, but from access to him for interviews, an edict that, while washing over my head, presented my employer with a little difficulty.

How can you have a sports correspondent who isn't permitted to talk to the manager of the area's principal football team? The answer was to have someone else do the interviews till Fergie calmed down and I was reintroduced to the fold. Eventually I was ... about six months later.

On another occasion, I was left without a name as I entered the Pittodrie room where members of the press gathered at the end of games to hear the manager's thoughts on proceedings. He had been unhappy with an interview I had done with him on the aeroplane returning from Romania where his side had squeezed through in a European tie en route to the Cup Winners' Cup final victory over Real Madrid, before 10,000 drenched Dons fans in Gothenburg's Ullevi Stadium in 1983. Cathy, his wife, had expressed disquiet to her husband over his "performance" during the airborne interview and he blamed me for transmitting it.

Fed up with his verbal abuse, I proposed that it might have been better had he and I spoken quietly about the matter and without an audience. Otherwise, I joked, "I may have to make a comeback," a reference to my days as a Scottish champion and internationalist boxer. An apology quickly followed.

Such histrionics were not uncommon and the unpredictability of dealing with an exceptionally driven character meant you never knew what to expect when stepping into Pittodrie, as many of the wonderful players he had assembled would testify. But then we must recognise that there can be many sides to men and women at the top, or aiming for it, of their chosen professions. They will not be diverted from what they wish to achieve.

For me, the moment that underlined just how good Alex was at his job, and made him a manager not only lauded in his native land, came on the cold March night in 1983 in the Olympic Stadium in Munich when his tactical nous saw his provincial side draw 0-0 with Bayern, one of the best teams in the world, en route to that European Cup Winners' Cup triumph. That performance, followed by a victory over the Germans in the home leg two weeks later, signalled that by focusing as hard as he did on the job to be done, his players would not be stopped in their quest for greatness.

Sir Alex continued to deliver year after year. That is the mark of greatness.

Frank Gilfeather is football correspondent for the Times and the Herald, and a weekly contributor to Sky's Gillette Soccer Saturday programme. A former Scottish amateur boxing champion and internationalist, Frank has been a news and sports print and broadcast journalist for more than 40 years, and has additional credits as a playwright and author.

HAIRDRYER IN THE BATH – ALEX FERGUSON, ABERDEEN AND ME

By Alan Muir

For a moment a wave of unreality washed over me, prickling my scalp. I had just spent half an hour one-on-one with my hero, the greatest manager Britain has ever seen and possibly the world. The gaffer. The boss. The hairdryer.

Ferguson.

"Is that enough, son?" he barked over the line from his Manchester mecca, ready to hang up.

I froze – it was now or never, once in a lifetime, last chance, final minute, "speak now" I commanded myself, he's going to hang up, it has to be now…

"Sir Alex …" I began in a quiet, semi-detached voice …

To understand this pivotal point in my evolution we must travel back in time, back to a time before the Twitter-twatter of the internet, jovial Jeff Stelling and his merry band of dements, freezing Friday night kick-offs, and Russian owners with no patience but plenty of roubles.

It was a time BM (Before Murdoch) so although brick-like telephones could rest easy with their secrets, there were only four TV channels and nothing on. This was an era when a team of red superheroes sat astride the league like hairy-armed Goliaths, their magnificent moustaches almost taunting the baby faces of the Old Firm, their skin hardened by exposure to North Sea winds and deleterious nights of drink and docks. Of course, we've raced past Pro Evolution and sailed by Sensible Soccer, so there was naff all for kids to do except kick a ball about or beat each other sadistically for supporting 'The Sheep.' That and a felt cathedral of football.

I speak, of course, of Subbuteo.

I had never been the first pick for football at school – I hadn't even been the last; many of the girls were given a game before me. No matter – here, at last, was my chance. My dad bought the game and we selected our teams (Aberdeen, Motherwell and the Scotland squad). We decided we weren't going to play like savages – not for us the constant unfurling of the mat and trying to smooth out wrinkles. No, my dad decided we would buy a full-size piece of plywood on which we could paste the pitch. It sounded magical, a field of dreams over which I would control my beloved Aberdeen like a pre-adolescent giant.

We duly took over the living room, pushing the entire contents against one wall, and pasted up the pitch. "It's a bit big, Dad," I ventured tentatively as we looked down.

My dad sighed heavily. It was indeed a bit big. In fact, it was the full size of the living room. It was impossible to either enter or exit the room without standing on the board and scattering the formations.

We had one aborted match, ball and men repeatedly pinging off the walls, before the game was abandoned at 0-0 (when my mum came home and demanded to know, "how in the name of the wee man" she was going to watch Coronation Street on a TV turned to the wall?).

As I watched my dad snap the plywood pitch in twain in order to get it out of the living room, it was my first lesson in fantasy not really translating to reality (the felt pitch ended its days in disgrace in the hall cupboard, crushed amid the wreckage of the plywood and buggered board games).

Despite this devastating childhood blow I maintained a love of football and the Dandy Dons. It was a love forged in the glory of Gothenburg, of a bronzed moustache of a man, clutching a European trophy with chimp-like arms and a grin like that of a caveman who had just discovered fire.

His name was William Miller. His manager was Alexander Ferguson.

I was never an obsessive fan, I must admit. On one occasion my dad took me to see Falkirk v Aberdeen at Brockville. I began by leading us into the wrong end. Then I asked my dad who the black player was for Aberdeen. He sighed heavily (he was growing used to it by then; I was 13). "That's Willie Miller," he replied in a weary voice, looking at his watch.

Later, I would flirt heavily with becoming a real fan – joining a Central Scotland supporters' bus and enduring six-hour round trips to Pittodrie with the cast of Neds. This lasted two years – including a memorable match at Ibrox. We lost, of course, but the experience was livened up at half-time when there was a near-riot at the pie kiosk. I clearly recall the bald psycho who ran the bus yelling we were probably going to have to fight our way back to the bus.

"Can't we get the train?" I pleaded.

"No we bloody can't!" he shouted.

I also remember going to the Scottish Cup final in 2000 (the so-called Orange Final) which ended as a contest after a few moments when Jim Leighton was clogged and carted off. His replacement was mercurial winger Robbie Winters.

"Do you want to get the train home?" I joked to the bald bus convener.

He sighed heavily and looked at his watch (unlike my dad he had never grown used to me and often spent the long bus journeys staring at me and shaking his head).

My time with the Aberdeen urchins ended after I experienced a moment of clarity on the bus – peering through a fug of bong smoke and swearing, I realised no-one here had read a book since school and even then it probably had pictures (or at least a phallus drawn in the margin).

Fast-forward a few years and Miller is now denuded of moustache (and Harry Ramsden's), just as Aberdeen have been denuded of cups and their greatest manager. I'm still a fan of both though and that was why I was so nervous in 2003 when I rang Old Trafford and was put through to Sir Alex of Ferguson. I was interviewing Sir Al to pick over the bones of his Falkirk playing days (Brockville was in its final days before the bulldozers and the bland horror of Morrisons moved in). I had prepared my questions, but also secretly harboured a couple of ambitions – one was silly (to get Sir Alex to say "vewy pwoud"), the other deadly serious – how to communicate my enduring love for Aberdeen and the Ferguson era?

Not many get a one-on-one with the great man and I was nervous, but we were soon flying (I was even relaxed enough to drop the "Sir" and call him "Alex" – something Wayne Rooney can only dream of). He fired off more anecdotes than Peter Ustinov huffing lighter fluid. It was gold.

There was only one thing left.

"Is that enough, son?" he barked in a slightly Taggart tone.

I hesitated. Here I go, I thought: "Can I just say, as an Aberdeen fan … thanks."

There was a silence.

"Aye. Whatever."

Alan Muir has twice been voted Scotland's weekly newspaper journalist of the year. He is also an Aberdeen fan who has experienced a litany of failures, shattered dreams and hairy Scotsmen over the last two decades (he's also been to a few Aberdeen games). His is a story of faded glory (journalism career), occasional beauty (wife Amanda) and promising youngsters (sons Jack and Ben) – much like the Dandies.

A DAY OF DRAMA AND TRAGEDY IN THE NORTH-EAST

By Roddy Forsyth

The insistent beep of the pager – this was in the days before mobile phones – signalled something urgent was brewing while I was driving near Stirling on the afternoon of Thursday, November 6th, 1986.

I stopped at a telephone box to call the editorial desk at Radio 2, which was the BBC's main sports network in the days before Radio Five Live became the corporation's first rolling news and sports channel. The editor was excited. "Get yourself to Glasgow Airport," he ordered, "you're booked on the next flight to Aberdeen. We're sure Alex Ferguson is going to be the new manager of Manchester United. We think he's still in Aberdeen, so see if you can find him."

By the time I arrived at the airport a good many journalists had already checked in. Most of them, though, were newsmen, flying to the oil capital of Europe on the first leg of a journey that would take them on to Shetland, where a Chinook helicopter carrying workers from the Brent Field had crashed into the North Sea just short of its destination at Sumburgh, killing 45 passengers and crew.

Three others on the Aberdeen flight were sports reporters – veterans who travelled together and who were not likely to offer a junior colleague much assistance on a story of this substance. When we arrived at Aberdeen Airport they bolted for the exit in search of a taxi while I went to a car hire desk to pick up a vehicle that had been pre-booked. I asked the girl behind the counter if I could use her phone while she filled in the paperwork. The first call was to Ian Taggart, the Aberdeen secretary, who said that Ferguson was not at Pittodrie and had not been there all afternoon. "He's not at home, either," Taggart added conspiratorially. After a little more chat he said: "Look, you could try one of the hotels at the airport – Martin Edwards might be there, too."

On the car hire desk was a card with a list of useful numbers – including those of all the nearby hotels. The first call struck pay dirt when I asked if I could speak to Mr Edwards. The operator asked, "Is that Mr Edwards from Dundee or Mr Edwards from Manchester?"

If it was Mr Edwards from Manchester, she said, he was not in his room, but she was pretty sure he was in the restaurant. The hotel was close at hand and as I drove the hire car over it was gratifying to witness the little clique of older correspondents in a taxi heading for the city centre.

The restaurant was a typical hotel facility of the period, with heavy red upholstery and dark wood panelling. The tables were mostly obscured in alcoves. At first it seemed deserted – then I heard a familiar throaty laugh. And there, in a discreet corner of the otherwise empty dining room, was Alex Ferguson with Martin Edwards – and between them a bottle of champagne in an ice bucket. I walked to their table and said: "I believe I can congratulate the new manager of Manchester United."

Fergie grinned, shook hands, introduced the Old Trafford chairman and poured a little bubbly for me so that we could all toast the occasion. After a couple of minutes' chat, he said that he and Edwards still had some bits and pieces to discuss but that they would be around for a while.

I went to the phone box in the foyer to call Radio 2 and was put on air to break the news that this Ferguson bloke would indeed take charge of the Red Devils. After 20 minutes or so, reporters began to arrive in ones and twos, and eventually Fergie and his new chairman came out to brief the throng.

I saw him again in the hotel car park and we talked about his prospects. When it was time to part I remarked that it was a pity there was no European football for him because of the ban on English clubs following the Heysel Disaster. "There's enough to be done down there, believe me," said Fergie.

None of us – and that includes Ferguson and Edwards – could have summoned the imaginative leap needed to envisage the dazzling narrative the man from Govan would impose on English and European football over the next quarter-century.

The sheer scale of Ferguson's achievements almost hypnotically induces the belief that his has been an unbroken chain of success, from his earliest days at Pittodrie to the present day at Old Trafford. Yet, as with virtually all stellar careers, timing is crucial. Having turned down offers to manage Rangers, Arsenal and Spurs, Fergie chose the perfect moment to depart the north-east of Scotland. In the first instance, Aberdeen's form was unimpressive. The Dons had lost three and drawn five of their 15 Scottish Premier Division fixtures, and had been knocked out of Europe on a two-goal aggregate by Sion. The Scottish radio phone-ins of the time were not short of callers declaring that Ferguson's time was up. And Fergie, whose players had also been knocked out of the Scottish League Cup, was now up against Graeme Souness at Rangers, who had begun to unleash a far superior spending power.

Souness, of course, could sign England players such as Chris Woods and Terry Butcher because Scottish clubs were not quarantined from European competition after Heysel – but the very absence of the need to qualify for that arena also removed a substantial layer of pressure from Ferguson in his early years at Old Trafford.

Ferguson enjoyed good fortune but his genius was to take it at the flood, as he no doubt muses when he contemplates his astounding reign at United. Given the nature of the man, it would be no surprise if he also reflects that, on the afternoon that Edwards lured him from the shores of the North Sea, the same waters shattered the lives of 45 families, whose thoughts of that weekend must be imbued with far more sombre recollections of how life deals its deck of cards.

Roddy Forsyth has been Scottish football correspondent for BBC

Radio Sport since 1986. He also writes for the Daily Telegraph and has worked for, among others, the Times and the Sunday Telegraph. Roddy has been president of the Scottish Football Writers Association since 2010.

A FISHY TALE

By Michael Grant

The whole stupid idea was sold to me like this: every year Sir Alex Ferguson is presented with a giant box of fresh fish from Aberdeen market, sent to him at Old Trafford by some of his old pals up in the north-east. We think it would be a good idea, Michael, if you came away from covering the Euro '96 finals from Scotland's base in the Midlands and head across to Manchester for the day. You'd be there when the fish guys turn up with the crate of mackerel, halibut, or whatever it is he likes with his chips. And you'd get an interview with Fergie. Uninvited, unannounced, intruding on a shared moment between the great man and pals he doesn't often see any more ... as journalistic assignments go this was about as pathetically half-arsed as it can get.

Naturally the thing was as big a disaster as it deserved to be. A late-running train meant a missed connection between Leamington Spa, near where the Scotland squad were training, and Manchester. And that meant arriving almost an hour late for this doomed door-stepping job. So no Fergie, no photographs, no story, not even the fish guys. The Old Trafford receptionist politely went through the motions of calling his office on my behalf.

"Hi. Listen, there's a lad here from Scotland. Something about fish for the manager. Yeah, fish. He's saying is there any chance of a quick word with him. Yeah, with the manager. Oh I know, I know ..."

Plenty of journalists have their tale of the one that got away when it comes to an interview with Ferguson. For the past quarter of a century he's consistently been the biggest beast of all in the pool of football targets. He used to do 'one-to-ones' relatively frequently but as he piled more silverware on the heap, and Manchester United withdrew deeper behind wall after wall of corporate bulls***, he got busier and fussier. He would periodically turn up in something like L'Equipe, or a style magazine, or in the glossy pull-out of one of the English Sunday heavies. But run-of-the-mill football interviews with run-of-the-mill British papers? Gradually they became few and far between. To get Fergie you had to somehow catch his imagination, or you had to get lucky.

Early in 2001 we got lucky. It's burned on the memory all these years later; oh Lord it's there in black and white in the email from his secretary – Fergie's said "yes!" Every journalist knows the thought that comes next: "Please don't let me balls this up!" There aren't second chances with something like this. This was big. The newspaper, the Sunday Herald, wasn't yet two years old (I'd moved on from my old paper and its boxes of fish) and here was one of the highest-profile interviews it had landed.

This was a new batteries job. You don't risk possible equipment failure on a mission this enormous: you prepare notebook, list of questions, pen, spare pen, and new batteries for the tape recorder. Sony Microcassette-recorder M-540V: don't let me down now, you little bastard. This would be a conversation with Fergie and a simultaneous attempt to prevent him noticing the umpteen stolen glances to check those little tape spools were turning. Am I getting this? Please God, let this be recording …

Everyone tells you Fergie's at his work at 8am every morning, or 7am, or whatever time you want to believe. They say he's read all the papers, he's had his breakfast, he's bollocked four people down the phone and watched a full replay of United's last game before you've reached over to hit the snooze button. Well, not this day. At 9am, interview time, Fergie's car park space was empty and the workaholic manager of Manchester United was nowhere to be seen. He wasn't there at quarter-past either, or half-past. Tut tut, lazy Fergie. Eventually an update from his secretary: "He's running late, come back and he'll see you at 11am." This was good news because it would be the icebreaker. Fergie would feel a bit guilty about a messing around a fellow Scot, and he'd be friendlier and more open because of it. His 'apology' would come in the form of better quotes, some jokes, a bit of colour, a better interview. That's what I thought.

You look for a way in at the start of an interview, something to establish some sort of connection and get a foot in the door. These early exchanges can be crucial. It's when you're being sized up to see what you're made of. Unlike Ferguson I'm not into horseracing. I don't play the piano. I'd happily drink wine out of a Thermos flask, to hell with the vintage bottles. I haven't managed Manchester United for 25 years. But we have Aberdeen together. I'd tell him I was a Dons man who'd grown up to his teams spanking the Old Firm left, right and centre. We'd get on like a house on fire.

I've read the vast majority of big Ferguson interviews over the years. The one that stands out was by Michael Tierney in The Herald in 2002, which read like Tierney had just gone three rounds with Tyson. They didn't hit it off, and he perfectly captured what a hard, challenging bastard Ferguson can be in interviews, let alone in management. My own experience was more enjoyable, but even so …

He doesn't do small talk or pleasantries. No "how was the trip down?" No "did I find the training ground easily enough?" He couldn't give a sh*t. Two hours late he flew into the room, briskly shook hands, clapped his hands together and said, "right, fire away." No apology and not a single second's gap which might have been filled with some ingratiating you're-so-great Dons chat. The starting pistol fired and we were off, ready or not. Would he have time for the photographer when we're finished? "Naw, he can take some while we're talking …"

Ferguson might test, intimidate and even try to bully but boy, he delivers too. For the best part of an hour he took every question. Words poured out of him. Retirement (he was still in his 50s), horseracing, golf, how Rangers bought too many players every summer, how Celtic needed Martin O'Neill to sort out their perennial player problems, how United would react in adversity – "many people shrivel up and die, we wouldn't" – how it interested him to see how disparate personalities gelled to form a winning team, how everyone obsessed about United. "In the newspaper industry they've got to get something about Manchester United every day because it sells. It doesn't matter whether it's 'Roy Keane was seen on Mars yesterday', it definitely works."

But he's tough and hard-going. He keeps you guessing, and he can look cold and unimpressed, and he'll not fall for tired patter. And then suddenly it's all over. Another clap of the hands, as abrupt and unexpected as the first, and he's on his feet. There hadn't even been any tapping of the watch as a warning. He said, "well done" (a phrase he has a habit of using at the end of questioning) and then a tiniest morsel of chit-chat. "You driving back up the road just now?" At last! This was more like it, me and Fergie shooting the breeze and … oh, he's just said cheerio and the door's closing.

Every single interview is a breeze after that and they always will be. The ring is never worrying again after being in with Mike Tyson. Every journalist has their own Fergie: a hero, heroine, villain, favourite sportsman, artist or star. And if you're lucky enough to get them your pulse doesn't really quicken thereafter whenever you sit down with anyone else. You aren't fazed or worried by anyone once you've landed what, to you, is the biggest of them all.

And what's the first thing you do when the door's shut and he's left the room? You check the tape recorder.

Yeah, it's all there. Got him.

Michael Grant is chief football writer with The Herald and has covered Scottish club and international matches all over the world for two decades, including three World Cups and three European Championships. Over a pint, he may accept that Aberdeen FC aren't quite what they used to be.

SAVE US FROM THESE MINI SIR ALEX FERGUSONS

By Graham McColl

The man standing on the touchline this Saturday morning is a coach.

We know he is a coach because it says so on the back of his yellow fluorescent bib. He knows he is a coach because he is shouting, pointing, gesticulating incessantly. Sometimes he stands side-on to the pitch, all five fingers of one hand splayed out or with the hand turned into something resembling a hook and revolving to make a point to those on the pitch. All of this is what a coach does, isn't it? You've seen it on Match of the Day. So has he.

There are 14 players on the pitch – two teams of seven – this East Dunbartonshire morning; the Campsie Hills forming a magnificent backdrop to the action as these eight- and nine-year-olds play their weekly game of football, and the youngsters are not short of advice because the previously mentioned coach is not alone in his work. Taut to the touchline there are no fewer than seven others, all issuing, frequently simultaneously, useful instructions such as "Shout for it" and "Name the pass" or "Get in there."

The coaches are almost uniformly burly and bulky-bellied, wear jeans and training shoes below their bibs, and scrutinise every pass, kick and header with serious intensity. Nor are they themselves alone. Several parents also feel it is their duty to menace the touchlines and jab advice at the youngsters, prodding them on from various vantage points. "Take it quickly. You're too slow. Speed, speed,

speed." All this over a kick-in (not throw-ins at this age and stage) from the touchline, halfway down the pitch.

One fluorescently-bibbed coach edges into anxious desperation at seeing one of his players muck up a move. A choked squeal of "Come on!" emerges from his mouth as he abandons any attempt at coherent 'advice.' Another coach, arm extended horizontally, tells his "back three" to arrange themselves in a straight line and guides them into position as if his arm is an imaginary spirit level; this for a seven-a-side team with a goalkeeper and no offside being played.

"Hey! Hey!" The traditional west of Scotland call to rein in some-one about to cross a line of correct behaviour, peppers the air fre-quently as the youngsters weave and wind their way around the field, oblivious to their good fortune in receiving all this free personal tui-tion from the touchlines; the shouts of the young boys and girls on the field of play adding to the general Babel-like cacophony.

It is all quite different from the atmosphere at the Scottish Foot-ball Association's offices at Hampden Park where I visited Jim Fleet-ing, the SFA's director of football development, in early 2011 to discuss his radical plans for revamping youth football in Scotland. The carpets muffle even the slightest of sounds, there are no raised voices, and the atmosphere is restrained and civilised over coffee and biscuits. It is an unlikely base for revolutionaries but Fleeting was happy to share his plans for overturning entirely the way in which youth football is approached in Scotland.

A tall, refined-looking man, Fleeting had the air of a long-serving but still-enthusiastic, young-in-spirit schoolteacher as he enthused over how he and colleagues had visited Brazil, Argentina, Holland, Italy and France, among various other countries, to obtain a raft of information on how those nations develop young players. The result for Scotland was to be a radical one – for the first time ever, the SFA, in partnership with the Scottish Youth FA, had agreed that every child involved in youth football in Scotland would adhere to the same guidelines – four-a-side football up to the age of nine, followed by seven-a-side football; all on reduced-size pitches.

Even more radically, league competitions and trophies were to be scrapped for children up to the age of 12. "It's the first time right across the board that this must happen," Fleeting said. "We believe that people should express themselves in order to get better as a player, not express themselves to win a trophy or a medal. Through that intensity of trying to force someone to play their best to win a cup or a medal, I think we're doing a disservice to these individuals on a long-term basis. The kid who's been winning medals at nine, 10, 11, 12, thinks he's a player and doesn't go that bit extra; doesn't challenge himself in any way."

Given that youth football does not attract huge publicity, this radical step has gone almost unnoticed by those who follow mainstream senior football in Scotland but the SFA deserve, surely, encouragement and praise for introducing a venture that attacks at the root the win-at-all-costs mentality that has led to young Scottish players being forced to pursue prizes, points and wins at the expense of developing their skills.

It is one thing, though, to introduce a radical change, another to expect those implementing it to be tuned into the philosophy involved. The match with the oversubscribed number of coaches mentioned above took place in the spring of 2012, more than a year after Fleeting's plans had been implemented, and while the trophies and medals had been taken away, Fleeting's accompanying idea of non-intervention from coaches remains a mirage.

"We don't expect anyone to do any [touchline] coaching with the kids and that's the biggest problem we've had in the past," he said. "We all want to be Sir Alex Ferguson and if we can just get these guys to back off a wee bit and give the kids just a wee bit more space to be themselves and enjoy themselves the way we used to do when we played street games. There is no chance of street games coming back but most people do think they were beneficial to us so we're trying to recreate the street games."

One of the aims of the change is to encourage young players to express themselves more individually and to get away from the culture whereby passing is over-encouraged. Back at our Saturday morning match, a coach waddles on to the pitch after half-time and tells his charges to gather round him as if the extensive team talk at the break has not been enough for him to get across all his ideas. "Come into me," Mr mini-Alex Ferguson says, "what are we gonnae do second half?" "Pass," the boys tell him. "Cannae hear you." "Pass." "Cannae hear you." "Pass." "Still cannae hear you." "Pass."

Fleeting, meanwhile, can dream. "I've got this vision of me and my missus walking through the nice short grass – remember when you were young they used to cut the grass in the parks and you used to get the smell of the grass and you used to dive about – watching my grandsons and granddaughters playing in all these wee games and coaches just letting these wee kids play and hearing very little from the side of the park, and all the mums and dads sitting at the side of the park drinking their coffee and clapping their hands, saying, 'Thank the Lord someone's seen sense.' It is like football utopia but in my mind I had football utopia – those summer nights were my football utopia."

Visions, dreams, utopia; all fine until you drop the non-progressive Scottish male football youth coach into the middle of it all.

Graham McColl has been a freelance writer and journalist since 1994, and is the author of 20 books on football and one on golf. He has been a contributor to and editor on several other books. He has written for When Saturday Comes, FourFourTwo and numerous other magazines and newspapers, and is a regular contributor of features and match reports to the Times.

MAROONED ON THE ITALIAN RIVIERA

By Gerry McNee

A plaque on the wall of the Grand Hotel Miramare in Santa Margherita on the Italian Riviera boasts to the world that in 1933 from its marble terrace Guglielmo Marconi first transmitted short-wave radio signals to his yacht, the Elettra, moored below. The hotel has hosted, among others, a young King Hussein of Jordan, Vivian Leigh and Sir Laurence Olivier, and Fred Astaire and Ginger Rogers, who sang "I'm in Heaven" as they enjoyed exotic cocktails in the Barracuda Bar. And me!

Thanks to fellow Scot Alexander Graham Bell's own invention a dramatic telephone message flashed across that same stretch of water from the Scotland team World Cup HQ on the other side of the bay. It was the late Wallace Mercer, the embattled chairman of Heart of Midlothian, there with the Scottish Football Association on which he served: "I need to speak to you urgently. Can we have lunch tomorrow?"

We were based on the edge of the mountainous Ligurian coast just days into Italia '90, still in an era during which World Cup finals participation seemed Scotland's inalienable right. We were also just days after his attempted merger of Hearts and Hibs, which had ended in acrimony with threats against him, his family, home and business properties. What could he possibly wish to discuss? Wallace was always the best of company and a generous table host. He was also quite different to any Scottish football club chairmen before him. He was an interesting fellow, a maverick, and as it wasn't a match day, the answer, of course, was "yes." Next morning the phone rang followed by the trademark Mercer chuckle: "I'll pick you up by boat at the jetty in front of your hotel at noon. I think you'll approve of the restaurant."

On the minute a sleek motor-launch came into view and there was a beaming Wallace wearing the skipper's hat preparing to do a mock piping aboard. We sailed on and around the rocks into stunning Portofino, clambered on to the quayside and walked around to the far end before sitting in glorious sunshine. The food and wine reflected Wallace's excellent taste.

And now to business: "You're close to Alex Ferguson. I want him as manager of Hearts and you are the man to ask him."

The manager of Manchester United quitting to go to Hearts? Before you skip on by, remember Fergie had been at Old Trafford since 1986 and had failed to end a two-decade run without a championship. He had saved his job the previous month by winning the FA Cup, after hanging on round by round before at last triumphing in a final replay. He was, back then, no darling of the fans. There is no doubt he would have been sacked had United lost that final. The then sports editor of the Express in Manchester, Mike Dempsey, a fine man very close to Matt Busby, Bobby Charlton and the United board, advised me to quietly warn Ferguson of his impending fate late in that FA Cup run. I decided against as he had enough on his plate and had anyway grasped the gravity of his situation all by himself. He was in a vulnerable position, and by no means the wealthy man of today.

So this was no pipe dream of Wallace's, who hugely admired Ferguson's incredible record at Aberdeen. He gave a preparatory cough then rattled out the terms for me to deliver: Any title of Ferguson's choice including general manager; sole arbiter in team matters; a Hearts record transfer budget; a house of his choice to be built within a reasonable distance of Edinburgh; a substantial shareholding in the club and – if it didn't work out, provided Wallace was still at Hearts – a £200,000 golden parachute payment (Mercer's description).

After sailing back I shook hands with Wallace, stepped ashore, turned and said I would put it to Ferguson, but insisted that once he had given his decision the story was mine alone. He agreed and thanked me.

I contacted Ferguson, who was staying to the north near Genoa where Scotland played their opening game against Costa Rica, described the tone of the meeting and made the offer. He said he'd need a couple of days to think it over. And he did.

I called him at the agreed time: "It's some offer," he said, "thank Wallace very much."

Then he added a line which can only bring a smile when you think about what's happened since: "I still believe I can win the league with United."

As agreed with Mercer – when the decision was given – it was my story. I transmitted it in seconds from the Miramare to the UK on my brand new Tandy laptop, the first time such technology was available at a World Cup. Marconi would have approved.

Then I gave a line to Jim Traynor of the then Glasgow Herald and Andy McInnes who was with the Express where I worked at the time. My motive was to embarrass the Edinburgh-based Scotsman, the Herald's main market rival, as one of their reporters had some time earlier naughtily broken an embargo. Being beaten on an Edinburgh club story of this magnitude by a Glasgow paper was indeed a lesson he would never forget. Yes, we descended to these dreadful depths when necessary!

Obviously the Hearts incumbent manager, Alex MacDonald, was far from pleased to learn from the papers that his jacket was on a shooglie peg. As was Wallace when he received a furious call from MacDonald!

Mercer then phoned me. I picked up the receiver next to the shower and increased the water level as he shouted: "What's happened?"

After a couple of "Hello? Hello?" moments I shouted: "He turned it down Wallace."

The line went dead!

I had dared not tell Mercer Fergie's response before going to press, because he was close to an Edinburgh freelance who tended to pass such information to the high-paying Sun newspaper. That was why I had said that the story was mine, as soon as a decision was reached.

When Mercer later approached Joe Jordan for the manager's job he didn't call me. Joe was and remains a very good friend which Mercer didn't know. So he was peevish when he greeted Joe at Edinburgh Airport and I was there too.

We did laugh about it all in years to follow and I remember other splendid meals at One Devonshire Gardens in Glasgow's West End and the splendid Gothenburg Sheraton during Scotland's Euro 1992 campaign against Germany, the CIS and Holland in Sweden.

A 40-year career travelling at the expense of newspapers, television and radio was great fun. Interviewing players like Pele in Westchester, New York, Beckenbauer in Munich, Platini in Paris, Cruyff at the Amsterdam Arena, Baresi in Milan and so many others – was terrific. But for me above all was the daily cut and thrust. Getting the story and telling the readers/viewers/listeners something they didn't know.

Since Mercer unfurled his golden parachute in Ligure West German football has reunited with East. The Soviet Union's transitional CIS team (beaten 3-0 by Scotland in Norrkoping – McStay, McClair, McAllister pen.) is Russia once more. So much has changed over the last couple of decades.

But not so for the Grand Hotel Miramare. It sits original, aloof and sentinel above that same stretch of water. What would Marconi make of it all?

Gerry McNee is former chief sportswriter with Scottish Express Newspapers and former chief football commentator with Scottish Television. He is a former columnist with the Daily Express, Sunday Mail and News of the World, and is the author of The Quiet Man *(1990);* A Million Miles for Celtic *(1981);* The Story of Celtic – an Official History *(1978);* A Lifetime in Paradise *(1975); and* You'll Never Walk Alone *(1972).*

HOW JIM JEFFERIES GOT THE BIRD

By Kenny Millar

J im Jefferies has worked with some talented wingers over the years. Yet none of them could compare to a childhood feathered friend, 'Panda, the Sunday Post pigeon.' I confidently predict it's the strangest story I'll ever put to print.

Back in July 2011, I accompanied Hearts on their pre-season trip to the picturesque, sun-drenched Il Ciocco resort in Tuscany. There's never a dull moment covering the Jambos but, even by their standards, it was a turbulent week. Their young right-back, Craig Thomson, had just been placed on the sex offenders' register after pleading guilty to two counts of indecent behaviour. Back home, there was a clamour from the media and supporters alike for the club to clarify Thomson's future at Tynecastle.

A world away in rural Italy, the players shared their own views in private but the atmosphere was largely unaffected. That owed much to the renowned man-management of Jefferies, along with long-time lieutenants Billy Brown and Gary Locke. Make no mistake, the trio held that club together during the Thomson affair – and countless other instances of off-field unrest.

Jefferies couldn't have been more helpful over the course of the week, along with press officer Paul Kiddie, ensuring – despite the difficult circumstances – that I was well looked after on my first foreign assignment. After one typically expansive interview in the hotel reception, Jefferies swerved off on a bizarre tangent. He and his father, it turned out, used to keep a loft of racing pigeons – and one in particular stood out. 'Panda' – a distinctive black-and-white specimen – would never return to base on the same day, no matter where it was released. Jefferies recalled it would always reappear by the time the family copy of the Sunday Post dropped through the letterbox, adding, "My Dad won some money from a race in Rennes, when Panda flew back in record time – just because it was a Sunday. He turned up along with the paper – it was amazing!"

This revelation was tailor-made for a DC Thomson employee. After half-jokingly pitching the idea to my sports editor, I was charged with securing the coop scoop at Hearts' next press conference.

Egged on by a few sniggering Sunday colleagues, I decided to chance my luck with press officer Clare Cowan. Clearly bewildered by the out-of-the-blue request, she agreed to relax the club's no one-to-one interview policy and an equally bemused Jefferies afforded me five extra minutes to discuss his penchant for pigeons on the record.

Having fondly reminisced about bygone days, his facial expression changed when I asked him to hang about until my photographer arrived with a caged pigeon. I let it hang for a minute before putting him out of his misery. This blockbuster world exclusive hit the shelves on July 24, 2011.

As fate would have it, the original copy was gutted to accommodate news of Amy Winehouse's death. I'm told Jefferies was particularly tickled to have shared a page with the soul singer. The pair weren't exactly birds of a feather! Within a week he'd flown the nest or, more accurately, been ruthlessly sacked by Hearts' predictably unpredictable owner Vladimir Romanov despite a solid start to the new campaign. The selfish streak in me was delighted our piece had seen the light of day before it was too late. The journalist, however, bemoaned the unnecessary mistreatment of a genuine club legend and all-round good guy.

At least we'll always have Tuscany, and the tales of Panda. Oh, and contrary to popular opinion, we no longer file match reports at the Sunday Post via carrier pigeon – much to Jim's disappointment.

Kenny Millar is the Sunday Post's Edinburgh-based sports reporter and co-writer of Football Manager Stole My Life. *He is also a stubborn, sporadic defender of Scottish football for FourFourTwo and Champions magazines.*

HOW I FELL BACK IN LOVE WITH FOOTBALL

By Euan Crumley

When it became apparent that being a professional sportsman was not going to be a realistic career option for me, I turned my attention to the next-best thing. If I wasn't going to be on the pitch, I'd be in the press box instead.

As it has turned out, I've spent more of my career editing rather than writing sports coverage, but my working life has still let me fulfil certain childhood ambitions and meet people who would fall into my personal category of sporting heroes. I may not always have done myself justice when meeting them, but I've met them nonetheless.

For example, a turbulent helicopter ride through the Highlands with Gavin Hastings which saw me trying to hide the fact that I was vomiting spectacularly into a bag next to one of the greatest sporting figures Scotland has ever produced, was not my finest hour. Neither did I cover myself in glory as a young journalist during a Test match at Lord's when I was hosted by a very pleasant man called Bob Taylor. He had asked me if I played cricket at all and we had a brief chat about the game in Scotland. When I turned the conversation to him and asked, "And who did you play for?" there was an awkward silence while he weighed up this enquiry. The reason for the silence became apparent when his reply came. "England," he said. "You know the famous Ashes series from 1981? I was the wicketkeeper." Oops.

Then there was my first 'grown-up' assignment as a very young sportswriter. I was to go to Tynecastle and interview some of the Hearts squad. Since childhood I've been a Hearts fan and idolised those wearing the maroon shirt. Now I was supposed to not just meet the players, but speak to them with some authority and knowledge as well. I was ready to do just that as I stood in the corridor in the old stadium – then the players trooped in from training. John Robertson was one of the first through the door and I fear any professional façade I may have had dropped. I remember getting some interviews, but I doubt it was the toughest grilling any of that squad ever had.

When I was younger I used to feel a wide-eyed, all-consuming excitement about sport, and football in particular. Sport can still hold me very much in its thrall but after more years than I care to remember now of being involved in sports journalism and finding out how things can actually work behind the scenes, the hopelessly romantic view inevitably fades. There are times when you simply can't help it and with Scotland's national sport in such a critical condition, too, I feared that falling out of love with football completely was a genuine possibility. But something interesting happened recently that has already changed my outlook and taken me back to my younger self – I took my two young sons to Tynecastle for the first time.

My eldest boy Callum is five and this was not his first game – a Challenge Cup match between Stirling Albion and Dundee took that particular honour a couple of years ago – but this was his SPL, and Hearts, debut. His three-year-old brother Sam, meanwhile, was getting his first glimpse of live professional sport.

I wasn't entirely sure how the expedition would go but, when Callum shouted, "Wow!" as we turned off Gorgie Road and he got his first glimpse of the stadium, I began to feel a little more confident. St Johnstone were the opposition and, though the ground wasn't exactly at capacity, there were enough at the game to generate a decent atmosphere.

The boys were fascinated, by the crowd and the setting as much as the game itself. When Rudi Skacel opened the scoring right in front of us, they were at first bemused by the celebrations but, when they worked out that this was a place where you were positively encouraged to shout as loud as you could, they soon got the hang of things.

The best moment of the day came, however, a couple of minutes later. By scoring, Skacel had become an instant hero to Callum and he began to track his every move on the pitch. Hearts began to break forward and, with no encouragement from me, Callum was off his feet with scarf in hand and shouting them on. It was like a switch had been flicked and he suddenly understood how it all worked.

There he was, with that wide-eyed excitement and he has had a ball at his feet at some point during just about every day since. Sam, though he doesn't understand quite as much yet, is a more than willing accomplice when it comes to matches in the back garden and the park.

I hope they hang on to that feeling for as long as possible and that playing sport, whatever form that may take, is a big part of their lives. I, too, was energised by that day.

As for the finer points of stadium etiquette and fielding queries from Callum such as what was it that the Hearts fans were singing when Derek Riordan came on as a substitute for St Johnstone, I'll leave them for another day.

Euan Crumley started as sports reporter for Central FM, covering Stirling and Falkirk teams in the early '90s. He started in newspapers in 1996 as a sports reporter and sub-editor for the Weekly News and the Sunday Post before moving to London to become sports editor of the English titles at Metro. He moved back to Scotland to join the Daily Mail as a sports sub-editor before taking up his current position of sports production editor for the Scottish Mail on Sunday.

THE WRATH OF LEVEIN

By Paul Kiddie

When asked if I cared to contribute to this wonderful tome, I was only too happy to oblige. But no sooner had I given the thumbs-up to participating, than I began to wonder just what I was going to dig up from the past that would make it worthy of inclusion.

It soon became apparent, however, that having spent the best part of six years from 2000 reporting on Heart of Midlothian Football Club for the Edinburgh Evening News – during which period the club endured some of its most turbulent times – the Tynecastle outfit was going to be a reliable source of material.

My first tale of the unexpected dates back to the end of May 2004 and the official opening of Hearts' state-of-the-art football academy at Heriot-Watt University's Riccarton campus on the western outskirts of the capital. Years in the making, the impressive facility was the envy of almost every top-flight club in Scotland with its indoor arena, all-weather outdoor pitches and expansive training area for both the first team and under-19s.

No-one was more delighted with the academy than then manager Craig Levein, who, like his predecessors, had previously been forced to make best use out of the playing fields at Pinkie Primary School in Musselburgh and Musselburgh Juniors' Olive Bank ground. When former Scotland manager Andy Roxburgh helped to officially open the new facility on the morning of Monday May 31, the Hearts management team and players suddenly had a training HQ to be proud of, a base which would cater for their every need – rain, hail or shine.

While the national media descended on Riccarton in their droves to cover the much anticipated event, I was content in the knowledge the Evening News would already be running the story that day, complete with exclusive photographs thanks to access we had been given on the Friday. After regular coverage in the months building up to the big day, this was the moment everyone had been waiting for. As I was due to be off on the Monday, over the weekend I had left a newsline for the back page as well as a two-page spread inside the paper extolling the virtues of the magnificent complex.

It came something as a surprise to me, therefore, later that day when an incandescent Levein rang my mobile (it's never a good sign when a manager calls you directly) to express his displeasure at the manner in which the paper had handled the story. It had been brought to his attention that the opening hadn't commanded the back-page lead, and he was quick to pass on his displeasure. To make matters worse for those of a maroon persuasion – and to rub salt into the wounds – the main sports story of the day in the Evening News was a youth tournament success on foreign soil for Hibs. The decision was certainly the wrong call in my mind, although my boss argued we had been covering the academy story regularly and were now just rubber-stamping the opening. When Levein went on to question why we hadn't used one of the many photographs we had taken on the Friday on the back page, I tried to explain that while extremely grateful for the access, empty dressing rooms, gymnasiums and treatment rooms bereft of any life whatsoever could not carry a back page (there were seven or eight, if I recall, in the spread). I supported that decision by the editorial staff but did think they had possibly struck something of an own-goal with the choice of lead – and Levein, or perhaps more accurately chief executive Chris Robinson, wasn't going to let the paper off lightly. The manager promptly informed me that I was banned from speaking to him or the players for at least a month, and until such some time as he received an apology from the paper.

Under normal circumstances, a suspension of communications

with the club at that time of year would not have been a huge issue for a local journalist – except for the fact Hearts were planning a three-game pre-season tour to glorious Vancouver on the west coast of Canada that summer. This was the sort of pre-season trip hacks dream of, and I knew I was now in real danger of missing the great adventure.

However, the eight-hour time difference was to prove my saviour as my editor was happy in the knowledge we would be first with the result and match reports of all three friendlies, including the head-line encounter against Millwall at the Swangard Stadium in the International Pacific Soccer Series. Armed with a few features already 'in the can,' I left wife Margaret and one-year-old daughter Caitlin to jet across the Atlantic from Edinburgh via Amsterdam a little apprehensive as to what the nine-day trip would have in store.

As I recall, Levein flew into Vancouver a day after his squad due to SFA coaching commitments but as luck would have it we both arrived at the stadium for the opening fixture against a Canada select at the same time. Greeted with a warm smile, I asked, "Hi Craig, how about an international amnesty and then you can ban me again when we get back to Edinburgh?"

"No" came the terse reply. As good a working relationship as I had with Levein, I can't say I was surprised by his refusal to back down.

As luck would have it though, a number of good pals including the Sun's Robert Grieve, Neil Cameron of the Daily Record and John McGarry (News of the World) were also on the trip and were only too happy to furnish me with quotes from the manager on a daily basis – in return for a few refreshments, of course. Their service was so good, in fact, that on my return to Edinburgh, the Hearts media department claimed they would not have known I was banned.

Another anecdote, which this time brought a smile to Levein's face, involved the Jambos' 2004 Uefa Cup clash with Dutch giants Feyenoord.

Having qualified for the group stages with an impressive victory over Portuguese side Braga, Hearts were paired with Schalke,

Ferencvaros, Basel and Ruud Gullit's outfit. With the opening Group A game against Feyenoord in the De Kuip Stadium, spirits were high as the media assembled at Edinburgh Airport for the morning flight over to Rotterdam.

Arriving in plenty of time (for a change), I was called forward to check-in and handed over my passport. The gentleman glanced down at the passport, glanced up at me and then down again before showing me the page causing him some concern. To my horror it was my year-old daughter Caitlin's face staring back at me! Now while we may have shared a similar style of hairline, urgent action was required to get me on the flight.

Thankfully, wife Margaret was still home with the wee one and after a quick call, she was good enough to make a rapid return journey to the airport, this time with the correct document. Needless to say, by the time I was through security, word had spread and there was a warm welcome awaiting me from Levein and the squad as I eventually joined up with the travelling the party.

Paul Kiddie began his journalism career straight from school in 1984 when he joined the Weekly News as a sub-editor in Dundee. He moved to the Evening Telegraph in 1989 and remained there until 1996 when the Edinburgh Evening News came calling. After 10 years in the capital, he worked as a freelance in Florida for a year (it's a tough life!) before moving to the 'dark side' with a transfer to Heart of Midlothian FC as communications manager in January 2007.

THE DARK BROWNE ARTS

By Darren Johnstone

I n football, just like in every other sport, players like to indulge in the dark arts of gamesmanship as teams vie for any possible advantage on the pitch.

The levels of deception can vary, with deeds so subtle that they're barely noticed. But it was one very cruel and premeditated act away from the field of play which I stumbled upon, that led to my first-ever back-page story.

As I was learning the ropes at Capital City Press, I was tasked with keeping in touch with lower-league teams and regularly spoke to the then Arbroath manager John Brownlie. It was crucial to my early development as a journalist but in reality it was copy that had no chance of making headlines. That was until one day in June 2003 when Brownlie revealed that his defender, Eddie Forrest, had been the victim of an elaborate hoax that – if it wasn't so ruthless – could almost be admired for the perpetrator's ingenuity.

Forrest had successfully pleaded with the Red Lichties to terminate a recently signed 12-month deal after learning of interest from full-time Raith Rovers in a phone call from then Stark's Park chairman Danny Smith. Or so he thought.

As Brownlie went out and signed an immediate replacement in Paul Browne, it transpired that the hapless Forrest, a veteran of administration at Airdrie and Motherwell, had fallen for a convincing prankster purporting to be Raith chairman Smith.

"It's something very bizarre and weird and I cannot believe it has happened," said a shocked Forrest. "I asked him about travelling arrangements and he even told me not to worry because their striker Andy Smith travels through from Cumbernauld and I could come through with him."

Incredibly, Browne was unmasked as the hoax caller, although the former Aston Villa trainee, who briefly went into hiding in England following the revelation, later claimed a friend had made the call. Browne's reputation was irreparably tainted but when the dust settled on this extraordinary tale, Forrest signed for Partick Thistle, while the culprit at the heart of the deception managed to somehow keep his job at Arbroath.

A far less sinister act of gamesmanship occurred during Hibs' pre-season tour of Holland in 2010.

Easter Road manager John Hughes, aware there were representatives from forthcoming Europa League opponents NK Maribor at their final friendly on the tour, attempted to lead the spies up the garden path.

At first glance, there seemed nothing unusual in the Hibs side that was named on the official team-sheet for the friendly against Vitesse Arnhem. But it soon became clear that the numbers listed didn't correspond with the jerseys worn by certain players.

The press guys watching the game discovered that Maribor assistant manager Ante Simundza was sitting behind us and he too became aware that something was amiss. My peely wally Scottish skin was an obvious giveaway as he looked for assistance in resolving 'teamsheetgate' at half-time. It was hardly betraying your country stuff but my moral conscience got the better of me and I reluctantly helped him out. In hindsight, would it have helped if I had deliberately allocated striker Anthony Stokes the No.1 jersey?

In the end, trying to disguise his team from the enemy hardly seemed worth it, as only five of the side that started that friendly were in the line-up that lost 3-0 to the Slovenians in the first leg. Hibs eventually crashed out 6-2 on aggregate.

Darren Johnstone has been earning a crust at Capital City Press in

Edinburgh since 2003. He predominantly covers the east and central regions, including Hearts and Hibs, and has reported on Edinburgh's big two (while enjoying the local brew) in far-flung locations such as Latvia, Denmark, Holland and Hungary.

THE REDS' MILLS BOMB FROM BONHILL

By Charlie Allan

Willie Mills is the greatest Dons player I never saw.

The history books record him as one of the finest from Aberdeen FC's first 100 years. So I'm ashamed to confess I never really gave the man much thought until a cold rainy night in 1978, when I went to Aberdeen's Capitol Cinema for the gala launch of the book *The Dons* by Jack Webster, the north-east's greatest living author.

Like hundreds of other Dons fans in the audience that night, I was happy to get my hands on copies of Jack's book because it was the first real record of the club's history. As I devoured the words on the pages, I was particularly taken by tales of the partnership between Mills and Matt Armstrong, which helped Aberdeen terrorise defences in the 1930s. I didn't know it then, but Mills would flit in and out of my life until his own ended in 1990.

Mills, born in Bonhill, Dunbartonshire in 1915, played his last game for Aberdeen in 1938. His record of 114 goals in 210 appearances would make impressive reading in any era. As Webster put it in his book, he was the symbol of sporting glamour in the 1930s. Slicked hair and dashing good looks made him the Pittodrie pin-up boy of his day. But he matched those looks with a skill that once prompted Aberdeen manager Paddy Travers to say: "Just give me five minutes of the real Mills and I'm satisfied."

He was eventually sold to Huddersfield Town for £6,500, which was a sizeable sum in 1938.

Mills had retired from work, never mind playing football, by the time I was wallowing in Webster's words about his exploits alongside Armstrong as they helped Aberdeen – then still the Black and Golds – become established as a force in Scottish football.

Mills chose to stay in the north-east and became a machine operator while continuing to play and coach with Highland League clubs Lossiemouth, Huntly and Fraserburgh. And I can still remember the sense of excitement I felt when I found myself working as a postman in the 1980s and about to deliver mail addressed to a 'Mr W Mills' in a house just off Aberdeen's Urquhart Road. The first glimpse of the occupant at his door was enough to confirm it was indeed the great man. The legs that once helped Mills speed through defences were no longer as sprightly, he used a stick to get about, but even approaching his 70th birthday there was just something about the man that made you know he was no ordinary pensioner.

The postman and Mr Mills never built up a strong relationship, although he was always polite and happy to exchange the usual pleasantries. Our paths were to cross again in 1990, by which time I was working as a nursing auxiliary on the night shift at Aberdeen's Woodend Hospital. On arrival at work one evening, I discovered Mills had been admitted. By now a widower, failing health was making it difficult for the once famous footballer to simply get about. Or so we were told!

Mills may well have been a little infirm and slow on his feet during the day. But by night I would find my duties including having to escort Mills back to bed after he made surprisingly speedy dashes down the ward. It was all part of the confusion that sometimes hits the elderly when they are admitted to hospital. But old people can often compensate by also suddenly being able to recall events from earlier in their lives as though they happened yesterday. And softly spoken Mills kept his male nurse escort fascinated with stories of playing in front of massive crowds and of the big games his own mind was telling him he had coming up the following weekend. To some of my colleagues they were the ramblings of a disorientated old man. To me it was like a living history lesson. I had read about some of the games Mills mentioned, so it was a delight to sit and let the man himself add detail and a dash of colour to the tales Webster had written about.

Sadly, my time with Mills was all too brief because at the start of May 1990, the Evening Express took me on as a full-time sportswriter. And fate was to provide a cruel finale. I was into just my second week when the sports editor handed me a note. It informed me Mills had died at Woodend Hospital at the age of 75 and I was required to provide information about his career for an obituary.

Mills was gone and I regret to this day that I never got the chance to see for myself just how good a footballer he was.

Charlie Allan is sports editor at the Aberdeen Evening Express. He is a lifelong Dons fan and has been reporting on events at Pittodrie since 1990. Charlie is also co-author of the autobiography of Aberdeen's record goalscorer Joe Harper.

OCH AYE, DAVE MACKAY

By Douglas Alexander

How do you convey greatness to a reader when you yourself never saw the subject in their prime? It is a dilemma for any writer lucky enough to meet the icons of the Scottish game from the 1960s, yet too young to recall their on-field excellence.

My memory of football matches stretches back to around 1977, when I was six, and Scotland defeating England 2-1 at Wembley, a success quickly followed a year later by the misadventure in Argentina. I grew up with players such as Kenny Dalglish and Graeme Souness as my idols but soon became aware that they were part of a tradition going much further back. That Dalglish was chasing a goal record set by Denis Law and that Souness had equally combative predecessors in Dave Mackay and Billy Bremner. I always remember stumbling across that famous picture of Mackay grabbing Bremner by the shirt while the Leeds United man shrugged his innocence.

The chance to meet Mackay in person was one I never expected to arise, not even when I later became a sports journalist, yet it arrived early in 1999 when the Sunday Times asked Alex Ferguson and Hugh McIlvanney to put their heads together and come up with Scotland's greatest team of all time ahead of the new millennium. Mackay, of course, was part of their selection and I was dispatched to the picturesque Nottinghamshire village of Burton Joyce to meet him. It was to prove an unforgettable privilege.

Mackay was 64 back then and what immediately struck me was his vivacity as he described his morning routine, a five-mile walk around the village at 'Benny Hill pace.' He had shrugged off cancer in his lower lip, just as he had a shattered leg, a broken leg and several other serious injuries during his playing career. He sat animatedly talking about his own playing days and offered invaluable insights into current players, too.

He particularly liked Roy Keane and Paul Scholes, who would excel on Manchester United's run to the European Cup final that season. He loved Souness, whom he spotted playing for Scotland Schoolboys at White Hart Lane and advised Bill Nicholson, his manager, to sign immediately, which he duly did. It turned out that they had been raised in the same area of Edinburgh, Saughton. "Souness reminded me of myself," he said. "The way he strutted about. You have to have that confidence about you; you have got to strut about."

He also relished retelling the story behind that famous picture of his altercation with Bremner. "It was my first game back after about 18 months out with my broken leg. I pushed him in the back at a throw-in and he sort of fell over. It was nothing nasty, just a push, so he got up and came round the back and whacked me on the left leg. The bad one that I had broken, so that was it …"

Yet the picture was also misleading because it told only half of Mackay's story. It showed his aggression and competitiveness, but not his skill and subtlety. This brings us back to the difficulty with conveying greatness that you did not experience first-hand; the danger being that you fall for the cliché, such as Law's inaccurate, if amusing, portrayal on Only an Excuse, rather than providing a rounded impression for a reader. In this respect, it was particularly important to take in the testimony of those who had seen Mackay play and what came across consistently was he was rather more than another midfield enforcer.

Craig Brown, then Scotland's manager, told a tale of watching from the terracing at Motherwell one day as Mackay, as a Hearts player, contrived to hit the net with a back-heel volley from the centre circle. Other party pieces, according to his former Spurs team-mates, included flicking coins into his top pocket with his foot, deliberately hitting the crossbar in training before scoring with the rebound and keeping the ball up with alternate feet against a wall, setting a record that a young Glenn Hoddle later became obsessed with. Jimmy Greaves described Mackay as "Spurs' greatest-ever player," while Denis Law said: "Forget your Dalglishs or your [Danny] Blanchflowers, Mackay was the man. He made everybody play. He never took friendships on to the field, but off it he was a great character – a bit of a nutter, actually."

I remember that one particular stereotype, of him as the midfield muscle to Blanchflower's brain at the heart of Spurs' double-winning side of 1961, still rankled with him. "They always said Danny was the footballer and I was the hard nut but anything he could do with a ball, I could do better."

It was also an insult that the Scottish selectors, with a bias against Anglos, only gave him 22 caps in his career, a criminally low total for a player of his talent. Ferguson and McIlvanney were keen to remedy that injustice for posterity. Not only was Mackay one of the first names on their team-sheet, they also made him captain.

I eagerly told Mackay this, but he brushed aside the accolade with his towering self-assurance. "I was always the captain anyway, even when I wasn't," he replied. "If you are not doing your bit, you'll be hearing from me."

That gruff voice of his has stayed with me since. I never saw Mackay play, yet I left Burton Joyce that afternoon for the long drive back to Glasgow utterly convinced I had been in the presence of greatness.

Douglas Alexander has worked for the Sunday Times since 1994 and has been Scottish football correspondent since 2001. He lives on the outskirts of Glasgow with his wife and son.

The three lives of the footballer: Mr Marjoribanks scoring on his debut for Hibs v Hearts at Tynecastle. His football background won him a part in Doctor Findlay's casebook, and eventually a job at the BBC

Spoon botherer: Uri Geller

Legend: Diego Maradona (not deceased) scores a perfectly legitimate goal. Courtesy of Getty Images

Cry for me, Argentina: Ally MacLeod. Picture courtesy of Newsquest Media Group

Get a room: A graveyard yesterday

Dave Mackay invites Billy Bremner over for cocktails. Courtesy of Newsquest Media Group

Come ahead: The Bairns get their dukes up in Dwingeloo

In happier times: David Murray, scoop-of-the-century breaker Jack Irvine, Sean Connery and Graeme Souness

Ejected: Hugh "Clapped-out" Keevins

Seville dream team: Hamilton, Auld, Connolly and O'Neill

Bob Hope: Who are you calling a commie?
Picture courtesy of Newsquest Media Group

FAMILY FINAL WAS UNFORGETTABLE IN MORE WAYS THAN ONE

By Graham Clark

I T is hard to imagine that the first famous Scottish Cup 'Family Final' – the Motherwell-Dundee United Scottish Cup classic – happened more than 20 years ago. It seems like yesterday. But maybe that is because I played a fairly important part in proceedings that May day back in 1991.

Let's get one thing clear: I didn't influence the result in any way, shape or form and can't claim credit for Scotland's showpiece fixture producing extra time, seven goals and four red cards in one of the most memorable finals ever. I was The Sun's humble chief sportswriter at the time and, even though that tabloid was making huge waves in journalism in this country, its power did not extend to winning or losing football matches. Instead, my little moment of near-fame came immediately after the event.

But let's take a quick trip down memory lane to the game itself first. It was billed the Family Final because brothers Tommy and Jim McLean were rival managers of the two clubs. On top of that there was then, as there is now, something refreshing about the showpiece not involving the Old Firm.

And it was a remarkable occasion with Iain Ferguson giving wee Tam's 'Well the lead followed by Ian Angus' second before Dave Bowman scored for United. The late Phil O'Donnell grabbed the Fir Park side's third and Motherwell looked to be on easy street until John O'Neil scored and Darren Jackson made it 3-3 late on.

In the midst of all that, however, Motherwell goalkeeper Ally Maxwell collided with Tannadice star John Clark and, unsurprisingly, came off worse. Indeed, Maxie suffered broken ribs, a ruptured spleen and double vision but remarkably played on, and played his part, as Stevie Kirk's extra-time goal eventually settled the issue.

It was a truly astonishing game. And then there was a truly astonishing aftermath. I remember doing the usual round of post-match interviews before being collared by 'Well manager Tommy McLean in the Hampden foyer.

The wee man and I went back a long way and were as much friends as any manager and reporter could be – even if the McLean managerial family of Brothers Grim Tommy, Jim and Willie weren't always the easiest to deal with.

Tam pulled me aside to tell me the full extent of Maxwell's injuries and suggested it was a somewhat pressing matter that the keeper should get to hospital as quickly as possible.

But by then – at least an hour-and-a-half after the final whistle – medical staff and ambulances had long since left the national stadium leaving yours truly, with his trusty company issue Vauxhall Cavalier, as the only remaining transport option.

Even now, I can recall my first thought and that was that I had been a bit late getting to Hampden before the game and, basically, had managed it on a wing and a prayer because the fuel tank in my car had long since ceased to even register the presence of any petrol. I had vowed a garage would be my first port of call after the game.

Instead, though, I was faced with pouring a white-faced Maxwell into the back seat hoping I could make it to the Victoria Infirmary without either the car or him giving up the ghost! I recall pressing a motorcycle policeman into service as an escort and off we went the happily short distance to the hospital with lights flashing.

Not for a minute would I suggest this was a life-saving mercy mission but I'll tell you what – Maxwell was not a well man as the hospital bulletin later that night confirmed. I like to think I at least saved him from longer suffering.

Incidentally, in a further favour to McLean and Motherwell, I returned to Hampden after the hospital dash to collect Ian Angus who had had to wait behind for a statutory drugs test and ferried him out to Fir Park where, naturally, I joined in the celebrations. I felt I was due a glass of bubbly!

Graham Clark started his career in general news and sport at the Hamilton Advertiser before moving to: Scottish Football magazine, Scottish Daily News, Aston Villa FC, Ipswich Town FC, Leicester City FC, Evening Times, chief sports writer at The Sun, the Daily Record and Sunday Express. He has also been Scottish correspondent for the Belfast Telegraph, Daily Telegraph and the Guardian.

THE DARLING OF DENS PARK

By Alan Pattullo

H e has meant everything to Dundee fans, who consider him part of the property at Dens Park, even if he did leave to go and achieve perhaps greater success with Tottenham Hotspur. Alan Gilzean inhabits the consciousness of supporters of a club who associate him with better times.

Though I never saw him play – indeed, his career with Spurs was winding up by the time I was born in 1973, the year, incidentally, when Dundee last lifted a major trophy – I was always fascinated by Gillie's story. It helped that he was brought up mere miles from where I was from in rural Angus, and adding a strand of intrigue was the fact that he had made so few public appearances after the last of his football outings with Spurs in the mid-1970s.

Like many Dundee fans, I had grown up listening to tales of Gillie. The only difference is that mine involved his prowess with a bat rather than his ability to ghost in at the back post. My Dad was more of a cricket man and thrilled me with stories of Gillie playing at Coupar Angus Cricket Club, along the road from where he had opened the bowling for Meigle.

Even the name attracted me: Gilzean. Together with Jimmy Greaves, they were known as the 'G men'; glamour, goals and glory. When a rival Dundee fanzine to my own came out called Eh Mind O' Gillie, it annoyed me that they had the better title. When I started out as a sportswriter, my stated ambition, perhaps more so than covering World Cup finals, was to interview the great man himself.

I quickly learned I had handed myself a tough assignment. I did, however, attempt little nibbles at the Gilzean story, including a piece in 2009 when I made contact with his son Ian, whom I had watched play for Dundee in the early '90s, and Bobby Wishart, Gillie's delightful best friend and former Dundee team-mate.

Both politely listened to what I had to say and offered me some valuable titbits in return. Gillie, it was confirmed, was living in Weston-Super-Mare. While I also happily cleared up the persistent rumour that the great man was now a down-and-out in the West Country, I had to put to one side my hope of perhaps one day speaking with the man himself. I did still have my eye on the approaching milestone that was the 50th anniversary of Dundee's maiden title win in 1962, but what hope, really, was there that Gillie, the man of mystery for nearly 40 years now, would consent to an interview?

A well-received book, James Morgan's *In Search of Alan Gilzean*, was published in 2010, and Gillie had spoken to the author before declining to officially endorse the title. I attended the launch. Gillie, of course, did not. I remember speculating about what he might have been doing at the moment we were all in a cinema in Dundee, paying tribute to his understated brilliance. Walking the dogs in Weston-Super-Mare, perhaps? Getting another hit of the sea air at Carnoustie, where Ian, his son, stays?

But then, on Boxing Day 2011, came a stroke of luck. Dundee were hosting Morton, and, on a day off from reporting duties elsewhere, I went to Dens with my father to cheer on the Dees. We were both mildly interested in the half-time invitation to welcome a Dundee legend from the 1962 team. Ian Ure, perhaps? Goalkeeper Pat Liney? Remarkably, though, it was Gilzean who had been cajoled into waving to the crowd, alongside his son and grandson, Cameron. I resolved during the second half to hang around afterwards and speak with Gillie, so as to at least let him know the identity of the pest who has been writing about him for the Scotsman these past few years.

So there I was, in my late 30s and feeling terribly self-conscious about hanging around outside the Dens Park main stand, like a child hunting autographs. Gillie eventually emerged, woolly hat pulled down over the famously bald head that had proved such a deadly weapon in his heyday.

My father was sitting in the car, and got out when he saw Gillie. I introduced both myself and him before spending the next 15 minutes cast as a redundant bystander in a conversation between the pair as they reminisced about life in the agricultural badlands on the Perthshire and Angus border, trading stories of people they both knew in farming and cricketing circles. It even turned out that Gillie's aunt and uncle had lived on the farm where I grew up. He had visited regularly while I, oblivious, was probably up in my bedroom, hammering out articles for my fanzine which wondered where the hell Gillie was now.

Once Gillie and my father had finished, I nervously asked whether it would be possible to speak with him at some point prior to such a significant anniversary in Dundee's history, due four months' hence. Just over a week later I got a phone call: "Alan, it's Alan Gilzean." Less than 24 hours later we were sitting down in a hotel in Carnoustie, where I spent nearly two hours in the company of a bona-fide football hero for a piece published in the Scotsman, puffed as Alan Gilzean's first major newspaper interview in 40 years.

I almost blew it. Foolishly, I texted Ian (Gillie once claimed, rather proudly, that only seven people in the land had his phone number) to enquire whether his father would permit a photographer to attend. "Like every journalist, give them an inch and they want a mile," he sighed to me later (the answer had been "no"). He was, though, utterly charming, and revealing too. But Gillie was adamant about one thing. "I wouldn't have spoken to you if it wasn't for your father," he told me.

Thanks, Dad. And thank you Gillie.

Alan Pattullo was born in Dundee and his first steps in journalism came via the Dundee fanzine he set up in 1988 titled 'It's Half Past Four ... And We're 2-0 Down.' He read English at Dundee University and hung around long enough after a period of work experience

*at Scotland on Sunday to be offered a six-month contract with the
Scotsman. Fourteen years later, he is still there.*

TALKING ITALIAN ON TAYSIDE

By Tom Duthie

A sniff of coffee minutes into our first meeting was enough to tell me that whatever happened, Ivan Bonetti's time as Dundee manager would definitely be different.

It was May 2000 at a hotel in the centre of Dundee. Bonetti was to be revealed as manager that afternoon, but showing commendable co-operation and awareness of edition times, the club invited myself and veteran broadcaster Dick Donnelly to an early interview with the manager-in-waiting.

Being Italian, for Ivano it was unthinkable the sit-down wouldn't involve coffee. Having already worked in this country, most eventfully at Grimsby where a plate of sandwiches thrown by his manager had landed him in hospital, Ivano was also aware of the fact that what was sometimes presented as coffee here would not pass muster back home. So, before a notebook was opened or a microphone switched on, he signalled to a waitress and asked what brands the hotel served. With a charm that would become so familiar, he asked if a cup of each could be served. A few minutes later he was presented with two cups, each of which he sniffed before giving a polite grazie but no grazie. Such was his grace that the waitress seemed almost grateful for the rejection, and there started a relationship with the former Sampdoria star that would be at times exciting, at other times perplexing, but never dull.

Fast-forward a few months to a Sunday afternoon and a post-round of golf visit to Tesco to grab a microwave meal. A few aisles in

I spied the manager, accompanied by his future wife Erica – a former model and presenter on Italian TV. For once, Ivano was not his usual bouncy self. Days earlier a derby win over Dundee United had been blotted by an injury to Argentine striker Fabian Caballero.

The previous evening, after a defeat to Celtic at Parkhead, had come confirmation the damage to Caballero's knee was serious and he was not expected to play again that season. As we chatted I enquired if a replacement was to be signed and he uttered a name that stopped me in my tracks – Claudio Caniggia.

I was aware both Ivano and his brother, Dario, were on friendly terms with the Argentine great, but never did I dream I'd one day see one of the stars of the 1990 World Cup playing in the dark blue of Dundee. Noting my surprise and being aware of my profession, the manager quickly stressed there was still work to be done on the deal and I would have to wait for his say-so before I could go public.

There followed several anxious days before, true to his word, he gave me the nod and the story could be printed. I have to report that more stunned than myself in Tesco that evening was the charming Erica. As her fiancé told of his plan to persuade Caniggia to come to the SPL, in a state of shock she held out a can from one of the shelves, asking, "Macaroni in a tin – surely this is not possible?"

Not quite knowing how to confirm this culinary sacrilege, all I could do was paraphrase a line from Star Trek: "It's macaroni Erica, but not as you know it."

Caniggia duly arrived and while his stay at Dens Park was brief, he made a huge impression. As much a gentleman off the park as a class act on it, during a winter break trip to Riccione on Italy's Adriatic coast, the man who was both close friend and preferred national team strike-partner of the legendary Diego Maradona, agreed to a rare one-to-one interview.

Having answered my questions, this quiet but friendly man stayed and chatted, recalling that as a boy in Argentina he had memories of Scotland's participation in the 1978 World Cup. Owning up, I told him that when Ally MacLeod's squad left for South America I was one of those who naively believed the team could come back with the cup, or at least having gone close. Ever the gent, Caniggia apologised for his poor English, explaining he thought I'd said Scotland were genuine contenders in '78. On being informed by this embarrassed hack that his interpretation had been accurate, for once decorum deserted him and he laughed so much he had to wipe tears from his eyes before, in typical fashion, apologising for any offence caused.

After Claudio's departure for Rangers, the Bonetti brothers remained in charge at Dundee for a further eventful year and a bit. Both were better coaches than they were perhaps given credit for, though if Ivano had a failing it was his lack of attention to fine detail. That would be illustrated on a surreal day at Rugby Park, Kilmarnock, when he failed to list his brother among those who could be seated in the technical area. Ivano and the team had travelled on the Friday evening, leaving Dario to head west the following morning. Unfortunately, an accident on the M77 meant the assistant manager and majority of fans did not arrive until just after kick-off and to find no place for him at the side of the pitch. Not being able to take his usual place, the only man to have played in all the major Italian city derbies was forced to take a seat just in front of the press box, up at the back of the main stand.

Surrounded by Killie fans, much to their entertainment this imposing figure proceeded to kick every ball. Without realising, that is, that before his arrival his team had gone behind to an early goal. His frustration at a below-par performance was only eased slightly by Dundee grabbing a goal before the break, at which point he headed for the dressing room to tear a strip off the players and tell them they were lucky to be ahead. Informing us of this as he returned to the stand, it was left to injured full-back Marcello Marrocco to pass on the actual score – though not before a request to this local journalist to be the bearer of the bad news. Said journo being neither brave nor stupid, Marrocco was informed this was a score best delivered in Italian.

Tom Duthie is lead football writer with the Evening Telegraph in

Dundee. He has now covered Dundee and Dundee United for the best part of 25 years, and plans to mark that particular anniversary next year with a trip to the Dignitas clinic in Switzerland.

TALES FROM THE CITY OF DISCOVERY

By Jim Spence

A s the BBC's football reporter in Dundee I've seldom been short of interesting characters or stories to cover.

Reporting on two clubs who have a strong rivalry and are separated by only 100 metres of street, there has been a constant and fertile vein of stories to grip the imagination. Frequently the two boardrooms have supplied the liveliest tales, with Dens Park in particular having been a rich source of consternation and mystery to fans and journalists alike.

Short in stature but ebullient in personality, local property tycoon Angus Cook's dalliance with the Dark Blues in the early '90s saw him make a bid to buy United with a view to merging the two clubs. Local outrage by both sets of fans ensured the grandiose plan never got off the ground and shortly afterwards, the bold Angus had gone to be replaced by the even bolder Ron Dixon.

No, not the character from the late lamented Brookside TV soap, but a now-deceased Canadian with a grand vision of a new stadium including a state-of-the-art ice rink. Dixon did not deliver on the promise, instead coming up with the ill-judged and short-lived reintroduction of greyhound racing, which flopped spectacularly.

Mind you he was not a man to trifle with, as I discovered to my cost when he took exception to some comments made on radio by myself and colleagues Jim Traynor and John Barnes. He moved more quickly than any Dens striker since Gordon Wallace to issue a writ threatening to sue all three of us for defamation, promptly freezing my bank account as well as putting a legal stop to me selling my house.

The Marr brothers, Peter and Jimmy, were successful city businessmen, and had a bold vision of buying in quality players and selling them on at a big profit. Their stewardship of the club though, ended with Dundee's first bout of administration, but at least the fare on the park was often spectacular. With the rare talents of Claudio Caniggia, Georgi Nemsadze and Fabrizio Ravanelli among others all strutting their stuff at Dens, in an attempt to recreate the glories of a more illustrious past, the failure of the Marrs at least provided some terrific football viewing.

During the Marr brothers' reign, Scottish football was also treated to the arrival at Dens of Giovanni Di Stefano, friend to Arkan, the Serbian warlord. Di Stefano claimed to be a lawyer, although many disputed that claim. Regardless of his legal bona fides however, he certainly had a penchant for publicity. He called me one day to tell me that he was about to sign Dutch legend Edgar Davids. A far-fetched claim perhaps, but at Dens park in those days, with stars like Ravanelli, Ketsbaia, Caballero and others on show, nothing was beyond the realms of the imagination.

I had the sad task of breaking the story of Dundee's administration in 2003, when it became obvious that that the ambitions and outgoings at Dens far exceeded the capability of the club to meet them. Just seven years later I found myself again reporting on Dundee in administration. This time, after a brief flirtation with another colourful character, Calum Melville, Dundee fans endured further agony as the self-confessed Aberdeen fan pulled the plug on his investment at Dens, plunging the club's future into doubt. Fortunately the Dundee support has rallied magnificently and although the future looks likely to be one of financial struggle, the club has been saved.

You could take a long throw-in from Dens Park and hit the wall of the Shed End at Tannadice Park, so close are the grounds. If Dens had a revolving door for directors and owners though, Tannadice was a managerial carousel. The club which started life as Dundee

Hibernian had been very much the city's poor relations until firstly Jerry Kerr and then Jim McLean changed United's fortunes.

McLean in particular radically transformed the Tannadice club and brought them both domestic and European fame. However, 'Wee Jum,' as he was known, could not find a manager to meet his exacting standards after vacating the hot-seat himself, and in a seven-year period dispensed with the services of Ivan Golac, Billy Kirkwood, his own brother Tommy, and club legend Paul Sturrock.

McLean's time at United drew to a close after he resigned as chairman in 2000 for attacking BBC Scotland's Barnes in a post-match interview. Fortunately I had been sent to cover Dundee at Aberdeen that day for Caniggia's debut; otherwise I might have been the reporter face to face with the angry chairman.

McLean remained on the board as the major shareholder for another two years before selling out after a long and bitter battle with the late Eddie Thompson, who, backed by the protest group United For Change, had been trying to take over the club. Eddie poured more of his family wealth into United than was sensible, but the glory days continued to elude the United faithful. The managerial carousel continued to spin as Alex Smith, Paul Hegarty, Ian McCall, Gordon Chisholm and Craig Brewster were all unseated before Eddie's appointment of Craig Levein brought a sense of stability to Tannadice. Eddie sadly died after a long battle with prostate cancer, but son Stephen, who took over the reins as chairman, has seen some return on the family investment with a Scottish Cup win in 2010.

Twice at the invitation of Dundee's Lord Provost, I have had the honour of introducing victorious United Scottish Cup-winning teams from the balcony at the city chambers to thousands of cheering fans in the City square below. It would be nice to think that one day I might do the same for Dundee FC, who, although having suffered lean years of late, have a great history.

One thing I have learned covering football in my native city is that one never knows who or what is around the corner. Given the stories and characters I have encountered to date, I wouldn't want it any other way.

Jim Spence works with BBC Scotland and is based in their Dundee office. He is a regular presenter on Radio Scotland's Sportsound programme and also works for Sportscene on television. Jim was a law lecturer for many years, initially combining that career with broadcasting, before moving to the BBC full-time.

ACROPOLIS NOW

By Robert Thomson

A major part of the allure of playing in European competition for supporters and journalists alike is the prospect of venturing to a far-flung country for experiences the normal routine of life would usually not produce.

In 2010, when Scottish Cup-winners Dundee United were paired with AEK Athens the trip seemed, while having more than a smattering of glamour, entirely straightforward. Athens is one of the major cities in Europe, and the contest was to be held at a stadium which had hosted the Champions League final just three years before. Surely little could go awry? However, that all was not going to run smoothly became worryingly evident during the 48 hours before the contest was due to take place.

First, a problem arose with the playing surface at the Olympic Stadium, rendering the pitch unplayable and meaning AEK had to find another venue. After being refused permission by Uefa to play at the Peristeri Stadium, home of neighbours Atromitos on the grounds it was not up to standard, they eventually signed an agreement with local rivals Panionios to play at their Nea Smyrni stadium in time to beat the European deadline. Problem solved, travel plans tweaked, game on. Maybe.

This adventure really starts at another place beginning with A, and, while a lovely Clackmannanshire town, much more prosaic than Athens. And, to my knowledge, lacking an Acropolis. Attending Alloa v Aberdeen in the League Cup was to prove the starting point for a European jaunt like no other. Having watched the Dons dispatch their Third Division opponents with relative ease, securing a 3-0 victory to take them through, the journey home – where packing had to be done in preparation for a morning flight to Greece – was punctured by a text message out of the blue from United director Derek Robertson.

Derek, then the communications director at Tannadice, had spotted a report on the internet suggesting that Panionios supporters, enraged by their club's decision to give AEK the keys to their stadium, had broken in and vandalised their own ground. Further examination of these reports verified that this was indeed the case. A baying mob had scaled the walls, dug up the pitch and broken the goalposts. Panionios, it seemed, would not welcome AEK. Let the madness begin …

Word in Greece was that Olympiakos had emerged as the next option in the clubs' desperate bid to get the tie played. Uefa rules state that the visiting team must be in the country they're playing in 24 hours before kick-off, meaning the 9am Edinburgh-Athens flight was the final option the team had in order to get to their destination. Arriving at the airport, immediately visible was a stressed United chairman Stephen Thompson, phone pressed firmly against his ear talking to the authorities about whether Olympiakos were willing to host the event. Was the game on or was it off? He didn't know, neither did AEK and, it seemed, neither did Uefa. But with a plane chartered and their obligation to be in Greece, the decision was taken to board and set off for Athens.

Instead of wondering whether we'd see United overcome the Greeks, the question on everyone's mind – players, fans and club officials – as the plane took to the runway was, "Is this game even going ahead?"

Upon landing, Thompson resumed his phone calls, and confirmation was finally given that Olympiakos were willing to hold the game but on the strict condition that no AEK fans would be allowed in, despite over 13,000 tickets having been sold.

That satisfied Uefa and, to an extent, United – but AEK's

supporters, with their deep hatred of their Athens rivals, were then the bigger problem. The Greek authorities suspected the hardcore among the AEK fanbase would try to disrupt the match and even prevent it going ahead, so we feared for the safety of the 500 United supporters who had flown from the UK.

A press conference had been arranged for the Wednesday evening, at which the manager and usually the club captain give their views on the game. This time, however, it was Thompson who took centre stage and, as it dragged on into the late evening, he gave assurances to the travelling fans that the Greek police had given him guarantees of their safety. After discussions with the SFA's head of security, buses under armed guard would be sent for fans at pick-up points to bring them to the Karaiskakis Stadium. The whole event had taken a sinister twist.

On the day of the game proof arrived of how serious the Greeks were taking the security threats. Having been picked up by bus at our hotel to travel to the match we were afforded, much to our amusement, a police escort through the early-evening traffic towards the stadium. However, the police presence was more and more visible the closer the bus got, until we reached an exclusion zone one mile away. The traffic suddenly vanished and the only vehicles were those containing riot police armed with machine guns. There were 600 of them in total – more than one for every supporter due to attend the match.

After being driven into the ground, the Scottish press alighted into a corridor of armed police and, ridiculously, shuffled past the ranks of television reporters while being shown live on Greek television. Having been spirited into the arena, seeing not a furious fan in sight, we watched the busloads of United fans arrive amid similar security while the streets in the background remained entirely lifeless on account of the massive police presence. United's 500 supporters, tucked away in a high corner of the ground, were vociferous in backing their team – and launched the obligatory taunts at the lack of home support in the ghostly surroundings.

The game itself, which had been completely overshadowed and

warranted only scant mention in the build-up amid tales of 'warring Greeks', ended in a 1-1 draw with a goal from Jon Daly, but Peter Houston's team were unable to progress as a result of their defeat at Tannadice.

Dundee United's European adventure of 2010 had been short but it is never to be forgotten.

Robert Thomson was born in Perth, and after an uneventful football career playing for North Muirton and Letham boys' clubs as goalkeeper and lumbering centre-half, he embarked upon an even more plodding career in journalism. He covered Dundee and Dundee United as a freelance for 10 years but has recently been released to bore a wider audience as a staff football writer with the Scottish Sun.

THE BATTLE OF DWINGELOO

By Ed Hodge

'Dwingeloo.' It sounds like that 1998 song Vindaloo, the boisterous anthem recorded for the World Cup and a cult classic amongst England fans. Those imaginative lyrics, "nah nah nah" and, "we all like vindaloo" were belted out in noisy, over-exuberant, party-time fashion. It's a song that represents everything that Dwingeloo is not.

For those not versed in Netherlands geography, let me enlighten. Dwingeloo is a quaint, small, eastern village, population circa 2,500. Farming dominates, save for a tourism element attracted to the Dwingeloo Radio Observatory, formerly the largest radio telescope in the world. One can relax in the quietest surroundings imaginable; only the passing cyclists breaking the silence. Yet, one baking day in the summer of 2006, the town didn't know what had hit it. On the local public park, 'The Battle of Dwingeloo' raged – mayhem on a football field, complete chaos. "I remember being asked by my wife, 'What am I going to do about this?'" recalls George Craig, Falkirk's ex-managing director. "But there was nothing we could do, it was crazy."

The initial contrast in circumstances could not have been greater. It had been a relaxing, if hardworking July week for all. Handed my first foreign pre-season adventure as part of the Capital City Press (CCP) freelance agency, I had travelled to Holland with John Hughes' passing-orientated side, a manager whose 'football philosophy' was born from the Dutch school of 'Total Football.' "Holland is

168

a country very dear to my heart," said Hughes. "Not only is fantastic football played there but everything we could possibly wish for is in Dwingeloo. The facilities are fantastic."

'Yogi,' typically full of infectious enthusiasm, was spot-on. With the sun beating down during the hottest summer Holland had experienced in many a year, the former Celtic defender had his ideal training camp, as Falkirk prepared for their second season back in the Scottish Premier League. I was the only Scottish sports journalist in attendance and it proved a profitable week. I sat down with Russell Latapy, the brilliant Trinidadian, who had just graced the greatest stage of his career at the World Cup, aged 37. Falkirk spanked the local amateurs 16-0 in the opening game, the biggest mismatch you will ever see, but it made great copy. My lodgings at Hotel-Spier Dwingeloo lacked life, eerily quiet amid forests of trees, yet banter was never far away. Every day I hopped on a bicycle and pedalled two miles for my daily catch-up at the Bairns' base, kicking a ball around with Latapy, Alan Gow, Pedro Moutinho and Co. after their double sessions. These were genteel days, as happy and relaxed a football tour as you could imagine ... until the final afternoon.

Looking back now, CCP made a tidy sum in newspaper orders but it was far from my thinking as my phone buzzed frantically and sweat poured off my brow. Touring Turkish Super Lig side Rizespor were scheduled to face Falkirk in Dwingleoo, kick-off 3pm. Hughes was to again assess Udo Nwoko, a tricky Nigerian in the Latapy mould. Around 11.30am, my mobile phone rang. "Kick-off delayed, update to follow."

Already, I questioned why, the situation appearing odd. Soon after, a second call explained all. The Turks, citing medical grounds, were refusing to play in the fierce afternoon heat. Already I had a story, my journalist mind working overtime. While furious negotiations took place to finally agree a 5pm start, Craig and his team were enduring a logistical nightmare. Numerous Bairns fans had travelled for the game, yet many were now going to miss it to board pre-booked flights home from Amsterdam that night.

Come 5pm, matters escalated ... there was still no sign of the

Turks. "Every minute that passed there was more and more frustration from Yogi and the fans, many of whom had been enjoying a drink in the glorious weather," recalls Craig.

Displaying a total lack of respect for their opponents, Rizespor casually and belatedly, after a full warm-up, took to the field at 5.37pm precisely. Incredibly, they posed for a team photo rather than immediately starting proceedings. The Falkirk fans vented their displeasure, a 'friendly' affair already appearing unlikely. Indeed, it took just 22 minutes for the match to boil over as a mass brawl broke out in the Falkirk penalty area. The bemused officials wasted little time in simply marching off.

The bizarre scenes were far from over. The match resumed, and in the early stages of the second half a Falkirk fan, clearly under the influence of a beverage, streaked. He achieved only mild attention, but as he sheepishly returned to his mates behind the Rizespor goal, little Nwoko equalised for 1-1 after a superb solo run. It was the cue for the most remarkable scenes I've ever seen on a football field.

As said streaker celebrated in the six-yard box, the Rizespor keeper, Atilla Koca, didn't take kindly to a full view of the prancing Scotsman's bits. Koca kicked the ball at the intruder before he and his furious team-mates gave chase. Within seconds, Turkish players became embroiled with a posse of Bairns fans as the now-shaken referee failed to maintain calm. "I held my head in my hands before rushing down to try and placate things, but emotions were running so high," continues Craig. It was farcical stuff and the officials had little option but to call a halt to a game destined for trouble, after only 55 minutes.

'Falkirk's pre-season tour ends in farce' screamed the headlines back home from my feverishly filed copy. The fixture formed part of an official tour arranged using the services of an accredited Uefa match agent and was subject to Uefa rules. Craig feared a PR disaster: "I thought Falkirk would be kicked out of Europe before we had even qualified."

It didn't come to that, the mitigating circumstances understood by the authorities. The Bairns returned to Holland in future years, even securing a home pre-season match against Ajax as a spin-off.

Vindaloo raised the profile of British band Fat Les. Dwingeloo, ironically enough, did the same for Falkirk.

Ed Hodge is a golf-mad, St Johnstone-obsessed, family man. Formerly a sportswriter for Rangers News, Teletext Ltd and Capital City Press freelance agency, he is now PR & media executive for the Scottish Golf Union. Ed is also currently writing a golf book in association with the Gleneagles Hotel, host venue for the 2014 Ryder Cup.

JOY OF THE ROVERS

By Iain Macfarlane

I t was a memorable campaign involving puffin pie, whale-spotting, and a near-miracle in Munich.

The players geared up for the challenge with lazy afternoons on Burntisland beach, a forward roll competition down an airport departure lounge and a few prayers to God. In short, it was like no other European adventure I've ever been involved in or am likely to be involved in if I stay on in this game until I'm 70. Welcome to Raith Rovers' 1995 European odyssey. An experience never to be forgotten and most probably never repeated.

For all the Old Firm trips, their Uefa Cup finals and the Scotland adventures I've enjoyed doing a job I love for the past 18 years, nothing in football brings a bigger smile to my coupon than recalling the autumn of '95 spent with the Stark's Park crazy gang.

Led by player-boss Jimmy Nicholl, and involving fantastic characters on and off the pitch, this was a wonderful introduction for me to life on the road with a football team. It was my first foreign trip with the paper after just a few months in the job. It was exciting for that reason alone – but witnessing history and then a fantasy scoreline in Bavaria made it extra special. In truth, it spoiled me.

Truculent football players are the norm, not carefree kids lapping up the novelty of big games on the continent. Surly managers bogged down with the fear of losing a big game are more commonplace than enjoying the craic with a boss who still fancied himself as a player and definitely fancied himself as a comedian! Yet it was a fabulous feeling to be part of the Raith story in 1995 – a fairytale which had started the previous November at Ibrox.

An improbable Coca-Cola Cup win against Celtic paved the way for a sojourn into the Uefa Cup. And so the fun began – with a tie against Faroese giants Gotu Itrottarfelag. Yet it was a false start for players and press alike thanks to the mist which descended over Vagar Airport – an airport which requires the pilot to have the dare-devil skill of a Red Arrow if he's to avoid crashing into mountains either side of the runway, or plunging off the end of the landing strip and into the ocean.

Not that the Raith players were perturbed at the thought of a flight from hell and the dangers lurking in the rocky outcrop on the edge of the North Atlantic. Colin Cameron – a player who went on to represent Hearts, Wolves and Scotland with distinction – simply dumped his training bag at the ground, shrugged his shoulders and headed off to sunbathe on Burntisland beach until the flight was back on schedule. It was a carefree attitude embraced by the young players in the squad such as Cameron, Jason Dair and Stevie Crawford. There were old pros such as the late Ronnie Coyle and a character in Davie Sinclair – a man so tough he had tattooed teeth (not strictly true, but a nice line used by a fellow hack to describe his combative style).

The flight landed late at night, and after a bus journey and a boat trip to Torshavn the players spent a night in the famous Hotel Foro-yar, where you can be woken up in the morning not by a chamber-maid but by a handyman cutting the grass on the roof, which was completely turfed. Raith were a cut above the Faroese champs too over two legs – and a match report filed from a bedroom at the sta-dium in Toftir which doubled as a youth hostel told of a 6-2 Rovers aggregate win.

And so the bandwagon rolled on to Iceland. Icelandic champs Akranes were to be a tougher opponent, but the Raith lads were carefree and after a 3-1 first-leg win at Stark's Park the trip to Rey-kjavik was buoyant. The hour-long bus journey from the capital to Akranes was a winding one as we traversed numerous fjords until the town came into sight. It was another bizarre location for a game, with whales bobbing up and down in the sea behind the main stand. Not that Scott Thomson was whale-watching with the rest of us. The keeper had a blinder and Raith were through again despite losing 1-0 on the night.

This was now a journey that Nicholl and his players could scarcely believe. The mood at the airport for the return flight was one of incredulity. Dair and Crawford decided to do forward rolls all the way from the security desk to the departure gate while one of the players carried a ghetto blaster pumping out tunes. They were like kids at Christmas – genuinely excited by the thrill of winning big games and at the prospect of who they could land in the draw for the next round.

When Uefa paired Raith with Bayern Munich, you could hear the cheers of the chairman Alex Penman all the way back to the SFA offices in Glasgow. Jurgen Klinsmann and Jean-Pierre Papin were the Bayern front two – both former European Players of the Year. Class. And so it proved with a 2-0 win for the Germans at Easter Road – the game having been switched to a bigger venue than Stark's Park to maximise income.

The trip to the Olympic Stadium in Munich then was to be the final hurrah – but what a way to go. At the departure lounge in Edinburgh Airport, Raith's God-fearing winger Tony Rougier predicted a Rovers win. The Lord had visited him the previous night and told him to stay strong and have faith. We politely nodded, filed the story about God being a Raith fan and stuck our money on a Bayern victory.

Yet, incredibly, at half-time in the Olympic Stadium the dream was on. Danny Lennon's free-kick clipped Andreas Herzog's head and sailed past Oliver Kahn. Wee Danny was so stunned he didn't know how to celebrate. The massive electronic scoreboard behind the goal read FC Bayern 0, Raith Rovers FC 1. Myself and colleague Gary Keown – then at the Today newspaper – could hardly file our copy at half-time for chuckling at the madness of it all.

Soon after half-time it could have been 2-0 and level on aggregate

– only for Rougier to fluff a chance from close-range. When Coyle then trod on the ball and let Klinsmann in to level on the night, the fairytale script was ripped up. The Germans stepped up a gear and Raith lost a second goal to Markus Babbel and went down 2-1.

The press were invited back to the team hotel for a party and the European run was celebrated in fine style. Upon return to the press hotel the local hack from the Fife Free Press and now the chief sportswriter of the Scottish Daily Mail John Greechan, took to the grand piano in the lobby bar. He belted out 'Dignity' by Deacon Blue with a few off-key choruses from the assembled gang rounding off the European campaign.

Raith had certainly shown great dignity and class in the way they handled their Uefa experience. There have been bigger games in my career as a reporter, more significant events, more meaningful stories. But none quite as much fun as those three European games with Rovers.

As a few of us joked to devout Christian Rougier on the flight home: it was just a pity God turned out to be a Bayern fan.

Iain Macfarlane joined the Daily Star of Scotland as a reporter in May 1995 and has covered football and golf for all Express newspapers titles since becoming chief sportswriter in 2000. An Airdrieonian by birth, he now lives in Stirling.

METHIL NO MORE

By David Friel

The icy sleet hammered in on my head as I shielded a brick-like mobile phone from the elements and stared at a sodden notebook. Ink started to run down the page, the scrawls becoming harder to decipher …

"CAP D … e … SPACE … CAP B … a … r … r … o … s"

My voice was wavering with the cold. My fingers were turning a strange and worrying shade of blue.

"You what, love?"

The thick Yorkshire accent came booming down the phone.

"De Barros. Marco … De … Barros …"

"You what, love? Can you say that again?"

The date was December 18th 2004. The occasion was East Fife v Huntly in a Scottish Cup second-round replay – the first professional football match I ever covered as a journalist. I was 23 by then – probably a bit of a late starter in this game.

Some football journalists start as copy boys and work their way up. Others study journalism and then put what they learned to good use in papers. I took a different route. Four years at Uni studying history followed by a year of backpacking in Australia. I went there to find myself. I mostly found a fondness for Aussie beer. Tooheys Extra Dry. An absolute revelation.

Upon my return it was time to make inroads. As luck would have it, a traineeship was available on a local newspaper and I got the gig. I quickly made it known that football was my main interest, so the Juniors coverage was mine. Rob Roy and Petershill were on my patch. We needed a 350-word back-page lead for two different editions. My favourite 700 words every week without doubt.

My editor noted my obsession with football. He spoke to a mate on a national and I was offered the chance to cover Junior games on a Saturday afternoon. The only issue was that I was still playing football on a Saturday, still chasing the dream. I tried to juggle both for a while but it was impossible.

After suffering the ignominy of being a sub not used for Cumbernauld United in a 5-0 thumping by Dunipace, I stared at the four pound coins that passed as my expenses and realised I had to get out. I was never going to make any money playing football, but writing about it was the next-best thing.

I loved covering the Juniors. There were no airs or graces. It was gritty, raw and hilarious in equal measures. I travelled all over the west of Scotland and the people I encountered could not have been more accommodating. One Glasgow club was particularly welcoming.

"You from the Sunday Mail? Come on in son."

"You want a dram?" was the first question put to me as I entered the 'social room.'

"No, thanks. That's very kind though."

"Just a wee half? A wee Grouse? A Bell's?"

"Honestly, I've got the car. I'm good, thanks."

"Aw go on son … take a drink."

I looked around the room. People were staring at me, taking it in turns to cajole me into taking "a wee pre-match nip." It could have been a Chewin' the Fat sketch. I felt I was being rude but even the smell of whisky gives me the heave.

"If you don't like whisky we can get you something else. We don't have any beer, only spirits. Vodka? Gin?"

"You got any Smirnoff Ice?"

The stunned silence that greeted my drink order told me that alcopops were not common in Junior football grounds.

The post-match interviews with Junior managers were seldom

serene affairs, but always entertaining.

"Did you seen that f*****g penalty decision?" said one seething man mountain who decided he would lead the interview, not me.

"I did."

"What did you think? F*****g disgrace eh?"

I had two options. Be honest, tell him his 16-stone centre-half had basically committed GBH on the striker and wait for the offer of a square go. Or I could humour him slightly.

"Well, there maybe was a bit of contact."

"Contact? F*****g contact?"

I probably did a dozen Junior games before the call came from the sports desk: I was getting the chance to step up a level. East Fife v Huntly in the Scottish Cup. A real game. TV cameras, the lot.

I'd like to think this sudden elevation was due to the piercing analysis of the Juniors, but someone probably ducked out of the game for a Christmas party. I didn't care though.

"No problem."

I put the phone down and called the old man. "How do I get to Methil?"

Armed with a map and an insane amount of knowledge on Huntly, I set out on the trek. I took the wrong cut-off but got there eventually. You still phoned in copy to PA down in Leeds in those days but I took an oversized laptop to make some notes. A grizzled old hack stared at me and laughed as soon as I produced it from my bag.

"I wouldn't bother with all that computer s***e son. Just phone copy and busk it."

My immediate thought was, but I didn't bring my guitar.

The laptop lasted five minutes as rain, sleet and hail pounded down on it. My remit was 300 words; filed on the whistle, then up-dated with quotes. Not a problem. Sounds straightforward.

What transpired was an epic cup tie. Jerry O'Driscoll and De Barros – iconic lower-division names from Sportscene Scottish Cup specials of the past – gave Huntly a 2-1 lead but East Fife equalised in the closing stages. Extra-time was looming. Disaster.

I phoned the desk. They still wanted it in one hit. "Just sit tight," I was told, "but phone copy and start filing before the end of extra-time."

Russell Guild fired Huntly ahead again and with five minutes to go, I braved the elements and picked up the mobile. I found some shelter at the back of the stand – keeping one eye on the game and one on the drenched notebook.

Aside from the spelling of De Barros, the copy flowed. I was almost done when disaster struck again. Greig McDonald struck a last-gasp equaliser to make it 3-3. A journalist's nightmare. The game went to spot-kicks.

"Just scrap that intro please."

"You what, love?"

East Fife won on penalties and I filed promptly. Quotes followed. Within 90 minutes I was home. It was 8pm by then. I'm not ashamed to say the next four hours were spent waiting on the first edition hitting the local petrol station.

At just after midnight, I got my hands on a freshly printed copy and made my way to the Scottish Cup round-up. 'David Friel at Bayview,' instantly stood out. A lot of hard work was ahead but it was a start.

I'm lucky enough to have been to some of the world's finest stadiums since then and hopefully I'll get a chance to visit a few more in years to come. Whatever happens, I'll never forget my December day in Methil.

David Friel is a sports reporter for the Scottish Sun and has worked in journalism since 2004. He is openly ginger. And proud of it.

IL POSTINO AND IL PRESIDENTE

By Gary Sutherland

O ne of my strangest experiences as a sportswriter was the day I
didn't do any work and became a tour guide instead. The day
in question began with a phone call from an Italian postman
and ended with me in the Dundee FC boardroom, pretending to
be Italian and drinking wine with then Dens Park manager Ivano
Bonetti. In between, I showed the president of a Serie A club round
the sights of Glasgow.

I was sitting in the Scotland on Sunday Glasgow office mid-
morning when my phone rang.

"Ciao Gary!"

"Hey Paolo, how's it going?"

Paolo was the Italian postie in question. Best friend of Chievo
president Luca Campedelli, Paolo was in Scotland with the Verona
club who were on a mini tour of Scotland. The squad were staying
at the Carnoustie Hotel. I'd watched Chievo's Fir Park friendly with
Motherwell a few nights before and was heading up to Dens tonight
to see them take on Dundee, once I'd got some work done.

"We come to Glasgow!" shouted Paolo who sounded as if he
was on a train. "Luca want to see stadiums! Hampden! Ibrox! Celtic
Park!"

"That's an excellent idea."

"See you Queen Street station 30 minutes!"

"Eh?"

"You meet us at station, yes?"

"Er, sure. Of course."

"Luca very excited! Maybe we go to pub! Ciao Gary!"

What the heck just happened there?

I'd first encountered Paolo when I'd ventured to Verona to write the Chievo story for our paper's monthly sports magazine. It was, without doubt, my best-ever assignment, getting the chance to tell the remarkable story of Chievo's rapid rise from obscurity to the spotlight of Serie A. I travelled on a Chievo supporters' bus to Turin and saw the Flying Donkeys frighten the life out of Juventus. I had dinner with President Campedelli at his favourite pizzeria. And I got drunk with Paolo in the various pubs of Verona (Il Postino does like a pint). On my return home, I wrote it all up for the piece of sports journalism I'm most fond and proud of.

And now I had another assignment: to give Luca and Paolo a tour of Glasgow, when I was meant to be working. Ach well, they'd shown me a good time in Verona. Now it was my turn to look after them.

I phoned Rangers, Celtic and the SFA in quick succession, said who I was and – more importantly – who I was bringing, and they were all very accommodating. Yes, they'd give us a tour. I dashed to Queen Street to meet Paolo and Luca off their train.

The three of us jumped into a taxi and headed straight for Ibrox. On the way, my editor phoned from the Edinburgh office, asking what I was up to. I said something about setting up interviews for the following day. He was cool with that. It was midweek and we were a Sunday newspaper.

We walked in the front door of Ibrox, stated our business and were led up the marble staircase to the trophy room. Luca started checking out all the silverware and Paolo asked me who that man was over there. It was Derek Johnstone, who seemed to be doing some filming with a cameraman.

"That's Derek Johnstone," I explained and Paolo's eyes lit up. "Derek Johnstone!" He obviously knew who Derek Johnstone was then.

Before I could stop him, Paolo marched straight over to the former Rangers striker and slapped him on the back.

"Derek Johnstone!" cried Paolo. "I remember you – in the boat!" Derek Johnstone looked confused.

Paolo carried on, reminding Derek of the time he ended up stranded at sea in a rowing boat in the early hours of the morning after a hotel drinking session with his Scotland team-mates. Paolo was confusing Derek Johnstone with Jimmy Johnstone. First time for everything, I thought, as I managed to drag Paolo away from Derek so that he could continue with his filming.

We didn't meet any Rangers legends in the home dressing room, which was probably just as well, given what had happened in the trophy room. And we walked down the tunnel and on to the pitch, Luca, a quiet man (quieter than Paolo at any rate), seemed to be enjoying his tour of Ibrox.

Next we took another taxi across the South Side to Hampden where we spent ages in the Scottish Football Museum, Luca examining pretty much every item on display. And we did the dressing room and the tunnel and we sat in the main stand.

Leaving Hampden in the taxi, I noticed that Luca had a tear in his eye. Like Paolo, Luca is a massive fan of British football and British football history. Hampden had been an emotional experience for Luca and, as a Scotsman, I was touched by his show of emotion.

By now it was late afternoon and it was going to have to be a whirlwind tour of Celtic Park if Luca and Paolo were to catch their desired train back to Dundee for Chievo's evening friendly. Luca decided that it didn't matter that he saw Celtic Park. He had been before. And I remembered him telling me in Verona that he had shares in Celtic.

Paolo announced that we should therefore go to the pub. So I took the pair of them to the Mitre Bar off Argyle Street, a tiny pub (now gone, sadly) that was wall-to-wall football scarves and pennants from clubs the world over. Luca and Paolo marvelled at the football decor as they sank their pints. Then we ran for the train.

I watched Dundee v Chievo with my dad and sister who had driven down from Hopeman. And afterwards, Luca went to the away dressing room and got the shirt of one of the Chievo players for my sister. He'd already given the three of us Chievo scarves, which we'd worn throughout the game.

While we chatted with Luca, Bonetti walked past and invited us into the boardroom where we were handed glasses of wine. Luca and Bonetti talked away in Italian, and me and my dad and sister just sort of stood around smiling in our Chievo scarves. Bonetti seemed to have taken us for Italians. I'd never interviewed the man but had done the odd Dundee match report. He did give me this funny look, one of perhaps half-recognition, but I chose not to say anything and kept on smiling.

Looking back now, I can kind of see why I'm not a sports journalist anymore. A sports journalist might have introduced himself to a Premier League manager and, I don't know, tried to set up an interview? Whereas I just stood there grinning and drinking his wine.

Oh well. In any case, it was one of the best days I ever had in the game.

Gary Sutherland is a former sportswriter with Scotland on Sunday and the author of the books Golf on the Rocks, Great Balls of Fire *and* Hunting Grounds. *A former ice cream and candy floss maker, he once saw a panther on the outskirts of Perth and has danced on stage with Prince.*

OH CHOCCY, WHERE ART THOU?

By Andy McInnes

I thought I was getting a sunshine break on the company but instead it proved to be a busman's holiday from hell.

"We've booked you on a flight to the Costa Del Sol this afternoon. Enjoy the trip and oh, by the way, your pal Brian McClair is there with his family .We badly need a big exclusive. Find out if he's going to sign for Manchester United," said the sports editor, in that bend down to pick up the medal and I'll kick you up the backside tone.

"But I can't," I replied. "I'm going to a family wedding this weekend, and my wife, not to mention the bride-to-be, will kill me if I miss it."

Four hours later and somewhere over the English Channel with yet another vodka and coke in hand, my panic at missing the wedding waltz turned to real fear when I suddenly realised I hadn't a clue where then Celtic striker McClair was staying or the fact that the Costa del Sol stretched for nearly 70 miles between Malaga and Gibraltar!

This was June 1987, just two years after Vodafone had made their first 'mobile' phone call with a brick-weight contraption and journalists, never mind footballers, had never heard of tweets or emails, and were still relying on landlines, if not pigeons.

As I checked into my hotel in Benalmadena the brainwave finally arrived, although it was hardly a 'Eureka' moment. Brian's family and parents were neighbours of mine in Airdrie, so I should phone home

186

and ask Mrs McInnes – who was still unaware I wouldn't make the wedding in three days' time – to pop around to Mr McClair Snr's place and find out where his son was staying during his holidays.

"He hasn't got a clue but thinks he might be at a timeshare resort and is meeting up with Gordon Strachan who is staying at Rod Stewart's villa near Puerto Banus," said my wife when she phoned back. "By the way, your two young sons look great in their new wedding suits ... when will you be home?" ... Click.

The next day and with a staff photographer from Manchester who had flow out to join me we set out to find the elusive 'Choccy' McClair. It didn't help as we set off on a tour of Calahonda, Fuengirola, Marbella, Puerto Banus and Estepona, when my snapper (not the brightest of the breed) casually informed me he had flown over with a sportswriter and photographer from the Sun, who were also searching for McClair.

Anyone wearing a Celtic strip was accosted in the street. Folk in pubs and restaurants were quizzed as to whether they had seen my target. Even a trip to Rod's gaff was a waste of time as we only got to see it from behind 10-feet high locked gates. It was three days (and a missed wedding and potential pending divorce proceedings) later before the big breakthrough happened.

"He is staying in the Villacana Timeshare Resort in Estepona," was the tip.

With it being a timeshare, owners and holidaymakers alike came and went on a daily basis, and the reception desk had no idea who was in their townhouses or apartments. Even worse, they had never heard of Brian McClair.

There was nothing else for it. It was a case of starting in row A and working through to Z, knocking on every door and checking the many small swimming pools dotted around the vast complex. With sweat pouring down our backs and temperatures reaching the high 80s in the midday sun, I started to think of what my opening remark would be if and when we finally tracked the elusive striker down.

There were some highs and plenty of lows in the search, "Naw, I hivnae seen him but that wee blond-haired guy who plays fitba is four doors doon," said one helpful Glasgow pensioner. The "wee blond-haired guy" turned out to be Mo Johnston, but he had actually checked out a day earlier and the trail went cold again.

After about 100 knocks and several invitations to party (like all good sportswriters I made my excuses and left), we did what all good journalistic sleuths do and retired to the bar. And there, looking out from the terrace with a San Miguel in hand was Brian playing with his kids at the side of the main swimming pool.

Swiftly downing the beer and thanking the Lord of my newfound faith, we ran to the scene. "Dr McClair I presume," I ventured in a most unoriginal and pathetic opener.

I expected some signs of surprise but Brian being laconic Brian simply said, "Fancy a drink?"

Now at this stage I have to confess a vested interest in his transfer. A German football agent called Rudiger Bernd Killat, despite being a friend of Alex Ferguson, had promised me a brand-new Mercedes if I could secure my mate's signature for Cologne. That club was willing to pay the £2million asking price, whereas United would only offer £850,000. On one hand I was supposed to convince Brian that the Bundesliga was a better prospect for him than English football, but on the other it was always going to be a better scoop for me if he signed for Fergie and United.

McClair and I had been pals a long time, to the extent that he even drove me to and from Celtic matches at Parkhead and would go for a drink afterwards. His dad and brother were my guests when he picked up the Player of the Year Award, and he always had a kick-around with my kids when he dropped into the house for a beer.

There were further complications. One: he was, in fact, a guest of a Manchester United director who owned the Estepona townhouse. Two: Gordon Strachan had been paying him daily visits to sell a move to Manchester to him. Three: The Sun had offered him thousands of pounds for his story whereas I was only prepared to cough up another San Miguel or three.

It was a tough call for him to make but in the end the choice came down to family as much as football reasons. I knew Brian's wife, Maureen, hated flying and wanted to stay close to home rather than locate to Germany. After a few more beers I put him on the spot saying, "You will sign for United?" He gave me a nod and a wink to confirm and the chase for the story was over.

As I headed back to my room to file and earn a herogram from my bosses (who gave me another couple of days in Spain to enjoy a real holiday), I swear there was a thought-bubble above my head with a picture inside it of the promised Merc reversing out of my driveway, with my wife Irene throwing my belongings into it!

Andy McInnes switched from news to sports reporting 32 years ago, becoming chief football writer for the Daily Star of Scotland, then sports editor in chief of the Star and Scottish Daily Express. He has covered five World Cup finals and three European Championship finals, as well as Celtic and Rangers in their respective Uefa Cup finals.

THE STARS WERE BRIGHT, FERNANDO

By Scott Burns

E very football fan has one memory or incident from the World Cup finals that they will never forget, whether it be Archie Gemmill's wonder effort against Holland in 1978, Diego Maradona's Hand of God goal or his virtuoso effort in the same game as he saw off England in Mexico '86, or Roberto Baggio's shocking penalty shoot-out miss that went some way to handing the 1994 crown to Brazil.

The one game my mind always floats back to is the 2006 World Cup final between France and Italy.

Yet it has absolutely nothing to do with Fabio Cannavaro lifting the World Cup, the goals from Marco Materazzi or Zinedine Zidane, or even the pair's infamous clash that saw the legendary Frenchman sent off for butting the Italian defender in his final farewell to football. In fact, the mere mention of that game brings me back to a footballer who didn't even play in that match but still managed to wreck my afternoon's viewing.

Several daily Scottish newspaper journalists, including myself, had flown out to South Africa in advance to cover Rangers' pre-season tour, which was the first under their new manager Paul Le Guen. We were sitting in a local Italian restaurant near to our hotel in Johannesburg, watching the final and tucking into our bruschetta and pasta starters, enjoying the early exchanges from the game when one of my colleagues' mobile phones rang.

Sixty seconds later, our table was empty, our starters sitting half-eaten and our main courses still in the oven as money was thrown on the table and our utmost apologies were given to the restaurant owner as we raced out of his door, without even a second glance towards the television in the corner showing the World Cup final.

The phone call had come from the Rangers press officer who had confirmed that a certain Fernando Ricksen had been sent home by Le Guen, before he had even set foot in South Africa. The firebrand Dutchman had upset his new manager by drinking heavily and getting involved an altercation with an air stewardess during the incoming flight.

Suddenly our hopes of a leisurely afternoon watching the final were shattered and we had to scramble back to our hotel rooms to try and put some more meat on the bones of that particular tale. I eventually filed the story and fortunately managed to get downstairs to see the final fragments of extra-time just before the match went into penalty kicks, and I was able to see David Trezeguet miss for the French to hand the World Cup to the Italians.

That trip to South Africa was certainly eye-opening. Bloemfontein Airport was hijacked just 24 hours before we were due to fly up there with Rangers for their tour game with local side Bloemfontein Celtic, while on our return to Johannesburg we ended up in the same restaurant as former American president Bill Clinton.

The main thing for me, however, was that Ricksen incident and it is fair to say the Dutchman's six-year stint at Ibrox was a dream for every sports journalist in Scotland. Ricksen was never far away from the headlines whether it was late-night firework parties, liaisons with former Page Three models or his on-the-field antics. Whenever you interviewed him he was one of the nicest and most genuine footballers you could meet, but he also lived on the edge. I remember another pre-season tour, in Germany, where he claimed he had turned over a new leaf and had returned to training early that summer. It even led to Alex McLeish praising him for his new approach yet, unbeknown to the then Rangers manager, he had sneaked out of the team hotel to meet a local girl in a nearby restaurant the previous night. Fernando was always good value and even when I met up with him again before the 2008 Uefa Cup final against Zenit St Petersburg he couldn't have been more welcoming to me and the rest of the Scottish press corps.

Being in this game means you have more than your fair share of run-ins with managers and players. There was one incident after a Scottish Cup win at Forfar that McLeish cornered me in the Station Park boot room and tried to find out who had leaked the story that his friend and successor at Hibs, Frank Sauzee, had called in a sports psychologist to try and turn round his disastrous spell at Easter Road.

I also had a bust-up with Terry Butcher when he was in charge at Motherwell, who took exception to something I had written before Stephen Pearson's pending move to Celtic. We didn't speak for about eight months until Butcher finally broke the ice, ironically, just minutes after his Well team had beaten Celtic 2-1 to hand the 2004-05 title to Rangers on Helicopter Sunday.

Through the years I have done dozens of interviews. Some you come away from with a real buzz, while in others you wish you hadn't even bothered to pick up your pen.

There was one interview I did over the phone with the Scottish international Callum Davidson. He was at Preston North End and he got a long-awaited recall after an injury-hit spell at Leicester City. I was interviewing Callum and he was nice enough but at times it felt like I was pulling teeth before I finally admitted defeat and decided to call it a day, thinking I had the bog-standard, 'It's great to be back' line.

Sixty seconds later my mobile rang again and Callum's number flashed up again. He said his wife had been standing next to him and she had told him that he should come clean about everything and his injury hell. Callum then explained how his injury problems had been misdiagnosed and how he had feared he would have to hang up his boots before he finally got to the bottom of his problems.

There are also times when you are in a privileged position and asked to sound out players and managers about possible moves.

There was an incident when the late Eddie Thompson, supremo at Dundee United, asked me to see if the Preston manager Billy Davies would be interested in becoming manager at Tannadice, while there was another incident in which Michael Johnston, the chairman at Kilmarnock, asked me to sound out Jimmy Calderwood before they eventually went on to appoint him. I spoke to Jimmy via his assistant, Sandy Clark, and he confirmed he was interested. Jimmy then went on the radio the next night and confirmed he had been approached about the job. He had indeed been informally sounded-out, but there had been no official contact, and Jefferies and sidekick Billy Brown still had to finalise their Rugby Park settlements. It led to a bit of an uproar on the radio that Jimmy had been tapped up but nothing could have been further from the truth, and an official approach was only made after Jefferies and Brown had officially departed.

Scott Burns has spent the last 12 years as a sports reporter with the Daily Express and the three prior to that at the Press and Journal. He is also a part-time author and a full-time dad.

GORGEOUS GEORGIA

By Davie Provan

t was the summer of 1995 and I found myself in the spike bar of Kilmacolm golf club watching the draw for the European Cup Winners' Cup. Celtic were heading for Batumi in Georgia and I knew I'd be going with them as part of Radio Clyde's commentary team.

Batumi? Never heard of it. Sadly, this Georgia wasn't that of Magnolia Drive and the US Masters but its namesake on the edge of the Black Sea. My good pal and regular four-ball partner, the late Ian 'Dan' Archer, disappeared to make some enquiries. Now Dan was a socialist, albeit of the Dom Perignon variety, and tended to get excited by any visit to the old Soviet Union. Sure enough, 10 minutes later he returned clicking his heels. "We'll be following in the footsteps of Joe Stalin," he announced. "Joe lived there before the Russian Revolution. Batumi is the Venice of the east, a cafe society city where members of the politburo built their holiday homes. This will be a trip to remember." He wasn't wrong.

Normally the media would share a direct charter flight with the team but Celtic claimed we had to go via Istanbul, then use Georgia's national carrier for the flight to Batumi. Manager Tommy Burns reckoned it had more to do with chief executive Fergus McCann trying to save a few quid.

Either way, we got to Istanbul where the second aircraft awaited us. It was a Yak-40, of the type you see in aviation museums. The carpets were threadbare, many of the seatbelts missing and there was an overpowering stench of aviation fuel in the cabin. Never a great flyer, I thought of doing a runner but a stiff drink did the trick.

Somehow this relic of an aircraft screamed out of Istanbul and over the Black Sea where the turbulence started. Real turbulence. Down in the front rows players were turning chalk white. Further back journalists were using duty free for sedation. As we bobbed about like a cork the captain emerged from the flight-deck to offer reassurance. After he'd introduced himself as Sergei, Dan asked him if he knew how old the plane was. "Oh, 25, 30 years old. Ex-Aeroflot fleet, very good aircraft" he said.

Dan: "What about the engines – Pratt and Whitney?"

"Not Pratt and Whitney, but very good copy," said our friend. More large ones all round.

To be fair, Sergei got us safely into Batumi International Airport, a misnomer if ever there was one. It was an old military airfield with a couple of unloved MiGs rusting in adjacent hangars. More worrying was the sight of cattle grazing inside the perimeter fence and with runway lights on the blink we were told we'd have to travel back out of Batumi International in daylight.

On our way to the Hotel Sputnik, Batumi's demise became apparent. Previously a fortified prize of the Romans and Ottomans, the city had once been Russia's biggest oil port. Now it was on its knees. The splintering of the Soviet Union had seen the collapse of the welfare system and subsidised industry. Buses lay abandoned by the roadside having run out of diesel. Cattle grazed on the street while there were goats on the balconies of high-rise apartments.

Waiting on our bags, I mentioned to McCann that I'd never seen poverty like it. "I don't know about that," he said, "these people should be manufacturing." Fergus didn't do sympathy.

Yet amid the squalor the black economy was booming. As we took some sun at the hotel, a top-of-the-range Mercedes glided into the car-park. Four Versace-clad spivs took the table next to us. Next thing a litre bottle of vodka was put in front of us, a gift from the mob. On the label was a picture of Georgia's president Eduard Shevardnadze, whom they wanted us to toast.

Such requests are never a problem for Scottish hacks, and eventually the tables were pushed together in the interests of detente. Fine, until a well-oiled member of our group got aggressive with our hosts, jabbing a finger into the face of one. In the best traditions of the mafia this guy pulled a silver revolver from his inside pocket, saying, "Please sit down while you have the chance." Game over.

The next day Dan and I took a guided tour of Batumi's dachas where Brezhnev and Co. used to spend the summer. To Ian's disappointment we never did find Stalin's pad but he did get his hands on some Soviet memorabilia.

As for the game? Ten minutes into the first half, commentator Dougie MacDonald's microphone packed in and he had to use mine. It was a hell of a long way to go for 10 minutes' work, even to watch Celtic beat Dinamo 3-2.

By the time we got back to the airfield everyone had seen enough of Batumi but we weren't getting home yet. Airport security claimed the Scottish media hadn't paid for telephone calls at the stadium. It was extortion but with night falling we had to stump up. A whip-round raised a few hundred dollars. We were on our way.

I still remember that Yak-40 roaring down the runway at dusk, praying no stray cattle would wander out in front of us. As we climbed above the Caucasus we were told to lower the window blinds. It was to prevent us seeing the Armenians and Azerbaijani's shelling each other in the mountains below. It will be some time before I reacquaint myself with Batumi.

Davie Provan is a former professional footballer who played for Kilmarnock (1974-78) and Celtic (1978-86). He won 10 Scotland caps before retiring through illness. He is now a columnist for the Sun on Sunday and broadcasts for Sky Sports.

LOOKING FOR MARKO

By Gary Keown

O ne lucky telephone call is sometimes all it takes to find that needle in a haystack and allow it to knit together the most splendid little yarns.

Pat McElhinney, a salt-of-the-earth Ayrshireman living well and working hard in the Australian city of Melbourne, was the recipient of one such surprise communication on a sun-kissed morning many moons ago.

And, sweet Lord, how he beamed a ray of light into a stranger's heart when he picked up the blower and set up the killer moves in the chess game that is a worldwide media manhunt.

Back in December 1998, a Celtic player by the name of Marko (later to be rechristened Mark) Viduka went AWOL, just days after joining in a £3million transfer, suffering from depression related to a miserable spell at former club Croatia Zagreb. His eventual destination would be his native Oz, but a short trip back to the Balkans had led to him and his fragrant girlfriend Ivana being holed up in their apartment under siege from a host of camera crews.

At the same time, in one of North Lanarkshire's more tranquil hamlets, a Sun sports reporter called Gary Keown was happily slabbering on to the pillow on his lonesome when the shrill ring of the landline sent a perfectly normal day off on a decidedly abnormal tangent.

"Gary. Are you up and about?"

It's the gaffer.

"Erm, aye, aye. What's happening?"

"You're going to have to pack a bag. We need to go and get Marko Viduka."

"Right, aye. Erm, he's back in Croatia the now, isn't he?"

"Yeah, yeah, but his flat is surrounded. Do you think we should go there and join the crowd, or head out to Australia and wait for him back there?"

Now, no offence to Zagreb, a most noble city even in the bleak grip of winter, but it does not offer that sense of infinite possibility afforded by a spot where it's bikini weather and the ostrich fillets are sizzling on the barbie.

"You know, Steve," I ventured, "My mind is veering towards Melbourne."

"Uh-huh?"

"Well, he'll be spirited out of Zagreb under cover of night to avoid the cameras, no-one will get near him, and we'll be in Melbourne to cut him off at the pass."

"Good thinking. We'll sort the flights out. You get to the airport as quick as you can and we'll take it from there."

In those more auspicious times, newspapers felt an obligation to provide club-class travel for those venturing vast distances in the quest for truth. Yet a little extra legroom does not assuage the nagging self-doubt that comes from knowing what hell will rain from the sky should this gamble of zipping across the world on a four-grand ticket throw up next to nothing.

Fresh as a marsupial's dank pouch after a 30-hour journey punctuated by far too much chicken satay and lager, it was soon time to emerge blinking into the sunlight from Tullamarine Airport and fish out the mobile along with a crumpled piece of paper with some local fellow's number on it. There had been no time for homework in the rush of leaving Glasgow. No time to get a grip on where I might find Viduka or even get it rubberstamped that he was, indeed, on his way back to Melbourne at all. However, before flying, I'd made a quick call to a Celtic-obsessed pal to ask about Antipodean supporters' clubs and the name of Mr McElhinney, secretary of the Melbourne

Number One CSC, came back. Well, I thought, there's no harm in giving him a try before we get down to the business of digging through phonebooks, is there?

Two rings and, Allah be praised, an answer.

"Hello."

"Hello, could I speak to Pat, please?"

"Aye, Pat speaking."

"Hello, Pat. This is Gary Keown here from the Sun newspaper in Glasgow. I've just landed in Melbourne and I was wondering if you might be able to help me out."

"Aye, I will if I can. What's up?"

"Well, I'm here to get hold of Marko Viduka when he finally pitches up from Croatia. You wouldn't have any idea of where he comes from or where his folks are, would you?"

It's a stab in the dark, a question so random and speculative that the echo of the final couple of words on the line causes the gut to tingle with a mild sense of shame. Pat starts laughing. You're making a clown of yourself here, Keown.

"I can do better than that for you," says this personification of everything good and righteous in the world. "His mum and dad are coming to our Christmas party in a couple of weeks' time. Here's their address and telephone number. Tell Joe and Rose I'm askin' for them when ye go up tae the hoose."

Bingo! Within half an hour of hitting terra firma, I've hooked up with my photographer Joe Sabljak, a man's man from the local Croatian community, and we're standing on the front step of chez Viduka in an upmarket suburb to the north-west of the city.

Contrary to popular belief, schooled reporters have a particular modus operandi when arriving unannounced at someone's doorstep. It involves being unfailingly polite and totally upfront about who you are, why you're there and what you're looking for. Naturally, Viduka's sister Sonia took our telephone numbers, divulged the time of the flight he was returning on the following night and pointed us in the direction of his old colleagues at Melbourne Knights FC, who threw up all sorts of super background stories as radio silence reigned in Zagreb. With the time difference in our favour and no serious pressure to phone home, the lure of a royal welcome at The Blarney Stone in Port Melbourne from Pat and other great guys from the Melbourne Number One – such as Harry Duffy, Tommy Carmichael and Joe McNeilly – proved irresistible.

Imbued with the overwhelming kindness and humanity they would show throughout my stay, I decided it was perfectly natural to show up reinvigorated and exceedingly well-refreshed at the offices of the Rupert Murdoch-owned Herald Sun after 2am shutting-time and demand access to the computer system to send the first dispatches home to Scotland. To our eternal shock, they agreed and kept the place open until I'd finished typing my reports with one eye shut for the purposes of focusing and one finger feeling its way around the keyboard.

Viduka turned up as planned the next night and a quick interview in the airport car park kept the desk off my back and the paper that little bit ahead of the game. By the time the sun had risen on a new day, though, the Daily Record and Daily Mail had got with the programme and scrambled their 'stringers' from Sydney to join me in the battle for the next, headline-dominating exclusive du jour.

The arrival of newsmen Frank Thorne and Richard Shears, grizzled masters of the trade, introduced the spice of harsh competition and led to a faintly comic weekend of chasing each other all over town in the scramble for more words from big Marko. For all that, though, the three of us would make a point of meeting up in Chinatown for a Thai dinner together and a good laugh over our adventures at the close of play. Rivals by day, comrades by night; this is the misunderstood esprit de corps that still exists between frontline reporters to this day.

Although we had all spoken with Viduka off-the-record and sent back various photographs, both snatched and staged, it was made clear nothing more would be uttered publicly until a hotel press conference on the Monday. In order to hammer the opposition, severely restricted because of time constraints and the lack of a bona-fide sportswriter on site, the Sun kept everyone on duty until after one in the morning to make sure the final edition had every cough and spit on the story of the moment from that event. There was no mobile internet then. Talk of taking one's dongle out in public could lead to police charges. My remit was to steam in with the early questions, bail out after 15 minutes to a payphone and dictate 1500 ad-libbed words to our secret weapon Susan McLaughlin back in Glasgow, surely the finest copytaker to grace the world of Scottish newspapers.

The Sun trumped everyone that morning and there was more to come.

While enjoying a farewell tincture with Mr Sabljak in his front room just hours before catching my flight home, the mobile rang. It was Viduka. The groundwork laid on the front step of the family home that very first day had provided one final pay-off. He fed me the most exceptional exclusive about his grandfather Michael dying while he was in Croatia and how this emotional return had allowed him to visit the grave for the first time.

Viduka, just 23 at the time, was a good big spud and it remains pleasing that he and his family trusted us to handle such information with delicacy. How lovely it was, too, to catch the tail-end of an era which saw papers send their men routinely traversing the planet on the trail of the stories behind the stories with no expense spared.

Gentleman supporters, carved from your own background, would offer help and friendship to journalists while the PR industry, with its spin and obfuscation, was still pretty much in its infancy.

It all seems such a long time ago. And it is.

Gary Keown left school at 16 to begin work with the Sunday Post in 1989. He has since served as a staff reporter and columnist for the Daily Record, Today, the Sun, Sunday Mail, Daily Express and Daily Star.

HOW THE SUN SCOOPED THE STORY OF THE CENTURY

By Jack Irvine

The Scottish Sun has been a potent force in journalism since its launch in 1987. However, in the first couple of years under my editorship there was a degree of resistance to this 'English inter- loper' and its entry into the cosy world of Scottish newspapers then dominated by the Daily Record (please note this editor was actually from Shettleston and his deputy from Elderslie).

That all changed on July 10th 1989 with a Sun front-page head- line that read simply, 'Mo Joins Gers.' Since that day it's the one story that I am repeatedly questioned about and the one surrounded by myth and misinformation. Did I pay Graeme Souness £100,000 for the story? Was it Rangers owner David Murray or Maurice John- ston's agent Bill McMurdo who delivered the goods? Why did the Daily Record fail to pick it up when it hit their desks on the evening of July 9th? Well, the truth is much simpler and at the same time an example of good old-fashioned journalism and gut instinct tinged with the wee bit of luck that every reporter needs.

At the end of June I had attended a Press Fund Charity lunch at the Marriot Hotel in Glasgow. To my delight I won the raffle which was a week for two in Majorca. That evening I showed the hotel de- tails to my wife, who said, "What a dump, I'm not going there. Take one of your golfing pals." I arranged to do just that.

A couple of days later Souness called me. I had got to know him and (then Ibrox assistant manager) Walter Smith because of the number of stories we had broken about Rangers, and we had always got on well. Souness indicated that he had heard about my win and he would be visiting his kids in Majorca following the breakdown of his marriage. His former wife was staying with her parents who had been resident on the island for a number of years but he would only be able to see the children for a couple of hours a day and would have a lot of time on his hands. "How about we team up when I'm there," said Graeme, "and we can play golf and soak up some sun?"

Sneakily I then up upgraded our run-of-the-mill hotel to the five-star Sheraton Son Vida where Souness would be staying. Naturally, I didn't share that information with Mrs Irvine.

The pattern was the same every day for the next week. Lying by the pool (oddly, the place was deserted), lunch, golf for me and my mate (Graeme didn't play in these days), then out for dinner every night to the island's finest restaurants, where Graeme was instantly recognised from his days with Liverpool and Sampdoria.

Round about the third bottle of Rioja, Souness would always ask the same question, "Should Rangers sign a Catholic?"

Now remember Souness was married (albeit about to be unmarried) to a Roman Catholic and as an Edinburgh lad he had never really experienced sectarianism until he joined Rangers in 1986 as player-manager. He knew only too well that things had to change at Ibrox if only to give them access to top continental players, but I must stress that the questions and the conversations were non-specific and extremely general.

However, I had observed that every day as we lay by the pool Souness was repeatedly approached by a waiter to be informed that a "Mr Rodger was on the phone from Scotland."

Mr Rodger was the legendary sportswriter Jim Rodger of the Daily Mirror. I say 'sportswriter' but to be perfectly honest the then 66-year-old was probably the worst writer in the business. However, his contacts were legendary and he had access to every leading football manager in the world, not to forget the Pope and Prime Minister Margaret Thatcher whom he insisted on calling "hen."

Souness kept his cards close to his chest and I assumed that Jim was talking to him about some future transfer because the Daily Mirror man was notorious for acting as a go-between for managers and agents. Whether the Mirror ever benefited from this inside information is a moot point. They were certainly going to miss out in a few days' time!

I flew back to Glasgow on Saturday July 8th to be informed by my wife that we were buying a new house. I think that was my punishment for the Son Vida. Souness was flying back to Edinburgh on the Sunday. As I'd been skiving for a week I felt obliged to give my deputy the Sunday off and take the editor's chair. Early in the afternoon our young gofer, a 16-year-old schoolboy called Keith Jackson (yes, the very same!), nervously popped his head round the editor's door and asked if he could speak to me. The conversation was surreal.

"Mr Irvine, I was round at my girlfriend's house last night."

"Mmm, interesting."

"I saw a fax on her dad's machine."

"Yes."

"It had Mo Johnston's name on it."

"Yeah, so?"

"Oh, I should have explained, her dad handles all the insurance for Rangers players."

The world stopped on its axis. "Bloody hell," I shouted or maybe something fruitier.

I dialled Souness' mobile and as luck would have it he had just stepped off the plane at Edinburgh. "Graeme, remember you asked me if you should sign a Catholic? It's Mo, isn't it?"

Souness, a man of few words, simply said, "Call you back."

About 20 minutes later he called. "Print it," was all he said.

The Sun went into meltdown on that Sunday afternoon. The sports desk under the brilliant Steve Wolstencroft teamed up with the news boys and it fell to Derek Stewart Brown to write the front-page splash which was quite an achievement considering he had virtually no hard facts apart from the Souness confirmation, Keith's sight of the fax and my endless conversations in Majorca.

If memory serves me correctly there were 14 news pages alone devoted to the story and sport must have done almost as many. My Daily Record spies told me the next day that when the early editions of the Sun landed on the Record sports desk at Anderston Quay they almost collapsed before phoning star sportswriter Alex Cameron who was in his bed. When the late man on the Record sports desk explained that the Sun were claiming that Mo was about to join Rangers, Cameron grumpily said, "They're just taking a flier. Don't wake me up again with crap like this." The Record boys promptly went back to sleep and have remained that way ever since.

The next morning, Monday, Rangers called a press conference. Sun sportswriter Jim Black told me later that day that when the media pack arrived they were heaping derision on the Sun, and at the head of the detractors was one Alex Cameron. Suddenly David Murray and Graeme Souness were followed into the room by Maurice Johnston. Jim told me, "Alex turned chalk white. It was as if his life was flashing in front of him."

Apparently when I had called Souness he was on his way to David Murray's home where Mo and Bill McMurdo were waiting for him. He told them that I had been on the phone and had guessed what was happening. I knew all of them and they agreed that Souness could confirm the story.

From that day on we knew we had broken the Record's spirit and every big story dropped into my lap. How much did it cost me? I gave young Keith five hundred quid to go on holiday and that was the end of it. How he ended up on the day-late Record after such a promising start I'll never know. So, sorry to disappoint the conspiracy theorists. No bungs. No phone hacking. Just old-fashioned journalism. Oh, and of course, an editorial genius at the helm.

Jack Irvine founded the PR agency Media House International in 1991, after a highly successful career in British newspapers. He made his name as the editor of the up-and-coming Scottish Sun in the 1980s and he rates the Mojo exclusive – widely regarded as the most famous Scottish sports scoop of all time – as his proudest media moment.

A PORTRAIT OF THE JOURNALIST AS A YOUNG MAN

By James Morgan

You don't have to have played football to be a manager. You don't have to have a singing voice to be a pop star and, similarly, you don't have to be able to write to be a journalist.

This is the profession's great, untold secret. It's a revelation so staggering that an outsider might be hard pushed to believe it is actually true given that it seems to underpin the very essence of the job. One need not have a grasp of style, timbre or inner voice. One need not even understand sentence construction or simply making sense. There is at least one 'headliner' I know of who has his copy rewritten by the sports editor on a daily basis. But this guy is a shrewd operator, he has a public persona, he can speak to people and he brings in stories. The important thing to realise here is that just because he cannot write it does not mean he is unable to function as a journalist. No, instead he possesses just enough charisma to ensure he gets the story and thus remains a valuable commodity. Wearing many hats is one of the peculiar realities of modern journalism. You have to be a social butterfly, an individual, an organiser but a bit wacky too, an erudite listener and sharp interlocutor. Not all of these qualities are compatible and some of us have an abundance of one and precious little of another.

My own area of weakness is this: a craven inability to speak to famous people. I know all the cues: imagine them on the toilet; think of them naked; remember that they're just like you and me, and they're mostly insecure. And, all of that works, until the point of impact – when my throat closes over, my brain freezes and the words stick in the air like prisoners in a speech bubble.

Picture the scene. It was four months into my career on the sports desk at The Herald. Previous assignments for the local rag back in Northern Ireland had included interviewing members of a crocheting class for pensioners, speaking to a forest warden about tree felling in a country park and grilling a member of the local assembly about a new housing development. This was not Woodward and Bernstein stuff.

The phone rang one Friday mid-morning in February. It was the desk. They wanted me to get to Celtic Park immediately for a press sit-down with Martin O'Neill. I was just out of bed but as a newly appointed sub-editor this was my chance to prove that I could be a writer, too. Twenty minutes later my Peugeot 206 screeched into the Celtic car park. The butterflies were fluttering already, heightened by the feeling of inadequacy that parking one's clapped-out motor beside a brand-new Bentley brings.

"Morning, Mr Stein," I thought as I passed the bust of the legendary Celtic manager inside the main entrance. I half imagined Stein glowering back at me and growling: "And wha are ye?"

And then I was inside the building, my destination the Carling Suite. It seemed wholly inappropriate that a club with more than a century of history should be forced by sponsors to bow to such fripperies as naming a room after a beer. These were the thoughts I was thinking as I ambled about looking for the assembled presser. I knew I was lost when I entered a room containing several austere gentlemen in green blazers. "Downstairs, end of the corridor on the left, son," said one.

When I entered the suite, a television was blaring out Sky Sports News and a group of journalists clustered round a table were deep in discussion. One seat sat vacant.

"Now, everyone must ask a question," said one of the elders, as if it needed to be said. "No hiding," he added. It felt as if I had stumbled into a meeting of the Women's Institute as they waited for the local flower arranger to arrive to deliver the weekly speech.

And then I sat down at the empty seat.

"Erm, no, that's not for you," said the elder. "That's the manager's seat. You'll need to get another."

There was thinly veiled contempt for the interloper taking O'Neill's throne unannounced. I was eyed suspiciously by hacks who imagined me as some dilettante freelancer who was there to cash in on their probing questions.

Undeterred, I found another chair. This had been my moment to shine, to show the world that I could mix it with the big boys. Crucially, I still had a plan in place. In my head, the scenario would play out thus: I would introduce myself, O'Neill would hear my Irish accent and then I would inform him that I knew his nephews Niall and Shane, with whom I had attended university.

We would then fall into some kind of figurative embrace which took in the old country, Spain '82 and his Irish League days as a midfielder at Distillery.

As I daydreamed, O'Neill entered the suite, took his place in what had been my seat and scanned the table before alighting on a face he'd never seen before. He eyed me up and down, his bifocals giving his pupils a comic, Marty Feldman look. The press conference began with the usual smattering of pleasantries and superficial questions. And then I was up.

"Hi Martin, James Morgan from The Herald," I said, immediately realising this was a mistake. O'Neill fixed his gaze on me. I could feel my throat tightening and my heart pounding in the pocket of my shirt. All thoughts of nephews dissipated.

"Erm, eh, happy with last night?" I asked apropos of Celtic's 3-0 Uefa Cup win over Czech side Teplice. He stared at me again, and at that my hand started to shake. Not just any old shake, either. It was the kind of shake alcoholics refer to as delirium tremens. My pen shook so violently that it actually fell out of my grasp.

Martin O'Neill looked at my hand and then at me. He looked at my hand again and then at me. For a final time, he repeated the act and then answered my question.

I have no clue as to what he said. Not even now, as I attempt to read back the shorthand from my notebook.

James Morgan is deputy sports editor of The Herald. He writes the newspaper's weekly Tenner Bet column and is author of the critically acclaimed In Search of Alan Gilzean, *a biography of the Dundee and Spurs legend.*

JOURNALIST UNCOVERS NAKED TRUTH

By John McGarry

I n April 2000, I had the (mis)fortune to land a job as a sports reporter with the News of the World in Glasgow.

That's the paper that recently changed its name to the Now Defunct News of the World – and is the kind of history a journalist doesn't really want on his CV. It's a bit like a chef claiming he worked at a hotel that poisoned all of its guests, or a knighted banker admitting he recently presided over a financial institution's collapse.

Even now, a year after the closure of the 'Screws,' I don't actually know how I feel about working there. For all I became ashamed by being associated with it latterly as the phone-hacking scandal erupted, there were, as you might imagine, no shortage of moments of levity which raised it above your average nine-to-five job.

I'd only been in the job a matter of days when I was thrown into one such situation. After the editorial conference one Tuesday, my sports editor told me that the news desk had a story that Lionel Charbonnier, the Rangers goalkeeper, had confessed on a celebrity TV quiz in France to being partial to a bit of nude sunbathing. Would I, he asked with a wry smile on his face, fancy tracking him down and seeing if he'd play ball for what's unimaginatively known in the trade as a 'funny'?

Given that I'd just started in the job, telling him to go to France, or words to that effect, would not have been the wisest course of action, so I accepted the assignment (as if I had a choice). Already this was a long way from covering the rough and tumble of SPL football as per the job description, but never one to shirk a challenge I decided to give it a bash.

The story went that the bold Lionel had been on the Cote D'Azur on holidays and wandered off on his own one afternoon. After a few minutes he realised the beach he'd stumbled on to was, in fact, nude only. And rather than make a run for it, he'd opted to follow that old French saying – if you can't beat them, join them.

There were only a few small factors preventing me getting a successful re-enactment in that Sunday's paper. Firstly, Lionel himself. Apart from the fact I'd never met him, he'd a reputation for being extremely difficult and off the wall. As a member of the French squad that won the 1998 World Cup, he could pretty much do as he pleased.

Secondly, there was Rangers – or more accurately their press officer at that time, John Greig. Terrific player though he was in his day, Greig lacked one or two of the necessary skills to do the vital job of handling the hacks. If fact, he lacked all of them. He hated the media (a throwback to the criticism he received before being sacked as manager in the early '80s; here's a clue John: look at the results). Putting big John in charge of the media relations for a club like Rangers was like asking a claustrophobic to go potholing. Except the claustrophobic would enjoy their job more.

Thirdly, this was Scotland in April. Even if I could persuade Charbonnier to pose for a picture and do the story, he might become the first player in history to miss a game due to hypothermia.

Seemingly with about as much chance of succeeding as a lottery hopeful who doesn't buy a ticket, I trotted merrily along to Ibrox to chance my arm. After lurking in the shadows for a few minutes, my target finally burst through a side door. It was now or never. After quickly introducing myself and explaining the nature of my visit, I stood back expecting to be laughed out of the front door. To my utter astonishment, Charbonnier simply said: "Okay, fine. Come to my home tomorrow and we will do an article and some pictures no problem."

I was simultaneously staggered and delighted. I can't even

remember the conversation I had on the way out with guardian at the gates Greig, but as far as he was concerned if the player was happy to help me then there was no problem. It just wasn't meant to be that simple.

The following day then, I arrived at Charbonnier's city-centre flat at the appointed hour. Now with more time to explain myself, he laughed and suggested we take a trip to the Ayrshire coast. I phoned my photographer who agreed to meet us in Troon in an hour. Charbonnier insisted we take his motor – notably not some ludicrous ostentatious sports car but a little Citroen. Why, I asked him, did he settle for such a humble vehicle when his team-mates seemed to be in competition to collect to most expensive piece of tin? "It is simple," he shrugged. "It makes it easier for me to park outside my house." Clearly this was a man who marched to the beat of his own drum.

We arrived on Troon beach and without a moment's prompting, the man who had held the World Cup aloft just two years previously, stripped to his trunks. He gladly posed behind a beach ball which gave the impression he was, to coin a Scottish phrase, starkers. The job was a good one.

The following Sunday, as I analysed a spread in the paper under the headline 'Here's the Rangers nudes,' my mobile phone rang. Charbonnier's number screamed out at me. Now, as any journalist, will tell you, a phone call from a player or manager outside business hours is seldom of the congratulatory nature. So I braced myself for a barrage of abuse. "John, this is Lionel," he began. "I would like to thank you very much for the story in today's paper. It made me and my wife laugh very much. We would like to ask you and your girlfriend out for dinner tonight."

And so, that night my girlfriend (now wife) and I dined in style at one of Glasgow's top restaurants on the coin of one of the most famous goalkeepers France has produced. And all because he agreed to pose 'nude' on Troon beach. It is, as a wise man once said, a funny old game indeed.

But just to show what unpredictable beasts footballers can be, years later I phoned Charbonnier to do a piece on a goalkeeping issue at Rangers. I naively assumed he would remember me.

I'd no sooner got the words "Scottish journalist" out of my mouth however, and he released a verbal flamethrower at me. "You f*****g c***s. You f*****g made many problems for me when I was in Scotland," came the reply.

I thought it unwise to placate him with my recollections of the Ayrshire Riviera all those years before. He might not have remembered that day, but I certainly will never forget it.

John McGarry has worked as a football writer with the Scottish Daily Mail since 2011. Prior to that he worked for the Scottish News of the World for 11 years. However, he can hardly use a telephone let alone hack one. He's also managed to bluff his way through jobs at the Lennox Herald, Sunday Post, Sydney Daily Telegraph and Scottish Daily Mirror.

THE RESERVE GOALIE SAVED THE DAY

By Gavin Berry

I n the world of tabloid journalism it's all about trying to get the big names and that is never truer than when it comes to football, particularly in the last 20 years when players have taken on celebrity status.

But quite often the most interesting and relevant story can be found where you least expect it, and one such unlikely hidden gem occurred for me on a trip to Italy before Celtic played a Champions League last-16 tie.

It was early 2007 and the Parkhead side had qualified for the knockout stages of the competition for the first time in their history. Their rivals were none other than the mighty AC Milan, who would go on to win the tournament for a seventh time that season.

Myself and three other Sunday newspaper colleagues were on what's known in the industry as a 'spying mission,' travelling to check out the opposition in action in the game immediately before they take on one of our clubs in Europe. Needless to say it's one of the better parts of the job when you get the chance to visit other countries, often see some spectacular stadiums and of course speak to top players you've admired on television.

Preparation for such trips starts by analysing the squad and trying to establish a list of top targets who are likely to give you the best 'line.' You normally aim high for the sexiest name and try and find players who will have memories of playing against Scottish opposition, or with or against any of the players they're due to come up against. Of course, there is rarely a shortage of star names when it comes to the famous 'Rossoneri.' At that time they boasted the likes of Paolo Maldini, Andrea Pirlo, Rino Gattuso and Kaka, who would go on to score the goal that eliminated Celtic.

We travelled to the Italian club's famous Milanello training ground on the outskirts of Milan and seeing photos of some of the legends like Marco van Basten and Ruud Gullit made you appreciate what a privilege it was to be there. And it was another Dutchman who was to be our first target. Clarence Seedorf arrived for training and stopped at reception to sign some shirts and balls on his way. At that point we approached to ask if he could spare a few minutes for the Scottish press who had travelled over to chat about the upcoming Celtic game. Unfortunately he gave a polite "no" before a string of others declined – some hiding behind the "no English" excuse as foreign players often do as a get-out – before the panic really started to set in.

It's the phone call you just dread making as a journalist, particularly from a foreign destination where the company has paid good money to send you, to tell your sports editor that your notebook is empty. Yet it can happen so easily through no fault of your own.

After one knockback after another the situation was getting pretty desperate. That wish-list of top targets now became "anyone on the books of AC Milan who speaks English and is willing to talk to us." That man became Zeljko Kalac. After hearing a booming Australian accent from reception, we quickly referred to the squad list we'd printed off and established that the towering figure was in fact goalkeeper Kalac.

He couldn't have been more accommodating once we told him we'd travelled over from Scotland but as he hadn't been someone high on our list (he wasn't a regular starter) we had little time to do our homework on him. We just had to wing it but from the very first question it became apparent there was no need to worry.

"What do you know about Celtic?" we asked.

"I nearly signed for them," he replied, "but joined Leicester City instead … what a f*****g mistake that was!"

From that moment relief came over us all. Relief that someone had agreed to the interview. And relief that this was someone who was going to give us a good story. Relief we wouldn't have to make THAT phone call to the sports editor.

He went on to explain that as well as having had the chance to move to Parkhead he'd also played alongside Neil Lennon at Leicester and faced Shunsuke Nakamura during his time in Italy. It got even better because while Kalac was usually just a back-up goalkeeper for AC Milan, it transpired during the interview that he was certain to play in Glasgow in the first leg, as regular first choice Dida was injured, so his words were suddenly much more relevant.

As a sports journalist, you always look at players differently depending on your own personal experiences with them and Kalac will certainly always be remembered fondly for saving the day on that occasion.

It's funny how wide of the mark your preconceptions can be of players. On another spying mission to Italy, this time to Florence in 2008 before Rangers played Fiorentina in the Uefa Cup semi-final, we 'aimed high' again by asking for Christian Vieri.

Unlike Seedorf, the Italian striker agreed. Vieri had once been the most expensive footballer in the world when Lazio paid £32million for his services and had a playboy reputation following many high-profile relationships. Yet he couldn't have been more pleasant as he chatted away. However, he wasn't able to offer much in terms of knowledge or experiences of the Scottish game. Proof that the biggest name doesn't always guarantee the most relevant story.

Gavin Berry started out at the Rangers News before joining the Sunday Mail in 2002. Three years later he picked up the prestigious Jim Rodger Memorial Award for the best young sports journalist in Scotland. He currently works for both the Sunday Mail and Daily Record.

THE MAGNIFICENT SEVEN WAS ...
MAGNIFICENT!

By Stephen McGowan

P laying for Celtic or Rangers does strange things to a man. It elevates average Joes, content to chat in the street and drive a Ford Mondeo, to the status of a demi-god.

Within months of becoming part of the 'Old Firm' players become exponents of the thousand-yard stare. Of pinning a mobile phone to their ear while ignoring the pitiful pleadings of journalists in post-match mixed zones. Eye contact costs extra and an air of contempt becomes as much a part of their armoury as the latest high-tech boots from Adidas.

There was no greater practitioner of the Old Firm modus operandi than Henrik Larsson. His haughty distance in the company of pressmen was legendary, almost regal. The fans called him the King of Kings and in his bearing he lived up to the billing.

At least he walked the walk. Larsson is, by common consent, the best overseas import the SPL has witnessed. His haul of 242 goals in 315 appearances prompted a blast of the Magnificent Seven theme tune over the Parkhead tannoy every second week. All as the hero of the moment wheeled away like a dreadlocked Yul Brynner, tongue extended in trademark celebration. The tongue was a strange affectation for a man who, off the pitch, elevated an air of aloof disconnect to an art form.

Few, among those present, will forget the day in Orlando, Florida when – on a mid-winter break in January – Larsson sat in his throne high above his cowering media subjects. Asked the most innocuous of questions by an evening newspaper reporter – on nothing more offensive than a calf injury, the Scottish Cup or the state of Scottish pitches probably – he raised his Romanesque nose, looked down on his hapless inquisitor and barked: "WHAT?!" In the best journalistic traditions the hack in question mumbled his excuses and left. It was the only course open.

There was trepidation, then, as I arrived on the 10.08 from Malmo in the small town of Landskrona on Sweden's west coast on a bleak April morning in 2010.

A row of five cranes tower over an old shipyard and a grey fortress town away to the left. Like Glasgow this was a ship-building stronghold until the 1980s witnessed a collapse in the heavy industries of yore. The size of the town and the football club are incomparable with what Larsson was used to as a player, yet Swedish football's favourite son is now ensconsed as manager of the local football team BOIS.

His 21-year playing career had only just come to an end at local Allsvenskan rivals Helsingborg when the offer came to go into coaching. Larsson had always told his wife Magdalena that management wasn't for him. In recent years, however, his attitude had softened.

When he made the move it brought mixed reactions. Supporters of second division Landskrona could barely believe their luck, Helsingborg fans spoke merely of betrayal.

Beyond the sparse platform of the train station and the general store selling magazines and sweets, BOIS public relations man Kurt Lundquist waits in a Dodge crossover, painted zebra-like in the club's stripes.

We head for a small garden shed at the stadium gate. It's here that Lundquist, a former senior referee, keeps pictures of the club's greatest teams in neat frames on the wall. He shows off a sheet of A4 white paper with the club emblem printed large. Below in block capitals is the name, HENRIK LARSSON.

His wheezy chuckle is one of disbelief. A Swedish superstar, the most renowned international of the modern age, Landskrona had turned to this iconic figure as their new coach in December 2009. For three weeks they struggled to keep the news secret.

Finally, the day before his proposed formal unveiling on December 14th, approximately 30 pressmen arrived at the training ground to find Larsson already in situ.

"To us Henrik Larsson is a God," states Lundquist in hushed, reverential tones. "His arrival here means everything to the people in this town. Everything."

At his unveiling in December 2009 Larsson was asked why he had begun his coaching career at BOIS rather than his hometown club. "Because Landskrona asked," he responded matter-of-factly.

In Helsingborg they regarded the striker as one of their own, a hometown boy born and raised in the seaside town. Yet in the course of 45 minutes in the great man's company something becomes apparent. There may be affection for Landskrona, admiration for Barcelona – where he single-handedly tranformed a Champions League final – and respect for Manchester United; the one true footballing love of Henrik Larsson's professional career is to be found, however, in the East End of Glasgow.

His record and statistics are of the breathtaking variety. Four SPL championships, two League Cups, two Scottish Cups and two goals in Celtic's first European final in 33 years tell only half the tale.

A European Golden Boot, an MBE for services to Scottish football, an honorary degree from the University of Strathclyde and the accolade as the greatest Swedish player of the last 50 years go further.

Striding along the Landskrona stand, the first specks of silvery grey in his tightly cropped hair are the only clues to the drifting sands of time. Dressed in a designer white shirt with blue jeans, it could be a celebrity DJ in a Cypriot clubbing mecca. He is chatty and relaxed in a way he never allowed himself to be as a Celtic player.

The autograph requests are still as prolific as ever, but these days he signs them on a manager's desk in a black and white portacabin. Lifting a black marker pen Larsson scrawls his name on a glossy black-and-white picture of his smiling self in the scarf of BOIS Landskrona. Pausing only to clarify spellings, the autograph is signed in swooping letters before the briefest moment of hesitation. "I'll put the number seven up here," he adds, scribbling down his old number within the 'L' in his surname. If there is vanity in the gesture then forgiveness is swift.

We move to another room of the cabin where he sits, arms crossed, as if fielding every query. Yet, in the course, of a wide-ranging chat on Neil Lennon, his friend Johan Mjallby – "I have to swear here, I told him, 'F****** hell, you have to take the job!' " – and all things Celtic he is enjoyable company.

Larsson is proud of his place amongst Celtic's most adored figures. Beside Jimmy Johnstone he remains one of the two most influential players of the modern era to don the number seven jersey.

"I felt honoured to wear that number seven jersey," he states with a smile. "I had the pleasure of meeting Jimmy several times and he was like John Clark – a real legend at the club.

"He came in to the park to see John and I would sit in the laundry room doing my mail. We had good fun when 'Jinky' came in. It was a real pity when he left us."

Being understated is merely Larsson's way in a guarded situation. At Celtic he was diffident in media situations, professional yet distant. Here in his homeland he is a more laid-back figure, laughing and joking despite the new challenges brought forth by management. A mischievous, sharp and highly intelligent individual Larsson speaks best when discussing Celtic.

We break for pictures and I remind him of the days when he would order junior reporters on the Celtic club magazine – yours truly included – to fax their requests for interviews via the public relations department. "The same as everyone else."

The memory prompts roars of laughter and a Swedish translation for Kurt Lundquist.

"I had to keep these guys in their place," he explains, jerking a thumb in my direction.

Old Kurt laughs like the court jester – as if keeping a straight face might be akin to treason. The local freelance photographer snapping pictures is berated. "This is for a Scottish paper, don't sell it in

Sweden." There is mischief in the eyes as he speaks. He doesn't mean it, but kind of does.

Behind closed doors Larsson is amusing and sharp. Like Kenny Dalglish, another legendary Celtic goalscorer, his public persona is at odds with his true self. He preferred it that way and, fascinated by what little they knew of this god-like figure, supporters longed to scratch the surface of their hero. Like the media men, few got any closer than a garden gate in Bothwell.

Before we part he expresses concern for the financial state of the Scottish game.

"I hear people are not turning up at Parkhead the way they used to. We were used to playing in front of a full house week in and week out whether we played Kilmarnock or Rangers. That's not been the case lately."

Offer them a rewind button and the chance to see the old extended tongue routine and they'd be back in their thousands. But Henrik Larsson is a different person now. He left Glasgow and something happened. He became his old self again.

Stephen McGowan is chief football writer of the Scottish Daily Mail. Stephen began life with DC Thomson before spending two years working for newspapers in the Middle and Far East. He is the author of Flawed Genius: Scottish Football's Self Destructive Mavericks.

MAMMA KNOWS BEST

By Peter Jardine

Marvin Andrews only spent one full season with Rangers. He was signed, initially at least, as a 'squad player' by manager Alex McLeish and his arrival from Livingston in the summer of 2004 did not meet with the full approval of the Ibrox support.

Strong and powerful, the Trinidad and Tobago international could head the ball almost as far as he could kick it. He could by no means be described as someone who would 'build from the back,' in contrast to his immediate predecessor, who happened to be the splendid Frank de Boer (albeit in a trophyless Rangers team).

Yet anyone who bore witness to the reception afforded Andrews at a 2012 friendly 'legends match' with AC Milan old boys wasn't left in any doubt about Marvin's cult status down Govan way. Andrews partnered the likes of Richard Gough and Lorenzo Amoruso that evening and faced in opposition Italian superstars such as Franco Baresi and Paolo Maldini. For the man from the Caribbean to keep such illustrious company he must have been something special in season 2004-05, right?

He was involved as Rangers won two trophies that season as they claimed the League Cup and then snatched the SPL title from Martin O'Neill's Celtic in the dying embers of the campaign.

Marvin didn't play the final matches of the title run-in and was reduced to a cheerleader's role with his famous "Believe" mantra taken up by his team-mates and supporters. Most of them after Scott McDonald scored twice for Motherwell against Celtic, it must be said. His injury absence was a big story at the time and it was this that ultimately led me – with my brother in tow as a photographer – to knock on the door of a mother of nine on the other side of the Atlantic and ask her opinion on the Rangers medical staff, the Bible and the intricacies of cruciate knee ligament surgery.

Let's rewind first to one weekend in March when Rangers faced Dundee at Dens Park in an awkward fixture as a tense title race with Celtic built towards a crescendo. It required a goal from Andrews to break the deadlock late in the second half but only a few minutes later he was forced to limp off injured.

At the time, big Marvin was confident he would face Motherwell in the League Cup final a week later at Hampden but, during the week, bulletins from inside Murray Park indicated the season was over for Andrews and he would require knee surgery.

For boss McLeish it was a huge blow as an Old Firm derby loomed amid the run-in. And it transpired that there was a dilemma for the manager of the medical and the moral variety. Andrews, a committed Christian, didn't feel an operation was the right option and resolved to somehow carry on playing without one. His feelings flew in the face of the Ibrox doctor's verdict and a second opinion by an English specialist.

Your correspondent, meanwhile, was making final preparations for a fortnight's holiday in Trinidad and Tobago. My elder brother, Walter, and his family were Port of Spain residents in his role as an overseas BP executive. Slowly, I hatched a plan to interview Marvin's mum while on holiday and gauge her view on her son's dilemma. Somewhat reluctantly, Marvin himself gave me a mobile number for his brother Micah and the arrangement was made to meet him on Sunday afternoon in San Juan before heading to the family home.

We should have known that 2.30pm in Caribbean time means closer to 3.15pm. And so it came to pass that two milk-bottle white Scotsmen stood at the crossroads in San Juan under a baking sun … wondering if every 20-something Trinidadian who passed by happened to be the brother of Marvin Andrews.

The island's English-speaking newspaper had just reported the

100th kidnapping in Trinidad that year and we were barely into April. Hanging around waiting for Micah clutching a mini tape recorder, mobile phone and camera possibly wasn't the best idea. Eventually he sauntered along wearing a yellow Brazil strip and offered to take us to see his mother.

Cynthia Andrews wasn't out of her 40s at the time yet had given birth to nine children in a 14-year period and was also a grandmother. When she opened the door of a modest semi-detached home halfway up a hill, Livingston defender Oscar Rubio peered back at me over her shoulder. Rubio's photo, I should say.

As Walter and I stepped inside, pleased to escape the relentless sunshine and a couple of stray dogs hanging around the dusty yard in front of the house, we knew were in the right place.

Marvin's pictures dominated the walls of the small living space, in action for Livingston and in a Rangers calendar for 2005 which also featured Gregory Vignal and Paolo Vanoli. There was a picture of Buckingham Palace on her wall but none of the mod-cons many of us in Scotland would expect.

She immediately agreed to an interview with the Scottish Daily Mail and, although a mother's pride burned brightly, she gently advised her son to have the operation. 'Don't Leave This To The Lord, Son,' read the spread headline across our sports pages a couple of days later, in fact. She feared that should Marvin resist surgery – such was the depth of his Christian faith – that it could prove costly in the long-run. As it transpired, Andrews did play on without an operation – call it miraculously if you will – although McLeish had to leave him out of the final matches in the knowledge his knee was dangerously damaged.

Back in San Juan that day my brother enthusiastically took photos of Marvin's mother, his brother and the little house from which he made it to Ibrox. This friendly, Caribbean 'mamma' even posed holding the Rangers calendar.

It is worth noting that Andrews made it to the World Cup finals the following summer even though he was still troubled by the persistent cruciate ligament problem.

Writing the piece on the balcony of my brother's BP house in a gated community just outside the Trinidad capital, only a few hours after meeting Mamma Andrews, remains a special memory. As does the entire experience, from setting up the arrangement to waiting at the crossroads for Micah and then entering the Andrews home, it was all truly bizarre. It was with a little surprise, no doubt, that my bosses at the Mail received an email bulletin from Port of Spain with the customary 1000-word interview required for a major feature. But a reporter is never really off duty. And, happily, Walter's pictures made the paper, too.

Peter Jardine began his journalism career as a news reporter on a local paper before quickly securing a move into sport. In a four-year spell on Merseyside he covered Liverpool and Everton before moving back to Glasgow as the Press Association's Scottish sports correspondent. The Scottish Daily Mail beckoned in 1997 and in a 14-year career Peter estimates he has contributed 12.4million words, but who's counting ... Peter is now communications manager for scottishathletics, the governing body for the sport in Scotland, and he is looking forward to Glasgow 2014.

THE DALGLISH DISASTER

By Hugh Keevins

There is a school of thought within the journalistic profession that bans are good. This is true.

In 1999 I had the pleasure of being thrown out of the Celtic Supporters Association's premises in the shadow of the ground that then housed a team managed, on a temporary basis, by Kenny Dalglish.

My ejection was carried out by a man who went by the name of Finbar O'Brannigan, an alias which covered up his true identity and, as it later transpired, a private life of dubious merit.

The reason for my sudden dismissal before Dalglish's weekly pre-match press conference on a Friday afternoon was that I had been guilty of writing a number of pieces of a negative nature concerning Kenny's stewardship of the club. This was, and still is, a charge to which I readily admit absolute guilt, but with mitigating circumstances attached which ruled out malice aforethought.

Dalglish was, to any right-thinking person, a Celtic icon as a player. But only those of troubled mind and a congenitally stubborn nature would argue that his time as Celtic's director of football, leading to a battlefield commission as manager, was anything other than an unqualified disaster.

The price that had to be paid for pointing this out on what was an apparently irritating basis for the blessed Finbar was ejection from the supporters' premises and entry into the land of the banned.

Martyrdom is always a comfort to sports editors with an

appreciation of a good story, so the first instruction received from central command was to stay where I was until a photographer got there to capture the moment for posterity. This led, unkindly I thought, to one of my comrades-at-arms, Scotland On Sunday's Graham Spiers, describing me in print as looking "clapped-out" when the snap of me appearing as pained and aggrieved as possible was printed in the Sunday Mail that weekend.

The role of the columnist, as I was then, is to hopefully stimulate debate or, at the very least, provoke outrage among the readership. My weekly thread where Celtic and Dalglish were concerned was that one mistake was piling on top of another to the serious detriment of the club's dealings on the park, and its reputation off it.

Celtic's then chief executive Allan McDonald had appointed Dalglish while confessing Kenny had been his hero. Dalglish's appointment of John Barnes as first-team coach while having had no previous experience of working with any team at Celtic's level, was as ridiculous as it was shortlived. The marriage of inconvenience was eventually dissolved when Barnes' team was knocked out of the Scottish Cup by Inverness Caley Thistle amid shambolic scenes at Celtic Park.

Dalglish, by then known as the club's director of golf, had to be recalled, ever so reluctantly, from La Manga to take charge of operations as Barnes was sacked and the club went on to an emergency footing.

Anyone not writing about what a state of disrepair Celtic had fallen into would have been guilty of dereliction of duty, and the story that was a dripping roast continued to keep on giving.

Rafael Scheidt, the only Brazilian in captivity unable to play football, had been signed, sight unseen, in one of the costliest, and most catastrophic, errors of judgement ever witnessed.

And in the last act of a desperate man, Dalglish had decided to hold the first press conference ever staged by Celtic in a pub. Baird's Bar is a supporters' haven in the East End of Glasgow which would later have its opening hours curtailed by Strathclyde Police on the basis that the place was a threat to good public order. The press reaction to what was a dismal abuse of Celtic's good name saw the licensed premises experiment dropped after one week.

The now desperate attempt to keep the support on board in the face of a season that had long since capsized took everyone to the Celtic Supporters Association's premises on London Road.

The gentlemen of the press were asked to wait in an anteroom before the manager discussed his thoughts on the weekend in prospect. That is to say we went into the room off the bar where the patrons could play snooker and discuss why Scheidt had managed two starts in the first team in exchange for a reputed transfer fee of £5million, with as much again going on his payment package. But I didn't get to have social discourse with the manager because I was frogmarched out in front of his dismissive presence and left on the pavement to await collection.

It was the Daily Mail's Ian McGarry who pointed out to fulminating Finbar that he had done me a favour by making a small man with spectacles from Clydebank a cause celebre. The would-be Mister O'Brannigan's response was that he "Couldnae give a f***," because I was leaving, no matter what.

What followed was the wringing of hands and the gnashing of teeth, mine not his, and then the ultimate indignity. Most young boys born in the west of Scotland dream of hearing the Celtic or Rangers fans chant their name during a match. I got my wish at Dens Park when a briefly revived Celtic were 3-1 up on Dundee. "Hughie Keevins, you're a w****r," sang the Celtic fans with unconfined glee while Dalglish, soon to be relieved of his duties, exhorted them to increase the volume.

On the night that Caley Thistle humiliated Celtic in the cup some fans had gathered outside the ground to kick the cars of the players who'd embarrassed them as they drove away at speed.

Presumably, if they'd been given my job for a day those incensed supporters would have written a column so critical it would have needed to be legalled by the Sunday Mail's lawyers for fear of court action.

Personally, I always thought I was due a vote of thanks from the more discerning fans for force-feeding them the information that Celtic needed better management than they had, regardless of how brilliant Dalglish had been as a player two decades earlier.

But being banned is like being a one-hit wonder. No matter how much time elapses, and regardless of what you've done since then, that highly publicised moment of exclusion remains your signature tune. You are defined as the reprehensible person who dared to say that there might be a flaw in the idea of having someone in charge who was lurching from one disaster to the next with the unsteady gait of a drunk man chasing a balloon. And the opprobrium has stayed with me for 13 years.

But, there I was, a man knocking on 50 who'd toiled away to no-one's great notice for 30 years in newspapers suddenly thrust into the limelight. The man who had the ineffable cheek to say King Kenny's crown had slipped from his head and fallen round his ankles, caus-ing injury to Celtic.

One year after Dalglish had gone Martin O'Neill became only the second manager to lead Celtic to a treble. Now he's gone, and so are Gordon Strachan and Tony Mowbray.

But I'm still here.

Hugh Keevins began in journalism with the Sunday Post in 1970, moving to the Scotsman 10 years later. He has been with the Daily Record and Sunday Mail since 1997, as well as broadcasting on Radio Clyde from 1985.

THE CULT OF NAKA

By Anthony Haggerty

Gordon Strachan once famously labelled him a "genius." Japanese midfielder Shunsuke Nakamura came to Scotland as a virtual unknown in the summer of 2005, but by the time he left the Hoops in June 2009, he had long been lauded as a footballing deity.

In his first season with Celtic, Nakamura was signed too late to make his European bow against Artmedia Bratislava as Celtic tumbled out of the Champions League thanks to a 5-0 defeat in Slovakia on Strachan's debut, but he ended the campaign on a high, winning his first major club titles, the Scottish Premier League and Scottish League Cup.

And finally, on September 13th 2006, Naka – as he became affectionately known – made his continental debut for Celtic in a Champions League game against Manchester United at Old Trafford, and it was well worth the wait.

Naka scored a magnificent goal from a long-range free-kick to level the scores at 2-2, although Celtic eventually would go on to lose the match 3-2, and scoring spectacular free-kicks would become a trademark and speciality of the Japanese internationalist's stay in Glasgow.

To score once from a free-kick against Manchester United was special. To do it twice against Sir Alex Ferguson's multimillionaires on the Champions League stage, however, was verging on showboating. But that's what he did on November 21st 2006, when the most important goal of his career, a breathtaking 30-yard dead-ball effort, secured not only a 1-0 win over the English Premier League aristocrats but created a slice of history as the victory saw Celtic progress to the Champions League knockout stages for the first time ever.

And, barely a month later, on Boxing Day 2006, Nakamura added another to his collection when he chipped the ball over Dundee United goalkeeper Derek Stillie at Celtic Park as Strachan's team fought back from two goals down to draw 2-2.

Nakamura was the architect of his team's comeback in the final 20 minutes, and his point-saving contribution prompted Strachan to acclaim the little midfielder as aforesaid genius.

It was little surprise that when PFA Scotland came to hand out their prizes at the end of the season, Naka was in contention for Player of the Year and also the Goal of the Season award for that chip against United. With that in mind the Daily Record despatched me to the Hilton Hotel in Glasgow for the ceremony as Naka scooped both awards. My brief was to interview Naka for the now-defunct publication Record PM.

Naka spoke no English whatsoever, but his presence at Parkhead had rendered Celtic box office across Asia. Naka, and by association Strachan's team, were 'Big in Japan.' So big was the cult of Naka that every day he had a TV crew following him and filming his every move at training, as well as every match he played for Celtic. He also had his own personal English translator who just happened to be named Macca. That's right, Naka and his right-hand-man Macca. You could scarcely make it up.

That night at the PFA Scotland awards ceremony you could not move as it seemed that half of the Japanese and wider Asian media had descended upon Glasgow for a Naka frenzy. There was an incredible battery of photographers and an accompanying press entourage that would have befitted a Royal or Papal visit. The clacking of Japanese tongues and the popping of camera flash bulbs had to be seen to be believed. And after what seemed like an eternity, Nakamura was eventually made available for interview with the Scottish press corps. The daily papers duly did their bit and asked about his

Player of the Year award and Goal of the Season trophies. Naka, in typical humble style, his head bowed at all times and speaking via translator Macca, answered all the questions put to him without speaking a single word of the Queen's English.

As Record PM reporter, my beat was to get a different 'line' from the daily newspapers and having listened in on their Q&A session, I realised that there was one thing they had not asked Naka. So I gleefully told Macca to ask Naka, "What was your favourite-ever goal?"

The answer to that question has lived with me to this day. So allow me to share with you the transcript of my interview with the newly crowned PFA Scotland Player for the Year for season 2005/06 and the recipient of the Goal of the Season award.

Anthony Haggerty: "Macca, can you ask Naka what his favourite-ever goal is?"

Macca: (Translates my question to Naka in Japanese.)

Nakamura: (Replies in Japanese.)

Macca: "Nakamura says that his free-kick goal against Manchester United at Parkhead is his best-ever goal. It holds a special place in his heart because it took Celtic into the last 16 of the Champions League for the first time ever.

"He also says that to have achieved something like that for a club like Celtic was very special and that it is a feeling that he will never forget. And also that he feels privileged and proud to have scored such a massive and historic goal for this great club."

Me: "To be fair, it was a f*****g beauty!"

And at that point, Nakamura, who has not lifted his head or spoken a word of English yet, suddenly looks at me, smiles and says, "Aaah, yes, 'Ya fooking booty!'"

Me: "Macca, did Naka just say what I thought he said?"

Macca: "Yes, I think he did."

Me: "I thought Naka does not speak any English?"

Macca: "He doesn't."

Macca then turns to Naka, shrugs his shoulders, and asks him a question in Japanese. Then the two of them collapse laughing and the translator gave me the following explanation.

Macca: "Nakamura does not speak any English but after he scored that goal against Manchester United, everybody who came up to congratulate him said the words, 'Ya f*****g beauty' to him. He thought at first it was some kind of Scottish phrase and that it was culturally significant. And Naka wanted to learn the words and how to say it properly. As you can imagine, the Celtic players took great delight in telling him how to pronounce it and, eventually, what it meant. But those seem to be the only English words Naka speaks and it has become a bit of a party piece at Celtic."

Cue mass hysterical laughter as Naka repeats the phrase again and again in front of his delighted audience.

Shunsuke Nakamura carved an indelible mark on the Scottish game, grabbing his share of exceptional goals during his four-year stay at Parkhead. But none was better than that deadly swish of his gifted left boot that felled the mighty Manchester United on that memorable Champions League evening under the floodlights in Glasgow's East End in 2006.

It was, to all intents and purposes, a "fooking booty" in anybody's language!

Anthony Haggerty has been a sportswriter for the Daily Record since 1999. He has also worked on TV and Radio, and his list of credits include being a regular sports pundit on Scotsport.

I THOUGHT I WAS SMIRNOFF ICED

By Ronnie Esplin

t is half-past midnight and I'm in the back seat of a stranger's car somewhere in Moscow, clutching my laptop and hoping I have re-membered enough karate to help prevent what I am beginning to believe could be my imminent demise.

I am being driven through dark, dingy, desolate streets, flanked by stereotypically unattractive eastern-European housing which dominate large parts of the Russian capital. My mind flashes back, for a moment, to my daytime visit in the summer sunshine to the cosmopolitan, westernised city centre with its historic Red Square and its new hotels, restaurants and shops.

This is the real Moscow though, I guess, and I'm not liking it.

The taxi journey from my hotel to the Arena Khimki for the second leg of Celtic's Champions League qualifier against Dynamo Moscow hours earlier was mostly through well-lit main roads and motorway. As we disappear further in to the high-rise jungle, I'm wondering why the taxi driver has avoided using the same route on my return. In fact, I'm now wondering if the big, bulky and unshaven man at the wheel, aged around 30, with dead eyes, like a shark, is ac-tually a taxi driver. He is on his phone the whole time and I can't un-derstand a word he is saying. I try not to let my imagination run riot but I'm failing. Is he informing friends of fresh tourist meat? Will this be a simple robbery of my laptop, phone and wallet – or worse?

I can't phone anyone. Who could I phone – I don't know any-one in the city. I don't know where I am. And what would I say?

Seconds seem like minutes. I know we will stop at one point so I start thinking about how to escape and I decide on a simple plan of action. I will go for his throat. No matter what he does just keep going for his throat. One well-connected punch is all it takes. What if he pulls a knife? Easy – run like f**k. A gun? Easier – run like f**k whilst zig-zagging. But deep down I know that only in the movies do knifemen and gunmen get disarmed without causing some serious damage first.

How did I get myself into this situation? It was a typically late finish following what was a routine European match. On these occasions, you have to get both managers at the post-match press conference – not just the boss of the Scottish team – and then get to the mixed zone to get quotes from the players. Sometimes you manage it, sometimes you don't. This time I did and sat inside the main entrance filing Tony Mowbray's dissemination of Celtic's surprise 2-0 win while the stadium emptied.

In Mogga's second competitive game as Gordon Strachan's successor, substitute Georgios Samaras had scored in injury-time to secure a dramatic 2-1 aggregate win. It was Celtic's first away triumph in Europe since 2003 and the Parkhead club had overturned a first-leg defeat for the first time.

"Over the two 90 minutes I think the better team came through the tie," said a strangely unexcited Mowbray and I typed away enthusiastically.

The win, ultimately, became the highlight of his Celtic career which ended the following March after a 4-0 defeat in another dark and dangerous city: Paisley.

I realise I am now sitting on my own. The media bus has long since left for the airport, where they will fly home with the team. Colleagues will be filing on the bus, hoping the airport is sufficiently far enough away to get their work done before they are whisked on to the official flight. On this occasion, I have travelled independently and will be going home in the morning.

I come out the stadium hoping there will be taxis waiting but there are none, which is unusual. A few stragglers are still milling around.

I try to explain to one of them that I am looking for a taxi to take me back to the hotel by using two words: "taxi" and "hotel." He speaks to a guy who nods his head. There is no taxi sign on his car that I can see. I hesitate, but then get in. I ask the driver if he speaks English but he ignores me and the journey begins. As we weave our way through the urban jungle, with me starting to fear the worst, I can't remember if he had acknowledged me when I told him the name of my hotel. Sh*t.

I recognise that I am now in fight-or-flight mode. It is a feeling I try to control. I recall my training: confident, controlled aggression. Don't panic. Go for the throat and be prepared to take a few in return.

"Right, you Russian bastard, stop this f*****g motor right now," I am about to shout when all of a sudden, we take a left then a right on to the main road where my hotel is. He pulls up outside and when he points down at his meter, which I couldn't see from the back seat, I pay him and get out. I berate myself as I go up to my room but my relief is real. My karate days, after all, were a long, long time ago.

The receptionist has pre-ordered a taxi to take me to the airport just several hours later. The traffic is crazy in Moscow even at 6.30am and my driver is evidently acting out his grand prix dream.

He catches my eyes in his rear view mirror after he makes yet another emergency stop, this time within millimetres of a lorry. He turns round and laughs loudly, manically. He has a perfect set of teeth. All of them gold.

I remember well, Moscow, August 6th 2009.

Ronnie Esplin is a sports reporter for the Press Association in Glasgow. He is also an author who has written books related to both sides of the Old Firm. Ronnie lives in Glasgow and has three children; Kirsty, Alex and Mhairi.

I PREFERRED PSV TO EBTS AND CVAS

By Fraser Mackie

O n February 14 2012, Rangers were placed into administration and the job description of a Scottish football writer changed forever.

The announcement triggered a series of events that stripped bare the way a sporting institution had been run by Sir David Murray then, for nine devastating months, Craig Whyte.

The crash course in financial skulduggery dragged us out of the comfort zone cycle of transfer stories, player interviews, match reports and injury updates – into writing about a world we toiled to understand. From reporting on action in the SPL and SFL, all of a sudden the priority became the complexities of EBTs, HMRC and a CVA, as the paths of a multitude of entangled stories changed direction on an hourly basis for many months.

It was thanks to PSV, in 1998 as the Ibrox regime approached the peak of its largesse, that I stumbled across some supposed 'top-secret' work of Murray and Rangers.

The Eindhoven club's president, Harry van Raay, handed me a page hot off the fax machine at the Philips Stadium with 'Rangers Football Club' at the top and Murray's signature at the bottom. Van Raay thought so much of its contents that he motioned as if to drop it in his office bin.

The adventure began three days earlier when the Daily Mail decided, with rumours escalating that Dick Advocaat had signed up to replace the outgoing Walter Smith as Rangers manager, that having a man on the ground was necessary. I packed for three nights – and was ordered to stay for 10.

I arrived on the Sunday night for local journalists to inform me that Advocaat had batted away questions after their game. It was vital I got to Advocaat the following morning and that's when the club's dashing press officer, Pedro Salazar Hewitt, took over. "Mr Advocaat will talk with you as he walks from the training pitch to his office," said Pedro. "Then I will bring Arthur Numan to speak with you."

What a way to start – exclusive words from the next Rangers manager and his captain. Then, as the 'Little General' paced towards the facility, I heard the screech of a taxi's wheels followed by the even higher-pitched sound of Rodger Baillie's voice. The vision of the veteran Sun man scuttling towards me confirmed this was exclusive no more. Advocaat's brisk stroll to the sanctuary of his office was interrupted by our questions. He was guarded but said enough for a back-page story. Numan was a delight, spending 20 minutes discussing his manager's methods and the prospect of him leaving. Rodger's brief was 'in and out' so he returned to Glasgow that night.

Staying close to the action paid dividends. The next day Pedro fixed me an interview with the hulking figure of Jaap Stam. This 6ft 5in defender would apparently weigh in soon at £15million and he offered me a run-down on Advocaat's disciplinary style. His insight was gold for the paper. Ever since that week, I've believed it should be compulsory for anyone wishing to work in football PR to spend a week shadowing Pedro. He grew up in Chile but grandfather Hewitt was from Liverpool so he was fascinated by Britain and learned English from an early age. He moved to Holland in 1977, joined PSV 20 years later, has worked for the Dutch and Russia at major tournaments, and is in a different league to his peers.

Many British clubs make it impossible to speak to the manager or a top player on a one-to-one basis – even when there is positive news to break. Some derive pleasure from being obstructive. Here, PSV were on the brink of losing staff to Rangers yet were a pleasure to deal with. Pedro also knew how best to use me to carry his club's message. When I asked to speak with Van Raay about Advocaat, to gain a different view of the coach, he clearly sensed the opportunity. I was surprised Pedro phoned to confirm, once I'd finished with Stam, the president wanted to see me that afternoon in his office.

Fortunately, my gentle initial approach, inviting Van Raay to tell me about his relationship with Advocaat, was abruptly brushed aside. Shaking his head, Van Raay brandished a fax that arrived earlier that day. Murray had informed him in writing that Rangers did not contact Advocaat directly, that initial discussions had taken place although nothing had been contractually agreed and that there was intent on both sides. According to Van Raay the message just happened to be the first contact – after weeks of newspaper speculation in Holland and Scotland – that Rangers had made with Advocaat's employers.

Van Raay said: "This is damaging to football as a sport. If you behave as a gentleman then, between two clubs and for good relations, it's much better to inform the club first of interest in their trainer."

Cue fury back in Edinburgh the following morning when Murray read our 'The Fax Of The Matter' headline and story which, sadly, lacked a copy of the fax itself as Van Raay stopped short of letting this mischief-maker take a print away! The Murray-friendly Daily Record were informed by the Rangers chairman that he'd sent another fax to Van Raay to request any future dialogue took place "between PSV and me – and not the media."

Meanwhile, Murray told the Scotsman: "I find his action of showing a confidential fax to a journalist as unprofessional." Great fun!

Ridiculous fortune continued the next day as Utrecht, complete with on-loan Borussia Dortmund striker Scott Booth, came to my Dutch doorstep for a midweek game. A terrific tale fell into my lap when Booth spun Stam inside out and scored a goal to stun the Philips Stadium. I grabbed a few quotes from Scott to support his bid for World Cup inclusion by Scotland and then took the train to Utrecht in the morning for a full interview. Booth starred on the local radio station's sports broadcast from the stadium. So I watched as he went out live in a show with strike partner Michael Mols and manager Mark Wotte – two men who'd go on to become big names in Scottish football. In Wotte's case, our meeting spawned a Scotland spying trip for the coach to see out-of-contract Dundee United defender Steven Pressley. However, the only logical next stage of the Rangers story was Sunday's PSV and Ajax match. So the days dragged.

Advocaat had shut down chat on Rangers, Pedro ran out of future English Premiership stars, and Van Raay and Murray stopped trading verbal blows. The greatest joy of the football reporter's lot is the camaraderie and adventures shared with colleagues on our travels across the globe. This lonely trip certainly lacked that as midweek evenings in Eindhoven were spent playing darts alone in the Irish bar. I turned into Fraser van der Partridge. Like Steve Coogan's chat show character Alan, the hapless inhabitant of Linton Travel Tavern, I cut a sorry figure around Holiday Inn Eindhoven. I learned the menu in the bar backwards, knew the hotel staff names and rotas. I think I unwittingly invented Steve McClaren's ridiculous Dutch voice 12 years before he did! My three-day clothes supply and the laundry service weren't on the same wavelength so the dwindling cash advance was spent on new gear.

With Advocaat promising an announcement on Sunday, the press pack from other newspapers finally arrived from Scotland for the game. The inevitable was not confirmed, though, until a statement on Monday. That evening, a besieged Advocaat didn't expand a great deal on the move at the training ground. A Celtic match was on Sky Sports that night and he politely declined the invite to join us in the Irish bar for an early spying mission.

What did become clear was that Advocaat had used an agreement with Van Raay that he could speak to clubs offering him a better deal with a year of his PSV contract left. Rangers had simply taken full advantage. But as Murray announced he'd got his man, Van Raay was still upset about Rangers and the coach. "They both informed me, in my opinion, after the contract was signed," was the president's parting shot.

Whatever the truth, it was quite a thrill to spark some squabbling between two powerful men in European football. Devastatingly for

Rangers and unfortunately for confused football writers, the ramifications of Murray's work at Rangers that he did manage to keep secret for so long turned out to be far more serious …

Fraser Mackie is a football writer for the Scottish Mail On Sunday. He started out on weekly papers in Barrhead and Paisley before joining the Rangers News in February 1994. After 18 months reporting on first-team affairs, he moved to the Scottish Daily Mail. In a rare act of foresight, Fraser's wish to cover at least one Scotland campaign at a major tournament prompted a timely and brief switch to the Scotsman six weeks before the 1998 World Cup in France. He returned to the Associated Newspapers stable in February 1999 when the Mail On Sunday relaunched in Scotland.

IT'LL BE ALL RIGHT ON THE NIGHT

By Tony Hamilton

Those of you who have read the Celtic View's 'Final Word' will already know that my writing technique is never going to threaten the positions of dominance long-enjoyed by the nation's favourite sports hacks.

However, as a long-term card-carrying member of the NUJ, I still take enormous pride in the journalism we create at Celtic, a lot of which these days comes in television, DVD or online format, in addition to the traditional print medium which the club has rolled out for many years.

I've learned the hard way, and back in 1996 I took on board a valuable lesson from former chief executive and principal shareholder, Fergus McCann. We were officially opening the North Stand in front of a packed Celtic Park. When I say 'we,' I actually mean McCann and Rod Stewart were doing the honours. I was merely there to serve up live introductions and commentary to the assembled masses within the stadium. McCann asked me what I was going to say as we stepped on to the pitch from the tunnel, as the capacity crowd, themselves proud of their own contributions, waited with anticipation for the ceremonial rebirth of the club in its new home. I tried to waffle him and he reminded me, in no uncertain terms (as was his wont) in that crazy Scots/Canadian accent that: "The best ad-libs are written down." I've carried that advice forward in everything I have done in terms of presentation from that day to this.

However, to paraphrase the Bard of Ayrshire, there is a significant chance that even the best planning won't be good enough and one needs to be adaptable to the situation. One such instance in which adaptability would play a huge role came in 2003, in a wee Spanish town called Jerez (famed for its sherry industry) just two days ahead of Celtic's Uefa Cup final in Seville. Jerez was the team base and was also the venue for what would be our first live TV pay-per-view event which didn't include a live match. We had previously produced and presented around 15 or so live matches throughout Europe and North America, and while the main focus was the football, mistakes were often forgiven or overlooked, so long as the team performed.

But this was different. We had put together two hours of live chat and video. And I'm no Michael Parkinson. Margot McCuaig, these days a successful MD of a Gaelic TV company, was my co-host and interviewer, while our main, ever-present guest for the duration was the inimitable Bertie Auld.

I asked Lisbon Lion Bertie to join us mainly because he can talk the head off of a stamp and I knew the conversation was never going to die. I also knew that he, more than most, enjoys the Spanish sunshine. We had prepared several VT inserts of the run to the final, some pre-recorded interviews, a few anniversary pieces such as the night 10-men-won-the-league some 24 years earlier, and we also had a couple of 'emergency' videos, just in case …

'The best-laid' plans were, therefore, in place. What could possibly go wrong?

We had the rehearsals in the morning – many of our own technical people who work on these things had made the trip but the main broadcast and satellite facilities came from a Spanish crew out of Madrid. I realised quickly that even when I shouted really loudly in English, there was still a communication problem.

However, we ran through what we could, double-checked timings, tweaked the running order and once I had picked Bertie up from the edge of the pool at the hotel (after he'd been told that the show was two hours in duration and not 30 minutes), we were all set.

That afternoon taught me a few things. I wanted my mammy. I had too much time to worry about things that couldn't possibly go wrong. I felt physically ill at the thought of being the front of this programme (and trying to co-produce it) especially when sales of the PPV event were at an all-time high.

The plan was to have live guests to join Bertie and me 'on set,' while others would join Margot at an adjoining set. Martin O'Neill, Billy Connolly and John Hartson – who had been ruled out of the final through injury – were all lined up. But 10 minutes before air, none of them were to be seen. Connolly was spotted strolling, nay, wandering around the outside perimeter of the team hotel by John Clark as the titles rolled while MO'N and Big Bad John were AWOL. I really, really wanted my mammy by this point.

As things transpired it all went very well. The journalist in me had penned my autocue links but there were gaps where I had to ignore Fergus' wise words and ad lib, like all good journalists and presenters can and often have to do.

For me journalism has changed. It has certainly changed since the 10 years I wrote a column for the Irish News in Belfast. My long time at Celtic has taught me that creative journalism doesn't have to come in the form of a newspaper. I know that there are many mediums, which can engage and captivate an audience, and live, edgy TV production has its part alongside the more traditional forms we once all signed up to. And it is evolving again with social media set to play a major role in news dissemination in the coming years.

That night in Jerez, however, is one of the best in my career. We desperately need to get to another European final so I can see if my nerves have steadied any in the past nine years …

Tony Hamilton has been at Celtic since time began. These days he manages the club's digital and publishing output. He is married, and has six weans, some of whom have weans of their own. Most of them see things the Celtic way.

THERE IS A TIME AND A PLACE FOR GIANT FOAM HANDS

By Mark Wilson

T here is a time and a place for giant foam hands. This can be counted among the many valuable lessons learned from the strange travelogues that are pre-season tours.

These summer odysseys are the kind of thing that make people outside the microclimate of football journalism ask, "When you are going to get a real job?" Crossing countries and continents with either half of the Old Firm – what's not to like?

And they are often right. A fortnight of planes, trains and automobiles can transport reporters to exciting destinations and grant a level of access denied in the stuffier atmosphere of the regular season. But the dynamic changes when the press pack ends up at loggerheads with the subject of their attention. Then the whole affair becomes more like a highly dysfunctional family holiday, with the hacks in the role of annoying children trailing along after increasingly irate parents.

This was pretty much how things worked out during Celtic's epic adventure of 2006. The bags hadn't even been collected after the first of many flights when the bonhomie began to unravel. In an interview with sportswriters conducted beside a luggage carousel in Warsaw Airport, midfield man Alan Thompson offered the opinion that the hectic summer plans – encompassing Poland, the USA and Japan – were 'far from ideal' preparation for their SPL title defence. The straight-talking Geordie had delivered an obvious back page story – just not a particularly positive one. By the time we caught up with Gordon Strachan's squad for their second match in Krakow, the temperature outside was touching 90 degrees. Inside the media room, it was somewhere south of zero as Celtic's PR man made it clear the coverage given to Thompson's criticism wasn't going to have them throwing open the dressing room doors for further interviews.

After a brief return to Scotland, the now not-so-merry band crossed the Atlantic to Boston, which would be the club's primary stateside station. The collapse of part of a key tunnel in the city added a layer of travel problems. Perhaps fittingly, relations remained as gridlocked as the traffic.

Celtic had lost both their matches in Poland without scoring a goal, increasing the scrutiny on their schedule. First up in the US was a game against DC United in Washington's RFK Stadium.

It wasn't pretty. One-time wunderkind Freddy Adu scored the opener in a 4-0 defeat that also saw Kenny Miller sent off for a rash challenge on one of the DC defenders.

Homer Simpson is at least partly to blame for what happened next. Inspired by the great man's antics in the peerless cartoon sit-com, a colleague had purchased a huge red-and-black foam hand as a joke before kick-off. The slogan 'Go DC United' was written across the palm.

Having filed my copy for the evening, I decided my turn at re-enacting some of Springfield's funniest sporting moments had now arrived. I donned the hand – just as a grim-faced Gordon Strachan emerged around the bend of the concrete concourse to head for the post-match interviews. Instantly recognising the need to conceal a comedy item in the colours of a team that had ransacked the Celtic defence, I attempted to thrust the foam hand inside my jacket. Unfortunately, the protruding index finger still jutted out like a beacon of inappropriate mockery as Strachan strode by without a second glance. A witty if somewhat irascible character, the former Scotland midfielder's general opinion of the press tended to hover not that far above the particular disdain he reserved for radio phone-ins. Clearly, this ill-timed japery was not the best way to try and win him round.

New York was the next stop, where a goalless draw with Mexican side Chivas further extended the scoring drought before it was back to base camp in Boston. Celtic's hotel, swish but under renovation, was at the harbour. The media hotel, not swish and in need of renovation, was situated across town in Cambridge. And it was while sitting in a diner midway between the two that we discovered the headline-making Thompson had been sent home.

A club statement said the midfielder had a thigh injury, but the player's agent, Tony McGill, moved to refute that with a memorable line. "Alan wasn't injured when he left the team's hotel in America so unless he injured himself carrying his luggage on to the plane that situation is still the same," claimed McGill, who effectively accused Celtic of trying to ease his client out the door.

Strachan was having none of that when we finally located him on one of the numerous Harvard training pitches the next day. Unhappy that McGill's words had been given prominence, he flatly insisted Thompson was suffering from a niggling injury and had actually thanked him for the opportunity to return home.

By now, the manager's limited patience with the media had worn to a microscopic thickness. Thompson, meanwhile, only played for Celtic once more – and was there perhaps a hint of revenge in the fact that his only other appearance in the Hoops before leaving Parkhead was on another stamina-sapping far-flung jaunt, this time to Japan to play an August friendly against Yokohama Marinos?

One small mercy did arrive when Rocco Quinn finally scored Celtic's first goal of the summer in a 1-1 draw with New England Revolution, before press and players boarded their respective planes home. It had been far from an auspicious tour.

That, however, merely brings us round to the most important lesson of all from pre-season. Never, ever make predictions of any kind based on what you see in these bounce games. The following campaign turned out to be a glorious one for Celtic. They won the SPL at a canter, added the Scottish Cup and reached the last 16 of the Champions League for the first-ever time, losing narrowly to AC Milan.

It was a sequence of achievement that meant Strachan truly deserved a big hand. Of applause. Not foam. Definitely not foam.

Mark Wilson has been in football journalism for the past 15 years, most recently including spells at The Herald and the Daily Mail. The timing of his stumble into this career means he has never covered Scotland at a major international tournament. He has, however, shaken Diego Maradona's hand.

MY MAIDEN FLIGHT ROCKED

By Graeme Croser

With apologies to Alex Salmond, Scotland doesn't have any proper celebrities. Those music and movie stars who ascend from our little country to world fame tend to flit to the action-packed super-cities of London or Los Angeles or, in the case of Sean Connery, retire to where the weather's nice and they don't have to pay much tax.

So, in the absence of genuine star names what are we left with? Footballers. And it's up to the Scottish sports hack to try and make the superstars of the SPL sound interesting.

We do our best but for all the honest toil which goes on in our top league we are not awash with colourful personalities. That's why my ears pricked up when I learned the identity of the pilot on a flight chartered by Rangers for a Uefa Cup trip to Israel in 2007. At the controls was Captain Bruce Dickinson, lead singer of heavy-metal heavyweights Iron Maiden, a band who have shifted 80 million records worldwide.

As I settled into my seat on the Astraeus flight to Tel Aviv I resolved to try and engineer a meeting with our pilot during our three-day stint in the Middle East. Sure, the chances of procuring an interview suitable for the sports pages of the Mail on Sunday were remote, but that wasn't the point. I just wanted to pick the man's brains. Here was not only a bona-fide rock star and part-time aviator, but a man who had represented Great Britain internationally as a fencer, and dabbled in writing and broadcasting. A true polymath.

On these flights the usual practice is to keep the press as far apart from the players as possible. Typically, the squad and staff sit up front, then comes an extensive buffer of corporate clients, with the journalists shoehorned in at the rear.

The chatter among those at the back of the plane revealed a common first impression – as a pilot Dickinson made a pretty good rock singer. Approaching Tel Aviv across the eastern edge of the Mediterranean the aircraft bobbed up and down with a ferocity which suggested the captain and his cockpit crew were all head-banging, Wayne's World style, to Bring Your Daughter … To The Slaughter.

We made it on to dry land with a thud and a bump to rival any rollicking drum fill, but the cockpit door remained firmly shut as we trudged off, and meet and greet opportunity number one was lost.

Attending Walter Smith's pre-match press conference at the team hotel the next day, I spied the cabin crew huddled in a corner of the reception area and, sensing my chance, strode over. This would count as the only time I have asked a girl for her telephone number in the hope of meeting a man. A loose arrangement was made to get everyone together that night – writers, stewardesses and rock royalty, and so it came to pass at a beachfront bar soon after sunset.

Dickinson was a delight and his star quality stemmed from the fact he was so normal. He graciously accepted all requests for autographs from fans in the bar and a couple from the Scottish press corps. Conversation came easy. Flying, he explained, was his true love.

"There's nothing like it," he explained. "Performing to 60,000 people in Rio is a thrill but your feet pretty much stay on the ground. When you're up in the air you realise that you're in an environment which we're not really supposed to inhabit."

The ageing process had eroded this swordsman's prowess in the world of fencing but music and flying remained his two great passions, and he combined them by taking the controls of Maiden's Ed Force One jet while on tour. He also explained that the descent into Tel Aviv is often a bumpy affair due to air turbulence. At this point I thought it appropriate not to mention Wayne's World.

Keen to catch the game, Dickinson and Co. procured tickets for Rangers' 2-1 defeat to Hapoel (they would go on to turn the tie round with a 4-0 win at Ibrox a couple of weeks later) and afterwards, while waiting for the daily newspaper men to file their post-match copy, I caught up with the crew in the stadium car park.

We were due to land back in Glasgow the following afternoon and, once emptied, the aircraft would return to the Astraeus base at Gatwick. By coincidence, I too was making an onward journey the next day which would take me through Gatwick and one of the girls joked that they could keep me on board thus averting the hassle of waiting and checking in for my next flight.

It wasn't until I got to Ben Gurion Airport the next morning that I realised the idea had actually been taken seriously, but I was to be ultimately disappointed. Looking faintly ridiculous with his bejewelled ears taped up as per flying regulations and wearing a uniform that was at least two sizes too big, Bruce marched over and offered an apology.

"Sorry, but the rules state we have to unload your baggage at Glasgow so we can't take you to London. Good luck with your trip."

"Thanks," I mumbled, ever so slightly humbled.

As it happened I had to settle for typing up a Charlie Adam interview as I waited for EasyJet to cart me south from Glasgow. Distracted, all I could think of was my own narrowly missed opportunity to sample the rock n' roll lifestyle on my own private jet. With respect to Charlie, that really would have been a story to tell.

Graeme Croser started his career with DC Thomson in 1997, working on the Glasgow sports desks of the Sunday Post and Weekly News. He moved to the Edinburgh Evening News in 2000, covering football in the Lothians before transferring to the Mail on Sunday where he has spent seven quick years. In 2011 he became the first middle-aged recipient of the Jim Rodger Memorial Award for 'young' sportswriters.

BAD BHOY ROY SPOILED THE SCOOP

By Alison McConnell

I t was quite a coup for a relative rookie.

Roy Keane. The then Manchester United and Republic of Ireland captain. Notoriously spiky, opinionated and not known for being particularly media friendly. The man had agreed to a one-on-one sit down interview at United's luxury Carrington training base with Yours Truly, then of the Celtic View.

My remit with Keane was a blether about the forthcoming 2002 World Cup campaign in Japan. It would, of course, go on to become the most infamous chapter in Keane's colourful career. But more of that later.

Since the interview with Keane was early morning, I'd driven to Manchester at leisure the day before and booked into my hotel with no hiccups. United were playing Bayer Leverkusen in the semi-final of the Champions League that evening at Old Trafford and I'd decided to get a bite to eat and watch the game before retiring to organise myself for the next day. So when the call came from Diana Law, United's press officer late that afternoon, my stomach lurched. Dear Lord, surely not a call-off at this late stage?

I answered nervously. The news was good; would I like a press pass for that evening's game if I was in the city? A natural worrier, I grew concerned that things were running just a little too smoothly. I watched the game – United drew 2-2 with a Leverkusen team who would later progress to the final against Real Madrid at Hampden

– and headed back to the hotel. Bright and early I turned up at Carrington. David Beckham hobbled around on crutches and a trendy beanie hat, smiling, autographing for all. His broken metatarsal had been back-page news for around three weeks by then. He looked as though he was bearing up.

Keane was late and, not entirely wet behind the ears, I started to wonder just how many exits the Carrington base held. My concerns proved unfounded. Keane sauntered through smiling, offering handshakes, small talk and coffee. He was relaxed, chatty, co-operative. So easy, in fact, that I wondered what all the fuss was about. In his gentle Cork brogue, Keane talked freely and engagingly and I made up my mind that talk of barroom brawls and explosive dressing-room rows were nothing but the stuff of urban myth.

Still, after all the chat of Ireland and the who's who at the World Cup, I had to ask him about Celtic. I had enough smarts about me to keep it to the end of the conversation just in case I lit a fuse. When we did steer the conversation there, I tried hard not to give the game away when Keane handed me 'the line' – and more besides – on a plate. Yes, if they'd have him, he'd finish his career at Celtic. Yes, he loved going up for the Old Firm games. Yes, he loved the Hoops and Henrik Larsson was ridiculously underrated. I nodded encouragingly and even managed not to break into gleeful applause at the thought of regaling said line down the phone to the View's office.

When we finished Keane enquired as to how I would be getting home – did I need a lift to the airport, the train station? He was charm personified and I was thrilled.

Back in Glasgow the copy wrote itself. Keane was part of a special World Cup edition of the magazine that had some fantastic exclusives in it – Michael Owen and Larsson to name but two.

Almost four weeks after my sit-down with Keane, the magazine went to print on a balmy May Monday evening. It would be Wednesday before it would hit the streets and we would get our first look at the finished article. The proofs looked fantastic. The magazine looked like that of one of the big hitters, a magazine with far more financial resources than we did. I was chuffed with how the Keane piece had come out and figured that the line about Celtic would be picked up everywhere else – something I've always seen as a compliment.

The Tuesday after the magazine had gone to print was a quiet shift in the office. We had just produced a magazine of substantial craft and pagination, and given there were but four of us on a View beat, we were quietly satisfied with our efforts. Pizza might even have been called.

My peace of mind was wrecked within hours.

The omnipresent Sky Sports screen that updated hourly with news from around the various international camps suddenly got louder, more hysterical. Keane had fallen out with Packie Bonner and Mick McCarthy in Saipan. By that evening – when the View was somewhere in media limbo, between office and printers – Keane had quit the World Cup. For the next 48 hours the circus would be the talk of every media outlet in the land.

I could barely look at the magazine on the Wednesday morning. Not even out of the printers' wrapper and my flagship piece was dated, stale and defunct. No-one gave a flying monkey's about Roy Keane announcing he'd finish his career in Glasgow with Celtic. Nor did it matter a jot what Keane thought about Germany and Cameroon, two of Ireland's opponents in the group. The man was at the eye of the storm and everything other than that moment was an irrelevance.

Four years later when Keane was paraded in the Hoops at Celtic Park I had the urge to refer all and sundry back to the May 2002 edition of the View. It wasn't quite as strong as the urge to tell Keane that he'd wrecked my piece with his bickering and sniping nonsense. Unlike Keane, however – and contrary to any urban myths of the time – I managed to restrain myself.

Alison McConnell began her football writing career with the Scottish Sports Agency, progressed to the Celtic View and currently writes for the Evening Times. She can be found in a musty old press box most weekends.

IT TOOK A LOT OF BALLS TO CHAT WITH BEEFY

By Allan Herron

The first ball removed six red slates from the pavilion roof. The second ball, with the same accuracy, took out another five or six slates. Ball three was struck with such ferocity that it disappeared into a nearby car park, where the sound of a lengthy ricochet had car owners gritting their teeth.

It surprised no-one that the pre-Test match work-out of Ian Botham was terminated abruptly before he demolished the Old Trafford pavilion and turned the car park into a spare parts scrapyard, not to mention causing numerous insurance claims.

From behind the safety of the nets I had watched England's greatest-ever Test cricket all-rounder loosen up before ripping the heart out of Australia in the fifth Test match of the 1981 series. My privilege. It was with pen and paper that I had faced this 25-year-old legend an hour earlier in a deserted locker room of the Manchester stadium. I did so with considerable trepidation, having been told by those who knew that he had no great regard for sports hacks.

Risking the possibility of being thrown down the stairs which led to the players' sanctuary or being bundled over the balcony, I knocked on the door, walked inside and introduced myself.

Ian, a very impressive athlete of 6ft 2in, slowly laid down the tabloid newspaper he had been reading, lifted his feet from a bench, gave me 'the look' and asked why I was there. Realising I was on a mission of peace, he stood up, shook my hand (ouch!) and told me to grab a seat. My heartbeat returning to normal, I then enjoyed a full 30 minutes natter which turned out to be one of my most memorable career highlights.

Botham had arrived early at the Old Trafford ground for a practice session well ahead of skipper Mike Brearley and the rest of the England Test team. Fortunately I too had arrived early to get myself an interview I did not foresee in my wildest dreams.

Right here I'll come clean. I had motored down from Glasgow that morning, hoping to get a word or too with Brearley (not Botham), as things were going rather well for his squad. I never did speak with him.

My difficulty was to get Botham to talk about cricket. Statistics? "No, I don't bother with that sort of stuff," he told me, and preferred to chat about his many trips to Scotland, where he relaxed with a rod around the Rob Roy countryside of Callander, fishing rivers Leny and Teith, and lochs Venechar and Lubnaig. To hear him talk quite so passionately about his love of Scotland was perhaps surprising when I was trying to get the full details of his remarkable innings of 149 not-out against the Aussies in the third Test at Headingley, which stunned the aficionados of the game and made the visiting bowlers long for home.

This was a win everyone, including the English nation, hadn't expected. A bookmaker had offered England, who had to follow on, at 500-1 against victory. The bet was immediately taken up by Dennis Lillee and Rod Marsh, a doughty Aussie duo, as a joke. Incredibly, it paid off. England won by just 18 runs, thanks to You Know Who and a bowling burst from Bob Willis (eight for 43). The Aussies collected £7,500, and there was no suggestion of hanky-panky regarding the bets. The match had been played above board.

To my surprise Ian (I was by now on first-name terms) revealed he was a staunch Rangers supporter and always looked for their results at the weekend. He then said he had an ambition to visit Ibrox to see Rangers in action. I passed this information on to John Greig, who was then manager at Ibrox. Greigy told me: "Tell him he is welcome to come to Ibrox at any time as a guest."

No, I do not know whether Botham took up the offer, but I know that I should have suggested to Greig that he might consider signing him as a central defender (Rangers were not at their best that particular season). Just think of the box-office appeal! And after all, Botham had made 11 league appearances for Scunthorpe the previous year as a centre-half. Colin Jackson and Botham as a defensive unit? Savour the thought.

My interview with Botham turned out to be the kind of 'exclusive' you might only contemplate. That weekend of the fifth Test he hit six sixes (a test record at that time) in an innings of 118. He hit three of his sixes off the bowling of Dennis Lillee, two of them in the same over. John Wisden's Almanack rated the heroics of Botham at Headingley as the fourth-greatest innings in Test history. Lillee said his century-plus to give England their third victory of that series that day was better. As a badly bruised bowler he should know! It was no surprise that 'Beefy,' as he was known around the wickets, was named 'Man of the Series' with stats of 399 runs and 34 wickets.

In a fantastic career, Sir Ian Terence Botham scored 5,200 runs, took a world-record 383 wickets and made 120 catches in 102 Tests. He was named BBC Sports Personality of the year for 1981.

And as for me, I just happened to be in the right place at the right time to meet a quite modest man who shattered the hopes of Australia off his own bat … so to speak.

Allan Herron was in newspapers for 56 years, the last 26 of which as chief sportswriter of the Sunday Mail. He covered three Commonwealth Games, three Olympics, five World Cup finals, six Masters tournaments, Open championships, Ryder Cups, world boxing titles, and saw Aberdeen, Celtic and Rangers win their European trophies.

THE POPE'S COCKTAIL PARTY

By Stuart Bathgate

T he Pope's cocktail party was a non-event, literally. But it still came within an ace of being presented as a factual occurrence in the intro to a piece about the first-ever match in rugby's Six Nations Championship.

Journalists from rival publications get on far better than is widely thought; our jobs would be next to impossible if we were cutting each other's throats all the time. But we also have a tendency to feed each other misinformation, and that was certainly the case back in early 2000, as Scotland, the last Five Nations champions, prepared to fly out to Rome to take on the Italians, who had just been admitted into the tournament.

It all started on the Tuesday, with a supposedly casual remark by someone who should remain anonymous: Bill Lothian of the Edinburgh Evening News. Myself and the Bonk (a well-known and fondly regarded fellow rugby scribbler) were sitting in a room at Murrayfield waiting for a press conference to start, when Bill walked in and asked me: "Got your invitation to the Pope's cocktail party yet?"

There was something about his manner which made me realise this was a wind-up. "No, I haven't," I replied. "But I haven't been in the office yet this morning so maybe it'll be in the mail when I get back."

"Should be," Bill said. "I just got mine this morning."

A mixture of suspicion and worry was on the Bonk's face. "Nah, nah, you're talking bollocks," he said. But the seed had been sown.

He was right to be suspicious, because since he had started writing about rugby for a national paper a couple of years earlier he had been subjected to more than a few wind-ups. There was the time in New Zealand, for example, when we got a taxi driver in one town to warn him about going out at night because of the problems with Eskimos at that time of year.

"Nah, nah, they live at the North Pole," the Bonk replied.

"Yeah mate," the taxi driver said. "But they come round the back way and sneak up from the south."

Back home, too, we talked such gibberish that the Bonk never quite knew what was real and what made up. So although sceptical about the Pope's alleged party, he could not discount it entirely.

At the next day's press conference, he and Bill and a couple of others were there first. "Got that invitation," I said to Bill on entering the room. "Should be good, as long as we get finished our work on time."

"Yeah, 7.30pm on the Friday. Start work early enough and we'll be fine."

Someone else asked why they had not received an invitation, a remark which might have ended the deception right there, but Bill explained that only a couple of journos had been invited, as a token representation from the press. The party was really for the Scotland team and management.

We all flew out to Rome on the Scottish Rugby Union's chartered plane on the Thursday and little or nothing was said about the Pontiff's impending party. And on Friday morning at breakfast it got no more than a passing mention, as one of us reminded the other that work would need to begin and end early, to allow us to trot off to the Vatican.

Work did indeed begin early, which for us meant 11am or so. And it ended early enough to allow us to trot down to reception and meet up for a drink before dinner. The Bonk wasn't there yet, but one of his colleagues from the London office was, and he was brandishing a fax that had been sent to him. "The Scotland rugby team were spending some time last night at a cocktail reception hosted by the Pope," he read. "They will certainly need divine intervention this afternoon if they are to avoid defeat by an Italian team hungry to get the Six Nations off to a winning start."

It was the Bonk's copy for the following day's paper. The deception had worked and he had actually included this made-up occasion in the very first sentence of his match preview.

I can't remember how Bill felt at this stage, but I began to feel more than a little guilty. We had only meant it as a joke, and had not thought it would go that far.

Fortunately, the guy from London had heard about the wind-up and had warned his paper's Scottish office. They had time to delete all mention of the party and write a new intro before printing the first edition of the paper, which was a relief.

It was also a relief when the Bonk, good-natured to a fault, did not take umbrage. And in any case, he had the last laugh, as his intro, though factually incorrect to a degree, proved accurate in one respect: Scotland were rubbish and lost 34-20.

Stuart Bathgate has been a sports reporter with the Scotsman since 1996. He was that paper's rugby correspondent from then until 2000, and has also covered Wimbledon and the Olympic and Commonwealth Games.

MURRAY BURNED BRIGHT AS A NEW STAR

By Martin Greig

The London summer of 2005 was hot. So hot that the tar on the roads had started to melt and travelling on the Tube was like descending through Dante's circles of hell. At SW19, ball kids were wilting like flowers and the plummy patrons took to mainlining ice-cold Pimms as they huddled beneath their parasols.

As the midday heat shimmered over Court Two, a stringy 18-year-old, all awkward limbs and shaggy hair, swaggered on court with his iPod in. The crowd roared. He raised his head briefly before arching an eyebrow in brief, bemused acknowledgement. Andy Murray was about to take his first steps on the road to greatness. I had a press pass and a front-row seat.

A front-row seat on an outside court at Wimbledon gets you close enough to smell the grass. So close, you feel like you could reach out and touch the players (you could, but it's frowned upon, apparently). Murray was playing a heavy-set Swiss player called George Bastl, who was ranked 146 in the world, 166 places above him.

Bastl had ended Pete Sampras' Wimbledon career three years previously, but had lost to David Nalbandian in the next round and failed to capitalise on that historic victory. Still, he was an established, experienced pro. He had enough about him to dispatch a scrawny Scottish teenager. Surely.

Murray had burned brightly in a thrilling three-setter against Thomas Johansson at Queen's a fortnight previously, before being cut down by cramp and exiting like an injured foal. File under 'promising talent,' expect nothing for a couple of years and get back to the real business of cheering on Tim, was the general consensus.

But Andy Murray has always been in a rush. A former colleague had been interviewing his mother Judy a few years previously, only for 15-year-old Andy to enter the room and enquire as to why the journalist wasn't interviewing him instead. I liked the sound of this kid. Added to the fact that he had taken the decision to move to Barcelona at 15, it was clear he was of a different breed, one who had chosen to break free from the often insular and parochial environs of British sport.

Murray looked accomplished from the start, taking the game to Bastl with an impressive artillery of cross-court passing shots and deft lobs. The Swiss soon started to suffer badly in the heat, tongue lolling, rivers of sweat pouring down his brow. Murray skated around court like a midgie on a loch, contemptuously caning shots past the Swiss. 6-4, 6-2, 6-2 read the scoreboard as the teenager stuck his earphones back in and trotted off court with the minimum of fuss. I had rarely felt so inspired, so personally involved, watching sport.

Afterwards, Murray met the media attention in a 'what's-the-big-deal?' kind of way. Here was a young sportsman who looked like he had finally arrived at a point where he had long been convinced his talent would deposit him. I liked his matter-of-fact style and his dry humour. I liked everything about him.

In the press bar that evening, there was a buzz. The tennis writers – the ones who covered the beat from Roland Garros to Roehampton – knew Murray was coming up on the rails. The debate was not whether he was going to be good or very good. It was whether he would be excellent or truly world class. But even the optimists dismissed his chances of beating Radek Stepanek in the second round.

I was making my Wimbledon debut that year, too. I was 26 and had been to the tournament as a fan, though never as a working journalist. I was used to the press boxes of Scottish football, where hacks are squashed together like sardines and tossed the very occasional scrap by press officers who wear permanent scowls and scrutinise interviews in case anyone dares ask a challenging or insightful question. Wimbledon was a different world. The press officers actually helped you do your job. Quotes were typed up and distributed. No ploughing through lengthy transcriptions. Every desk had its own TV on which you could watch any court.

It was exciting. So exciting, I found it hard to maintain a professional demeanour. My girlfriend phoned on the second day. "Sorry, can't speak for long, I'm off to watch Maria Sharapova then Ana Ivanovic." Long silence at the other end.

Even when I wasn't required to write anything, I spent every moment watching matches. Federer, sleek as a racehorse and graceful as ballet dancer; Nadal, all terrier tenacity and lion heart. Not just colossal sportsmen and women but patient and articulate, happy to field questions on all manner of subjects. After a season of trying to prise words out of monosyllabic footballers, it was like I had died and gone to hack heaven.

But Murray was the story. On the day of his second-round match, Court One – a stunning, atmospheric amphitheatre far superior to Centre, in my opinion – was bathed in early-evening sunshine. Stepanek was a burly Bond-villain type with a look in his eye that could open an oyster at 50 paces. He sized Murray up like the kid brother he could barely be bothered beating up on.

But Murray stole the initiative from the start. Stepanek looked bemused. He looked up at his box. He looked at his racket. He checked his tennis shoes. He didn't understand, but it was very simple. He was being outplayed.

The increasingly desperate Czech resorted to some strong-arm tactics, following up points with steely glares. At one point, Murray ripped a forehand down the line and held his opponent's gaze, long enough for it to be meaningful; an impressive, controlled display of masculinity.

6-4, 6-4. Final set. My colleague, who was ghosting a Murray diary for The Herald that year, gripped my arm for the whole of the set. We were wrecks. It all seemed so unbelievable. A Scottish kid, ranked 312, knocking out the 14th seed. But he did. 6-4, 6-4, 6-4.

Two days later, in the third round, he set about Nalbandian like a devouring flame before cramp caught up with his willowy frame and he slumped in five sets.

It was heartbreaking, but never before in my journalism career has the end felt so much like the beginning.

Martin Greig is a former sportswriter with The Herald. He is a freelance writer and co-founder of BackPage Press, a new publishing company which produces high-quality sports books. Martin is author of The Zen of Naka, *and co-author of novel* The Road to Lisbon.

FAREWELL, SMELLY DELHI

By Gareth Law

The gun-toting Indian soldier jabbed a finger in my direction. "Road closed," he steadfastly repeated.

We were outside the velodrome in Delhi. It was October 2010 and day one of the Commonwealth Games. But already the Scottish press pack had suffered through plenty of fraught bemusement at just how shambolically bad the whole competition was being run.

The omens hadn't been good. Before we'd left photos had been released showing the mess Scotland team staff had discovered on their arrival at the athletes' village. There were paw prints on stained mattresses, doors off their hinges and grimy bathrooms. Then, just days before jetting out, a spectator bridge next to the Jawaharlal Nehru Stadium had come crashing down. But surely everything would be alright by the time the opening ceremony was done?

As our bus weaved its way through the dusty streets from Indira Gandhi Airport, it was hard not to notice the armed military men keeping watch from high up on buildings. A motto of, 'why have one person do a job when you can have six' quickly became apparent. You had to speak to four different people just to buy a cake in the media centre.

Friendly staff were always happy to answer any questions, although most of the time they opted to give you the answers you were looking for, rather than the truth.

"Will the wi-fi be working tomorrow?"

"Oh yes sir."

Was the wi-fi working tomorrow? Uh, no sir.

We had already suffered frustration on our first visit to the velodrome for some pre-arranged press time with the Scottish cyclists before the games got underway. After being directed towards different press entrances, none of which we were allowed through, we eventually had to give up and go back. But just when we thought it couldn't get any worse, it did.

This particular day we'd been dropped at the same spot as 24 hours earlier, just a few hundred yards from the press entrance to the velodrome, only to find our path blocked. As the frowning officer ushered us away I casually assumed the journalist's universal response would solve things. "It's OK," I said, holding out the press card that hung around my neck. "Press."

"No sir. Road closed," he said again.

"Well how do we get in?" I asked.

"You must go all the way around the other way."

We looked at each other, baffled at what we were hearing.

"How far is that?"

"Maybe three kilometres," was the unflinching response. Arguing soon became pointless. If only it had been that distance, though. An hour later we were still walking. Down a three-lane motorway. With six lanes of traffic coming towards us. And the sun beating down. Sweat trickled down our faces as we took turns to hold each others' bags while slapping on more sunscreen. We diced with death darting across heaving roads, plodded our way through parks and followed the crowds up narrow streets. By the time we reached the velodrome entrance, weary and dehydrated, we'd missed the first two races. It was to become an all too familiar cycle of life during our stay on the sub-continent.

As was the theme of transport during our time at the games. The driver, who had dropped us off at the velodrome – I say driver in the loosest sense – was a guy called Pease Mohammed and he drove a tuk-tuk, a kind of motorised rickshaw. He'd picked us up on day one and told us he couldn't read or write English then handed us a business card with his Hotmail address on. He and his brother Mansoor had been ferrying us all around until they had a bust-up over how to split the profits. One day I asked Pease what size of engine he had in the tuk-tuk. He immediately pulled over on the side of the road and motioned me to get out. He took me to the rear of the tuk-tuk, flipped down a hatch and ushered me to peer inside. "Look sir," he said. "It's a very small engine."

Pease walked with a limp, a legacy of being knocked over by a car when he was younger. As he described what happened he rolled his right trouser leg up to reveal a skin-covered bone sticking out at an angle just above his shin. The money he earned from the games was going to go towards an operation, he explained. But he deserved a medal just for driving on Delhi's streets where the only rule was there were no rules. Yet as we cowered in the back, somehow everything kept moving like water flowing down a river as we headed towards our next venue.

The Jawaharlal Nehru Stadium was a place where you invariably had company at your press desk. If it wasn't a giant grasshopper on your seat it was a group of locusts crawling across your laptop. But the creepy crawlies hit new heights when Pease took us to the R K Khanna Tennis Complex on the edge of town as a gold for Scotland in the mixed doubles loomed with the clock nearing midnight. As we watched Jocelyn Rae and Colin Fleming charge to victory, we fought our own battles with giant grasshoppers dive-bombing down on us from the swarms that raged under the gleam of the floodlights. We were all still itching three days later.

And in a city famed for its stomach upsets the local cuisine was understandably treated with plenty of suspicion. Many food outlets were still being built as the games kicked off, so biscuits became a staple diet of the journalist who wanted to keep everything nice and regular.

When word spread that the food court at the main press centre had opened it was time to call Pease for a lift. To get to the centre – which from the outside resembled a warehouse from an early out-of-town shopping centre that needed a lick of paint – you had to pass a small slum. Little tents were crammed together with peoples' feet sticking out of them at angles as they slept. A stench filled the air. With millions siphoned off to support the games, these improvised dwellings summed up the inequalities in the city. As we expectantly turned the corner towards the entrance to the food court we were greeted by the sight of stray dogs scratching and licking as they idled around in the sunshine. Inside was an alley reminiscent of an old shopping arcade with steel shutters clattering upwards to reveal food-filled counters. And there was a choice too. Either you could plump for the delicacies in the glass display units that were dripping with condensation. Or maybe a nice cake once the swarm of flies had been wafted off? Needless to say we took the third option – one which had become the norm – and starved.

Getting the chance to sample Delhi's diverse and colourful culture, so far removed from the one I am used to, was an unforgettable experience. But I shan't be rushing back.

Gareth Law is a Welsh sports reporter who has worked for the Scottish Sun since 2002. He reports on football and has also covered two Commonwealth Games.

I THINK TYSON'S BITTEN HIS EAR OFF ...

By Ewing Grahame

Where to begin? Why, at the very start, dear reader. It was the summer of 1997 and, in newspaper terms, still very much the best of times.

Sports desks worked with proper budgets and deciding how to spend that money was invariably a matter for journalists as opposed to bean counters. Consequently, events were covered much more comprehensively than they are today.

Back then I was working for the Daily Record, then Scotland's biggest-selling newspaper, and I was about to realise a long-held ambition to cover a heavyweight title fight in Las Vegas.

Not just any old bout, either: this was the rematch between Evander Holyfield and Mike Tyson. Holyfield had upset the odds by stopping Iron Mike seven months earlier and the return was eagerly awaited.

For future contests in New York and Vegas, I would fly out on the Monday before the main event. That allowed me sufficient time to attend training sessions for champion and challenger, interview them individually and collectively, and also speak to members of the respective camps and other boxing celebrities present (before Lennox Lewis fought Holyfield for the first time at Madison Square Garden in 1999 I spent an hour in the company of veteran trainer Angelo Dundee, who enthralled the Guardian's Richard Williams and myself with anecdotes about Muhammad Ali, Sugar Ray Leonard and Frank Sinatra).

On that first visit to Vegas, however, I flew out on the Thursday, having left some preview features behind for Friday's edition. Fortunately, my dear friend and colleague Gary Keown, then with the Sun, had chosen to attend the fight as a spectator. His flight arrived 20 minutes after mine and, since we were staying in the same hotel – The Excalibur – I waited for him and shared a taxi into town.

After decanting our luggage, we met downstairs in the bar at 8pm, where we were entertained by a charming Mexican barmaid called Angela. She finished her shift at 2am and said her goodnights. Shortly afterwards Gaz and myself decided to tour the Strip in the manner of Hunter S Thompson and his Samoan attorney. Visits to Caesar's Palace and Treasure Island (among others) helped keep jet lag at bay until we eventually returned to the Excalibur at midday.

Angela began her next shift at 1pm. She was astonished and (I like to think) rather impressed to see the pair of us occupying the same seats from which we had waved her away the night before. Shortly afterwards we retired to our respective rooms, although I had asked for an alarm call for 3pm in order to attend the weigh-in across the road at the MGM Grand.

Feeling remarkably fresh, I was initially surprised to discover that none of my British colleagues were present, although it later became obvious that they had garnered more than enough preview material earlier in the week.

Of course, it's also the case that, in a heavyweight contest, it's impossible for either boxer not to make the weight so there is no potential for a news story there. In any case, apart from a few local reporters, I had the place to myself. I spotted James 'Buster' Douglas, who had become the first man to beat Tyson in Tokyo seven years earlier, and who had lost the title in his first defence against Holyfield. That gave him a unique insight into the mindset of both fighters and he couldn't have been more helpful when I requested a one-to-one. Another legendary trainer, Eddie Futch (sadly, no longer with us), was equally generous with his time and his opinions. Not for the first time, I was left wondering why journalists so often need to jump through hoops in order to provide free publicity for relative nonentities in football when major figures in other fields are only too happy to talk up their sport.

I digress. Buzzing in the afterglow of a couple of big-name exclusives for Saturday's paper (it's possible I may also still have been slightly over the legal blood alcohol limit for driving), I made my way back through the MGM Grand, pausing to enter one of their art galleries. While I was admiring a large portrait of Sinatra, the unctuous owner/manager sidled up, clearly viewing me as a potential shoplifter. "I think that may be out of your price range, sir," he sneered.

Well, I wasn't about to be patronised by this oleaginous half-man, so I asked how much it cost. "$3,000," he replied. Naturally, I proceeded to buy it, staring at my nemesis with the quiet satisfaction of someone who has just been done like a dinner. Oddly enough, my wife, the lovely and long-suffering Aileen, was less impressed than I had been with our new acquisition. Indeed, her disapproval only increased a few weeks later when I had to travel to Glasgow Airport to collect it and pay an extra £300 tax on our investment.

Anyhow, fight night arrived. Gaz took his seat in the stands while I headed for ringside. Holyfield out-boxed Tyson during the opening two rounds and then, midway through the third, I turned to the Independent's James Lawton, who was sitting beside me, and said: "I think Tyson's bitten his ear off."

Lawton, a lovely writer and an even lovelier man, replied: "I don't think so, dear boy" and, since referee Mills Lane allowed the fight to continue without taking any action against Tyson, I assumed I'd imagined the incident. As you would.

However, clearly looking for a way out of the fight, Tyson repeated the offence and this time he was disqualified. This, it hardly needs saying, did not go down well with the high-rollers who had spent fortunes to be there.

As Tyson and his entourage walked the narrow corridor to the dressing room, dozens of large black men in garish suits rushed down from their seats in the raised dais in order to hurl abuse, cups, bottles, cigarette lighters, coins and punches at the former Iron Mike.

For his part, he seemed more willing to take them on than he had been to engage with Holyfield, but he was eventually huckled away.

After attending the post-fight conference, Gaz and myself found ourselves walking through the MGM Grand alongside Donald Trump when we heard gunfire. Being naturally inquisitive (not to mention stupid), we decided to head towards the shots in order to establish what was happening.

As we did so, we were met with a human tsunami rushing in the opposite direction, screaming at the tops of their voices and, literally, running for their lives. Less than a year earlier, Tupac Shakur had been shot to death on the Strip after Tyson had beaten Bruce Seldon at the same venue. Discretion being the better part of valour, I dived behind a registration desk. Gaz, meanwhile, locked himself in a telephone box. A glass telephone box. I don't think he had fully thought that one through.

While the Vegas police and hotel security dealt with the Bloods/Crips nonsense, Gaz and myself made our way back to the sanctity of our hotel bar, where we toasted our survival, feeling – all too briefly – like Sean Flynn and Tim Page in Saigon.

As for the Sinatra portrait, it still hangs, like a war trophy, in the West Wing of Grahame Acres. It'll soon be paid off …

Ewing Grahame has been covering Scottish football for 35 years, and has high hopes that sons Dylan and Adam will be significantly less useless at the playing side than he was. His career highlight was winning the £1,000 sweep for first goal from his English colleagues at the England v Brazil World Cup quarter-final in Shizuoka, Japan, in 2002. He can't allow himself to trust anyone who dislikes Elvis Presley, southern soul or dub, and has nothing but scorn for followers of U2.

HOPE SPRUNG ETERNAL IN L.A.

By Archie Macpherson

I went to the 1984 Los Angeles Olympic Games with great expectations of being close witness to the greatest show on earth. The expectations seemed natural. In fact, I ended up with a lot more than I had bargained for.

We have to go back several months prior to the games to understand the context. It was then I was asked to interview American guests at Gleneagles to reflect on the continuing interest they had in playing Scottish golf courses. The man I met was Jack Hennessy; a dapper little fellow who made annual visits to the hotel and played golf every day. We filmed on the course, during which I noticed that on his bag there was a golf disc which contained a caricature. It was of a hooked nose. On it were the words, 'The Hennessy Bob Hope Desert Classic.' It turned out that I was talking to the sponsor. He told me to give him a ring if ever I was in LA.

Once in California for the games I did just that, and we arranged to go for lunch at the fabulous Lakeside Country Club in Hollywood. It was then I asked if Hope was in town. Jack said nothing but went to a wall-phone and after a few words there, beckoned me over and held out the receiver to me. "It's Bob," he said. So, there I was thinking of what to say to one of my idols from way back when I used to sneak into the Palaceum cinema in Shettleston to see all his movies.

"Hi, Bob," I said and within minutes he was talking warmly about his time golfing in Scotland. I steadied my nerve and asked the important question, "Would you care to do an interview for BBC

Grandstand's Olympic preview?" To my astonishment, he agreed. Of course, I hadn't checked with the BBC about this, and I was worried because all the camera crews were busy around LA doing preview work. But as soon as I told the office who I had nabbed, they rolled up a camera for me.

Hope wasn't in when we arrived at his home. He was off being fitted for his new Olympic uniform. Hennessy, however, took us right through the house, and showed us the pool in the large garden and the four par-three holes that Hope had constructed in the back. We set up for him and when the 75-year-old arrived he opened the french doors and ambled through with a wedge in his hand, swinging it like it was his constant companion. However, cameramen are no respecters of stardom. Mine suddenly complained to Hope that the shirt he was wearing was too white and would cause glare in the bright sunshine. I made a mental note to kick the cameraman in the groin when I got him back outside. However, Hope took it in his stride. "Quite right," he said and wandered back inside and returned a few minutes later with a multi-coloured shirt. This was enough intimation to us that we were dealing with a pro.

That feeling was enhanced later when he asked for the sound-man to change the position of the mike, as he was deaf in one ear and didn't want to be seen turning his head constantly to answer questions. The interview in itself was not earth-shattering. He talked of his continuing love of the UK, having been born there, of course. When we had finished and the cameraman was preparing his side shots for cutaways so that the piece could be edited, I went a step further.

He had told us his wife Dolores was in the UK at that moment visiting friends, so I ventured a proposition to him. Would he like to do a straight piece to camera, talking directly to his wife, and at the tail end give a plug to Olympic Grandstand which would be broadcast the following afternoon in London? To my astonishment, he agreed. So here we had a Hollywood legend plugging our programme. I felt that at any minute an agent would jump out of a bush and demand a few thousand dollars. But no, I only remember his first line, "Hi,

Dolores, just to let you know I've taken out the garbage and I haven't had the boys in for poker."

We then had a rush job to edit this in and send it back by satellite in time for the following afternoon. It was desperately tight. Des Lynam introduced that short plug, at the end of the programme, without knowing what was coming, and could only say, "And now we have somebody special from Hollywood with a message."

Phew! I will long remember that experience. And in case I would forget, Hope gave me a special Olympic cap as a memento. It had a political comment emblazoned upon it. The Soviet Union had boycotted the games and above the snap-up brim it said simply, 'F**k Russia.' On cold wintry days I put it on to remind me of the heat of Hollywood and the fact that once upon a time we had a Cold War.

Archie Macpherson was the principal commentator and presenter on Sportscene. In recent years he has worked for Eurosport, Scotsport, Radio Clyde, BBC Five Live and Setanta, and has written four bestselling books. In 2005 he was presented with a BAFTA Award for special contribution to Scottish broadcasting.

FEAR AND LOATHING ON THE RYDER CUP TRAIL

By Paul Forsyth

I n a Fulham pub, about a month after the 2004 Ryder Cup in De-
troit, Paul Casey chatted for a good couple of hours about what a
thrill it had been to beat the USA in their own backyard. Americans, he admitted, could be "bloody annoying," what with their par-
tisan chanting and historic reluctance to travel further than the local
7-Eleven.

He described how the Europeans had nodded in agreement when
his American girlfriend joked in the team room that she and her
compatriots were a bunch of "uncultured idiots." He said that the
vast majority of Americans simply didn't know what was going on
in the world, and that they had no concept of the United Kingdom.

That, though, was not the 'line,' as we call it in the trade. The line
revealed itself when I suggested to Casey that the sporting rivalry
didn't make sense. Given that the countries shared a language, and
fostered a so-called 'special relationship,' was the animosity between
their golf teams not just a bit contrived? "Oh, we properly hate them,"
he insisted. "We wanted to beat them as badly as possible."

The "hate" word is never advisable, especially in sport, but on
the whole, it was good knockabout stuff, naively articulated perhaps,
but in keeping with the Ryder Cup's rich history of hostility. Casey,
his manager, and several thousand readers had no objection to the
feature as it appeared that Sunday.

It should be pointed out that it was my first interview for the

Sunday Times, conducted just a day after I had started my new career as their golf writer. The way it panned out had been ideal: a good, colourful read that impressed the new boss, without causing too many ructions on the golf circuit where I had now to make a living.

Then the Daily Mirror came along. Neil McLeman, a friend and former colleague, called the next day, as a matter of courtesy, to say that he planned to use the quotes in Tuesday's paper. Fine, I thought. The words were already 'out there.' Might even be a feather in my cap. Journalists tend to measure the weight of their stories by the extent to which they are lifted. The complication is that quotes used in one newspaper can take on new meaning in another, due partly to the way they are spun, but mostly to the headline that announces them. The Sunday Times, bless them, opted for 'Big Hitter.' The Mirror was rather less circumspect: 'Americans are stupid, I hate them, says Ryder Cup star Paul Casey.'

You couldn't help but squirm uncomfortably. Neil had been faithful to the quotes, but the headline was mischievous. Casey had not actually said that Americans were "stupid," and his "hatred" had not, as the banner suggested, been aimed at the Americans as a species. Casey lived there for goodness sake, went to college there, had an American coach, and would later marry his American girlfriend.

By the time I pitched up at that week's World Cup in Seville, where Casey was representing England, it had all kicked off. The Mirror's story had gone global. Casey had been swamped by a flood of abusive emails. Scott Verplank, the American player, had told him to go home if he wasn't happy. On Friday, Amy Sabbatini, American wife of Rory, the South African player, wore a T-shirt emblazoned with the words 'Stoopid Amerikan.'

Casey admitted that he couldn't sleep. When he went into a restaurant, diners rose from their tables and left. By Saturday, just when it looked as though the story might finally give way to the golf, the international ramifications of his remarks began to take their toll. Acushnet, owners of Titleist, Footjoy and Cobra, world-renowned suppliers of golf equipment, released a statement saying that they would not be renewing their sponsorship deal with the young Englishman.

All of which was hugely disturbing. I must have looked troubled by it, because I remember John Huggan, of Scotland on Sunday, assuring me that it wasn't such a big deal, and that it certainly wasn't worth making myself ill about. Casey, to his eternal credit, stood by his words, saying that he had no problem with the Sunday Times interview, only the Mirror's headline.

That week, and in the months ahead, Casey repeatedly stressed that the "hate" word had been used only in the context of sporting rivalry, but it was a long, and often fruitless, struggle to repair the damage. When he set out to play on America's PGA Tour the following year, he was heckled by spectators. Pretty soon, it affected his game, as he plummeted down the world rankings, and according to one report, sought professional counselling. He said that he would regret those words for the rest of his life. Alan Campbell, golf correspondent of the Sunday Herald, teased me with a phone call in which he asked, "How does it feel to have ruined someone's career?"

The fundamental principle of journalism is to structure a story and its presentation in such a way that the juicy bits are highlighted. By sparking a reaction from the same quotes that provoked nothing in the Sunday Times, you could say that the Mirror did its job better, but it begs a question: are readers incapable of making their own judgement? Do they identify a controversy only when they are told it is one?

Casey, one of the world's leading players, didn't win a tournament in America until 2009, so he paid the price all right, but he was not the only victim. We, as sports journalists, complain about the number of athletes who either have nothing to say, or choose not to say it, schooled as they are by a growing army of media advisers. But when a charismatic young player comes along with a willingness to say only what others are thinking, he is punished for it.

Casey won't be so honest again, that's for sure.

Paul Forsyth is a freelance journalist, based in Edinburgh. A former sports feature writer of the year, he has been chief sportswriter for Scotland on Sunday, as well as golf correspondent for the Sunday Times. He has covered some of the world's biggest sports events, including the World Cup, Wimbledon, the World Series and the Masters.

A PARTNERSHIP OF EQUALS: ADAM HUNTER AND PAUL LAWRIE

By Alan Campbell

P rofessional golf is a cutthroat business. It's one which makes a select band of men, and many fewer women, serious fortunes. Hundreds more make a decent living from the game. But for every Tiger Woods, Rory McIlroy and Annika Sorenstam, a cast of thousands see their dreams ground to dust.

Unlike team sports, players don't get paid just for wearing the jersey. If a golfer plays badly over the first 36 holes of a tournament he will not play the remaining 36 and thus not be eligible for prize money. Such a tournament on the European Tour will cost a player up to £1,500 in plane tickets, accommodation and other expenses, so it doesn't take too many 'missed cuts' for the nerves to get frazzled – which in turn can have a disastrous effect on performance.

It's a vicious downward spiral, claiming the careers of a multitude of fine prospects. The minority who survive, and go on to prosper, are those who are the mentally toughest; the ones who can deflect the many blows, dismiss the cruel bounces and fully capitalise on the breaks which come their way.

It was my privilege to witness two such men from inside the ropes as a golf and sportswriter. I use the past tense, because one of them passed away last year. His name was Adam Hunter, and I hope he might have regarded me as a friend. The other is Paul Lawrie, who is not only alive but flourishing in his 40s; as I write he is on course to make the European Ryder Cup team for only the second time.

In an individual sport, Adam and Paul were as close to a team as you could get. Adam a working-class boy from Glasgow, and Paul his counterpart from Aberdeen. Together these unlikely lads won golf's greatest prize, the Open Championship, at Carnoustie in 1999. The name on the Claret Jug is that of Lawrie, but although it will never be inscribed, the name of his coach, Hunter, is there in spirit too.

Yet until Adam was diagnosed with leukaemia some two years ago, the relationship had sometimes been strained in the years following that Open victory. In golf, the player is always the dominant figure, while the coach is a member of his back-up team alongside the caddy, the manager and perhaps a sports psychologist. When the player snaps his fingers, the backroom team is expected to come running.

Curiously, when Adam and Paul first met, the positions were reversed. This was at Banchory Golf Club in 1987. Paul was a young club professional, selling chocolate bars and soft drinks in the pro shop while supplementing his income giving lessons to the members. Into this entirely modest environment swept Adam, the elder of the two and already a European Tour professional. His name adorned the doors of his sponsored Ford Escort XR3i, and as Paul recalled, "He was dressed like a pop star, he twirled his club after shots, and he was the first Tour player I ever saw close up."

When Paul later became a touring pro, he and Adam established a strong bond – both were struggling to survive on the circuit, they shared formidable work ethics and had similar interests. And each was single-minded and determined to succeed. When Adam won his only tournament, the Portuguese Open, in 1995, his position as the senior partner in the friendship was cemented. But all that was to change when he retired as a player, became a coach, and penned his pal a long letter, setting out in detail what he could do for his game and career.

The triumph which so quickly followed, when Paul won the oldest championship in golf, could not have been scripted. As it became apparent there might be a play-off for the title, Adam was the first to react, taking his friend away from the media and public circus to focus on the possible task ahead. When the four extra holes became reality, Paul was the best prepared for them, maintaining a superb focus to defeat Jean van de Velde and Justin Leonard.

Yet, inevitably perhaps, the huge win shifted the dynamic of the relationship. His sights raised, Paul became more demanding and there were tensions and fall-outs. Adam would drive at short notice from Glasgow to Aberdeen to attend to an aspect of Paul's game, and for a time the friendship became fraught. Not, it should be noted, that this is unusual in professional golf; if the player is going through a rough time he will often lash out at his coach, his caddy, or anybody else in the line of fire.

Yet, when Adam became ill, Paul reacted as only a true friend would. Now it was he who would drop everything and drive down from Aberdeen to Glasgow's renowned Beatson Oncology Centre. As so often happens, adversity and tragedy brought the two great friends closer together than they had ever been.

Delivering the eulogy at Adam's service of remembrance, Paul struggled to reach the end without breaking down. But, finish the tribute he did. "I have said many times Adam Hunter was the reason I became the golfer I am," he said between huge gulps of water and deep exhalations of breath. "Adam was my coach, sometimes my psychologist, sometimes my mother – but thankfully always my friend."

Two men, two minds working in harmony. A partnership of equals.

Alan Campbell is a freelance journalist who has worked for numerous Scottish newspapers. He has covered two Olympic Games, in Sydney and Beijing, as well as major football, rugby, tennis and golf tournaments. He has also edited a number of sports magazines.

THE IRISH SHEIKH-DOWN

By Alan Thomson

M y Arabian Nights adventure was going belly up. The Dubai hotel manager, a menacing skyscraper of malevolent muscle, glowered like a genie just condemned to a lifetime of solitary confinement in a Buckfast bottle.

"You will stay in your room until the bill has been settled. It's 600 British pounds. My security officer will be happy to escort you to the ninth floor," he barked, with an expression that didn't invite contradiction.

Banged up for the night in a hotel room. What would the office say?

A recent career switch to the Daily Mail in London (sports sub-editor) had certainly expanded my horizons, but, deep down, I suspected the first-class 'dream ticket' to the Emirates was an office politics hot potato, tossed like a Gulf War grenade in my direction by that most talented, cunning, provocative and Machiavellian of sports editors, Bryan Cooney.

Why send me? Surely this was a job for the Mail's venerable and esteemed racing correspondent, I hear you cry from the cheap seats. Agreed, but the marriage of sports editor and writer rarely runs smoothly. They were going through a bad patch and, inadvertently but oh-so-providently, I had been awarded custody of the Dubai baby.

Cooney had issued strict orders. His strictures were law. "Make sure you come back with two exclusive interviews – with Sheikh

Mohammed and Robert Sangster."

No big ask then.

The World Cup race comes hot on the heels of the Cheltenham Festival, the jump-racing pilgrimage that takes a debilitating toll on mind, body and bankbook. Apart from £100 in readies in my back pocket, I was skint. Potless. And funds for expenses were not paid in advance.

Back in my room, it was time to get the old contacts book out. Sangster's best friend was larger-than-life Tony Collins from Troon, the man who was warned off the turf after the notorious Gay Future betting scandal. Yes, Sangster was in Dubai for the World Cup and, yes, Tony would fix me up with an interview. A result at last. Unfortunately, Sangster was staying at Jumeirah Beach, several miles from my city-centre Alcatraz, which meant an expensive taxi ride eating into my meagre fiscal rations.

I had always admired Sangster, the Vernons Pools magnate and playboy who, in his day, was the world's top racehorse owner. There wasn't much he didn't know about brides and bridles. Hero worship is a dangerous indulgence, and often your sporting giants reveal feet of clay, but I was sure Sangster would measure up. Yet, how was I to escape my captivity? By chance the next morning, a Pakistani worker came to clean my room. Slipping him a fiver (British money), he sneaked me down the back stairs and out the kitchen door. Cry freedom!

It was the perfect interview. Sangster was urbane, polite, informative, amusing. He had the assurance of inherited wealth, but none of its arrogance. Twenty years earlier, Sangster, the revered Irish trainer Vincent O'Brien and his astute son-in-law John Magnier, were kings of the sales ring, a triumvirate of bloodstock titans dubbed the Ballydoyle Mafia. But their reign was under threat. Dubai's ruling Maktoum family, their cheque books gushing with petro-dollars, were preparing to shake the racing world to its very core with their profligacy.

Sitting in the Arab potentate's sumptuous and spectacular fiefdom, Sangster recalled for me the day he accepted his first dinner invitation from Sheikh Mohammed, who was desperate to learn the secrets of his rival's success.

"It was about 1979 and I travelled to the United Arab Emirates with John Magnier. We sat at a long table, with John on one side of Sheikh Mohammed and me on the other. There must have been 15 other Arabs down each flank and we were surrounded by guards toting Sten guns. It was a very interesting experience."

Sheikh Mohammed, by lineage a hunter, is a master in the art of falconry and he was setting bait for his quarry. But Sangster was keenly aware that his beguiling host was anxious to pick their brains. For several hours, the duellists verbally fenced over the silver service.

"The Arabs were very strict in those days and there was no alcohol. Perhaps that was their mistake. A drop of the hard stuff might have loosened our tongues."

In their pomp, Sangster's team had blown every other high-roller out of the water, but I was intrigued to pin down the defining moment their masterplan was hatched.

"John and I were having a quiet drink at Goodwood and an American-bred colt named Ace Of Aces had just won the feature event, the Sussex Stakes.

"John said: 'You could have bought him as a yearling for $30,000 and now he'll be syndicated for upwards of $2million to go to stud in Kentucky. Let's raid the American sales. We'll gut the yearling catalogues from Keeneland and Saratoga as if they were fresh haddock. Let's develop our own stallions, instead of being squeezed for a fortune.'"

The opening skirmish was at Keeneland. O'Brien's dazzling 1970 Derby winner Nijinsky had sounded a trumpet call for his father, Northern Dancer, who had smashed the Kentucky Derby record in 1964. O'Brien insisted they must buy Northern Dancer and Nijinsky yearlings "at all costs."

Sangster eagerly picked up the pace. "We flew to Kentucky. We were ready to set the place alight, but we got off to a nervous start. The first potential purchase was a three-parts brother to Nijinsky but you could have knocked Vincent over with a feather when the yearling walked out of his box. Vincent's brother, another great judge of horseflesh called Phonsie, burst out: 'Jesus, I've got a bigger Labrador at home!'"

His concern was well founded. Nijinsky was big, robust and dark. This was a flashy chestnut with a flaxen tail and four white stockings. Like Trigger. All that was missing was singing cowboy Roy Rogers.

"Vincent said nothing but stared into the yearling's eyes – and the horse stood rigid, staring right back."

Later, when this diminutive, spirited colt loped into the sales ring, the auctioneer's gavel knocked him down to Sangster for a bargain $200,000 price tag. Sangster named his new purchase The Minstrel and O'Brien's intuition was proved spectacularly correct – two years later the little horse with a big heart won the Derby on Epsom Downs after an epic duel with Hot Grove, the mount of Willie Carson.

"We owed The Minstrel's jockey, Lester Piggott, big style. That Classic success gave us lift-off. We were in business," said Sangster, as our collective minds floated back to that fateful afternoon.

The Minstrel seemed to be making little impression on Carson's mount as they passed the two-furlong marker. Then Piggott administered two sharp cracks of the whip, like musket shots, and his mount dug deep into his reservoir of courage. It became a dog-fight to the winning line, Piggott's relentless rat-a-tat drive with the whip playing a victory drum-roll across The Minstrel's flank. The margin was a neck and the Sangster gang could breathe more easily now that the noose had been slackened.

After two indulgent, heart-warming hours, my interview was over, reluctantly, and it was time to return to my cell. The confused hotel manager's face was a picture as I strolled through reception, but, when confronted, we called an uneasy truce as I assured him the money would be wired the following day, when the Daily Mail sports secretary resumed duties.

So, Sangster was in the bag, but how do you get to Sheikh Mohammed? A press conference had been called for the following day at Nad Al Sheba racetrack but the visit proved fruitless. I was invited back to Jumeirah Beach, where good fortune smiled. On the next bar stool was an old ally, Tommy Craig, a retired racehorse trainer from Dunbar. Tommy explained that one of his former jockeys was now lead work rider to Sheikh Mohammed. Tommy made the relevant calls and, within a few hours, I was sitting down with one of Sheikh Mohammed's inner circle. I gave him a list of questions, he disappeared for an hour or two, before returning with the Sheikh's considered replies. Enough for a 1,500-word spread and an exclusive news line that the Sheikh was going all out to win every English, Irish and French Classic, plus the Arc, the Kentucky Derby and The Melbourne Cup.

'I WANT TO CONQUER THE WORLD,' screamed the headline, and Cooney seemed pleased enough.

Alan Thomson has worked for local, regional, national and international newspapers in a career spanning 40 years, but is probably best remembered by Scottish racing aficionados in the '90s as Garry Owen of the Daily Record and Joe Punter of the Sunday Mail.

I HAVE NEVER, EVER SEEN ANYTHING LIKE THE DARTS

By Hugh MacDonald

I have watched the eagle descend at the Stadium of Light in Lisbon: part mascot, all extraordinary wonder. I have sat in the players' box at Roland Garros: part slightly bemused, all Possil boy amused by the strange byways in life's journey. I have stood behind Tom Watson as he hit that final shot to the 18th at the Open at Turnberry in 2009: part consumed by anxiety, all trembling with a hope that was to be unfulfilled. But I have never, ever seen anything like the darts.

The memory races through my mind. It runs like a tracking shot of a Martin Scorsese movie, a sort of Goodfellas with the heroes packing a carry-out. It is winter, Glasgow. The door from the VIP entrance opens on to a floor that would have Caligula demanding some restraint. There are guys walking around with barrels strapped to their back with attached hoses. They dispense lager into proffered glasses. More adventurous punters make a trip to the bar and return with trays bearing enough alcoholic units to inflict cirrhosis on a postcode, never mind a table. There are Muhammad Ali shuffles, Jinky Johnstone sidesteps as the barrelled-backed dart around the tray-bearing. It is a sort of manic dance, a Strictly Come Steaming. The near misses provide a slick of lager on the floor. The interior of the beer-sodden SECC in Glasgow is as dangerous as Monza in the rain. The odd, very odd accident occurs as punters try to slalom back to their seats. They are either carrying six pints or have consumed six pints. Or both. Mostly both.

Then the darts players enter. A disco track blares out and the barn shakes as if it is on an Iowa farm during hurricane season. The players march down as if they are gladiators in a Roman amphitheatre. But only if the gladiators had overindulged at the Forum buffet and the Colosseum was a place where lions would not have dared tread. The SECC does not take prisoners.

The matches are conducted with the sort of quiet decorum that accompanied the second half of the Battle of Bannockburn and only if Rab Bruce had called in massive air support. There is mayhem when the dull thud of dart on board is amplified. Then it becomes louder as the player zeroes in on a double. The end of each leg is greeted with the roars that once graced Hampden. Finally, the din reaches its crescendo and one player turns to the crowd, arms aloft.

He has won. The other guy has lost. And two more march towards the oche.

In a sort of gang hut in a corner perilously close to the madding crowd, sits Sid Waddell. He is to darts what Leonard Da Vinci was to painters and decorators during the Renaissance. He is to wordplay what the Royal Mint is to currency. He coins phrases.

How about this: "Bristow reasons ... Bristow quickens ... Aaah, Bristow." Or: "He's about as predictable as a wasp on speed." Or: "The atmosphere is so tense, if Elvis walked in with a portion of chips, you could hear the vinegar sizzle on them." Or his classical classic: "When Alexander of Macedonia was 33, he cried salt tears because there were no more worlds to conquer ... Bristow's only 27."

I clamber into the commentary box. It could double as the office of the Royal Society for the Prevention of Cruelty to Animals as there is no room to swing a cat. Waddell's right leg trembles, taps the floor incessantly as if some disco track is playing through his headphones. He delivers his words precisely with the sort of drama worthy of Harold Pinter on a good day.

It proves impossible to remember what he says. I am star-struck. It is like sitting next to Ayrton Senna in a Formula One car – yep, the commentary box is as tight as an Aberdonian on the night before pay day – and noting what gear he is choosing. All that remains in my mind of Waddell is the speed of his thought and the exuberance of his words.

I tumble from the box back into the mayhem of the arena. And a thought strikes me – I ducked but I could not avoid it. It is this: this is a sporting contest where everyone is having a good time. There might be just a hint of mild disappointment as a local favourite is beaten but that is swept away with a beer-sodden roar. This is sport as entertainment. This is sport as a night out. This is sport where angst, depression and post-match despair are not part of the deal. Being Scottish, I can only take so much happiness, so I head towards the exit.

A helpful media man leads me to a hidden escape route. The door opens and I am enveloped in a cloak of refreshing, chilled Glesca air. The television trucks sit in the night mist. And Eric Bristow – the erstwhile Alexander the Great, the King of the Arrows – stands in a corner. The Crafty Cockney is having a fly fag.

It is the equivalent of watching Lionel Messi slump in a mixture of exhaustion and triumph in the dressing room at the end of the Champions League final. It is a private view of a great at leisure. He drops the fag, stamps on it, and walks away.

I pause, take a breath, and head back to Planet Earth.

Magic darts.

Hugh MacDonald is chief sportswriter of The Herald. Educated at the school of hard knocks (failed), he has been a journalist for 40 years, working in total for about one of them.

Acknowledgements

My heartfelt appreciation goes to Martin Greig and Neil White at BackPage Press (gifted colleagues, good friends and, most importantly, fellow Alan Partridge devotees) for backing my idea from the very start and offering expert guidance and bucket-loads of positivity along the way. Also, to Charlie McGarry and James Porteous for their slick professionalism in putting the book together.

This project, of course, could never have happened without the talent and kindness of each and every contributing writer; while thanks are also due to the Scottish Football Writers' Association for their help in getting everyone on board.

Hat-tips also go to my colleagues on the Scottish Daily Mail sports desk for their advice and support throughout, and thanks also to Gary Stanway, Campbell Ramage and Tony Murray on the picture desk.

Those I also owe a debt of gratitude to are: Jim McCann and the SNS Group; Newsquest Media Group; Trinity Mirror Group and Matthew Lacey at Getty Images; not to mention ace photographers Gordon Whyte, Chris McNulty and Jimi Rae for kindly giving permission to use their excellent work.

On a personal level, for their invaluable support I'd like to thank Brian and Kathleen Marjoribanks, Allan, Jenny and Ava McFeat, Graham, Gemma, Lillian and Bethany Marjoribanks, Katie Marjoribanks, Margaret Cantwell, Johnny and Liz Fleming, and Ross, Lorraine, Chloe and Blair Munnoch.

I'd also like to express my love and admiration for my brave and beautiful wife Jennifer. I became a journalist to meet inspirational people and I ended up marrying one. Jenni and I would both like to thank our gorgeous rascal of a son Alexander (2) for keeping us occupied and amused, and our spirits up, with his constantly mischievous antics.

Finally, this book is dedicated to the loving memory of Baby Andrew Marjoribanks.

– *Brian Marjoribanks, July 2012*